SOCIAL SECURITY IN IRELAND, 1939–1952

Jochen

Thank you for all your
help – it was much appreciated
+ made this book possible,

Sylvia

For
my mother, Norma Carey,
and in memory of
my father, Joe Carey.

Social Security in Ireland, 1939–1952

The Limits to Solidarity

SOPHIA CAREY

IRISH ACADEMIC PRESS
DUBLIN • PORTLAND, OR

First published in 2007 by
IRISH ACADEMIC PRESS
44, Northumberland Road, Dublin 4, Ireland

and in the United States of America by
IRISH ACADEMIC PRESS
ISBS, Suite 300, 920 NE 58th Avenue
Portland, Oregon 97213-3786

© 2007 Sophia Carey

www.iap.ie

British Library Cataloguing in Publication Data
An entry can be found on request

ISBN 978 07165 3359 7 (cloth)
ISBN 978 07165 2860 9 (paper)

Library of Congress Cataloging-in-Publication Data
An entry can be found on request

Typeset by Carrigboy Typesetting Services.
Printed by Biddles Ltd, King's Lynn, Norfolk.

Contents

Acknowledgements

This book would never have been finished without help and encouragement from numerous people over far too many years. I would like to thank the Irish Research Council for the Humanities and Social Sciences (IRCHSS) for the post-doctoral fellowship which supported this work. Many people in the School of Social Work and Social Policy (Trinity College, Dublin) provided help throughout the years. Chief amongst them is Tony McCashin, whose generosity was exceeded only by his patience. Thanks are also due to Judy O'Shea, Eoin O'Sullivan, Jarlath McKee and Robbie Gilligan, amongst many other colleagues in Trinity. I am indebted to Mel Cousins for his observations and responses to many queries, and to Eunan O'Halpin and Jochen Clasen for comments, suggestions and valuable support.

The library staff in Trinity College was unfailingly helpful over many years. I would also like to thank the staff of the National Archives, University College, Dublin Archives and the Irish Labour History Archives for their generous assistance. The Most Rev. John Kirby DD, Bishop of Clonfert, was also helpful in allowing me access to the Archives of the Diocese of Loughrea. Brendan Delany was an extremely obliging guide through the ESB Art Collection. Thanks to my editor, Lisa Hyde, for her continuing support despite my leisurely progress.

Finally, my husband, Charles Tyner, has sustained me through the process of producing this work. He knows, I hope, how grateful I am for the love and support on which I have depended so much and so often.

Naturally, I alone am responsible for any errors or omissions in this work.

SOPHIA CAREY

Abbreviations

CIE	Córas Iompair Éireann
CORI	Conference of Religious of Ireland
DATI	Department of Agriculture and Technical Instruction
DD	Dáil Debates
DDA	Dublin Diocesan Archives
D/Taoiseach	Department of the Taoiseach Files
D/Social Welfare	Department of Social Welfare Files
ESB	Electricity Supply Board
ESRI	Economic and Social Research Institute
FRW	Federation of Rural Workers
IAOS	Irish Aricultural Organisation Society
ICTU	Irish Congress of Trade Unions
ILO	International Labour Organisation
IMA	Irish Medical Association
ITGWU	Irish Transport and General Workers Union
ITUC	Irish Trade Union Congress
NESF	National Economic and Social Forum
NESC	National Economic and Social Council
NHIS	National Health Insurance Society
NAI	National Archives of Ireland
OACP	Old Age Contributory Pension
UCDA	University College Dublin Archives

Introduction

This book is a detailed analysis of Irish social security policy, looked at through the prism of the lengthy gestation of the 1952 Social Welfare Act and its impact on subsequent developments. It is, to put it another way, about the ideological battles and debates about the distribution and redistribution of resources which culminated in 'the birth of social welfare in Ireland' (Cousins, 2003). The starting point for the book was an interest in some puzzling aspects of the Irish welfare state, viewed from both a comparative and an Irish perspective. The period has been seen as the beginnings of 'the golden age of the welfare state', ushering in a thirty-year era of expanding social expenditures, which underpinned increasingly comprehensive welfare provision in the industrialised Western nations (Pierson, 1991). However, in Ireland, the period is more usually seen as marking the limits to reform. Following intense and often acrimonious debate about social policy in Ireland, the 1953 Health Act and the 1952 Social Welfare Act inaugurated limited reforms which defined the nature of the Irish welfare state until the 1960s and 1970s and, perhaps, to the present. The failure of radical health reforms meant the continuance of a two-tier health system while, in social welfare, 'the Irish system remained essentially fragmented and showed little commitment to inter-class solidarity' (Cousins, 1995: 20). Explanations for these outcomes have usually focused on events in the health sphere, for the very good reason that aspects of the proposed reforms (known subsequently as 'the Mother and Child Scheme') proved intensely controversial, and exploded into the public domain in what still stands as the major Church–state conflict of that century. One puzzle is why contemporaneous events in social welfare (as social security is generally known in Ireland) failed to generate equal passions.

One reason might be that social security, which is essentially concerned with the various types of cash payments for unemployment, old age, disability and so on, is simply too dull an area to generate passion amongst any but the most actuarially minded minority. Yet in the UK, in December of 1942, 'queues formed outside the government stationary office as people waited to buy a densely written three hundred page official report' (Hills et al., 1994: 1). This best-selling document, the Beveridge Report, was fundamental in shaping the structure of the post-war UK social security system, and it would be the pivot around which much Irish debate would subsequently revolve. In general terms, social security is emblematic of the welfare state to an unparalleled degree. Historically, it has eclipsed other policy areas as a focus of study: indeed, the welfare state itself is often dated from the social security initiatives seen in a range of countries in the late nineteenth century (Flora and Heidenheimer, 1981; Pierson, 1991). Scholars interested in why welfare states arose and grew so spectacularly, in how and why they differ from one country to another, and in what their future prospects are, typically turned to social security to answer these questions (Cutright, 1965; Wilensky 1975; Rimlinger; 1971; Flora and Alber; 1981 *inter alia*). The dominance of social security in the field of comparative social policy has subsequently been much critiqued, but it remains an important testing ground for theoretical understandings of the welfare state (Baldwin, 1990; Bolderson and Mabbett, 1995; De Deken, 2002; Allan and Scruggs, 2004). There are then good grounds for wondering if our understanding of Irish social policy outcomes in the post-war period might be enhanced by shifting our focus from the dramatic events in health to the less considered area of social security.

A case-study of social security policy is thus a very conventional approach to exploring the debates which have been thrown up by the huge body of theorizing about the welfare state which has emerged over the previous three or four decades. This theorizing has generated a range of theoretical accounts – mostly competing, but sometimes complementary – to account for the nature of contemporary welfare states, and in particular, for why there is so much cross-national variation in how states deal with what might be seen as fairly universal social problems (Skocpol and Amenta, 1986; Quadagno, 1987; Amenta, 1993: Myles and Quadagno, 2002). Three perspectives in particular have dominated the field: functionalist accounts, in particular those which stress the processes of industrialisation, politics-centered accounts, and statist or institutionalist perspectives. A central question concerns how useful these are in explaining the Irish welfare state, which has been described as 'an incongruous, even irreconcilable, case' (O'Donnell, 1999: 85), and which appears to present particular problems in attempts to locate it in comparative terms. Chapter one explores these debates in some detail, and subsequent chapters explore these large theoretical questions about welfare states through the smaller policy field of social security.

Relative to the welfare state as a whole, social security is a small area, but it is not a simple one. In particular, it is a field where apparently small differences of detail can have major impacts, in wide-ranging distributional terms, or in terms of the lived experiences of individuals accessing particular benefits. Many of the chapters in this book discuss these small details at some length. Of necessity this book engages with issues of actuarial concerns, funding methods, governance structures, and other details which are, on the surface, rather abstract and esoteric. However, it has been said that 'the nuts and bolts of social policy testify to the heated struggles of classes and interests' (1990: 1). Thus, apparently unpromising discussions about the administrative structure of social security in Ireland is surprisingly revealing of Church–state relations, lurking within discussions of scope are heated ideological debates about solidarity, and exploring debates about contribution levels sheds light on often obscured distributive conflicts in rural Ireland. These deeper issues however, will be more easily understood if some general aspects of social security are first clarified.

Debating social security: the aims of the welfare state

Social security is best thought of as a subset of what is now generally termed 'social protection'. 'Expressed at its simplest, social protection is about the cover against adverse living circumstances that members of a society are willing to extend to each other and what they expect from each other' (NESC, 2005). Social protection, however, can encompass different kinds of provision, including the direct provision of a range of services, such as health, education and housing. Social security is a narrower concept, and is most commonly associated with income maintenance schemes. It might thus be thought of as 'public measures that provide cash benefits to deal with specific contingencies arising from the loss of earnings or inadequate earnings and to deal with the cost of supporting dependants' (McCashin, 2004: ix). Having said this, in some countries, social security can encompass non-cash benefits, in particular the provision of health care. The fact that the Irish social security system does not encompass health care is one of its distinctive features.

Income maintenance schemes are conventionally divided into three main categories: universal benefits (citizenship or category based), social assistance (generally means tested and financed by general taxation), and social insurance benefits (predicated on a record of contributions). While any given country may (and usually does) have a mix of these different types of benefits, it is common to construct ideal-typical classifications depending on the predominant mode of provision (van Kersbergen and Becker, 2002). The construction of these typologies is predicated on assumptions about the principles underlying different modes of social security provision. Perhaps the key assumption is that choosing between different modes of provision is not merely an administrative choice, but is also normative in a very fundamental sense. Thus the predominant mode of provision is revealing of the overall ethos and aims of social security, and of the wider welfare state in which it is located. Hence, generalisations about different social security models are frequently proxies for generalisations about different kinds of welfare states. Thus, for example, systems might be distinguished from each other depending on whether the general principle underlying them is a concern with equality, poverty relief or status maintenance. These principles are often deemed to map onto whether the social security system rests most heavily on universal, social assistance or social insurance payments respectively, but in reality the complexity of most countries' arrangements make simple distinctions like this difficult to apply in practice (Clasen, 2002; Bolderson and Mabbet, 1995). Nevertheless, it is clear that debates about different kinds of income maintenance schemes are revealing of the principles and aims of policy-makers. The central debate in Ireland in the period focused on the rival merits of tax-funded assistance programmes, and a particular (Beveridgean) variant of contributory social insurance. This book traces the processes by which the distinctions between these different modes of provision became clear to Irish policy-makers, and looks at the factors which influenced the choices leading to distinctive outcomes in Ireland.

On the eve of the Second World War, Irish social security ran along dual lines of provision. Means-tested assistance schemes dated from the Poor Law provision of outdoor relief and the 1908 Old Age Pension, while insurance-based schemes dated from the 1911 National Insurance Act. The 1911 Act introduced contributory provision for unemployment benefit for some workers in a limited range of industries, and also provided for sickness benefit to provide an income during times of ill-health (See Appendix 1 for a description of these key income-maintenance schemes). Subsequent developments continued along this two-track path: new schemes (both contributory and non-contributory) were added from time to time, in a largely *ad hoc* manner. There was no real conception of social security as an integrated system, and essentially no extended consideration of its central aims and principles. It is probably fair to say that this mode of incremental, piecemeal development is characteristic of welfare state development generally, and is not unique to Ireland (Kasza, 2002).

However, while social security development may generally be incremental, certain legislative initiatives have more centrality than others. From time to time, circumstances conspire to create periods of policy-making which make visible the fundamental issues which underlie social security and consequently, to make the choices taken have long-lasting significance. It is a contention of this book that the 1952 Social Welfare Act is one such formative moment. Decisions taken in the period laid the foundations for the subsequent structure of social insurance and social assistance services in Ireland (McCashin, 2004). The bulk of the book looks at the long process of policy formation which culminated in the Act, and it concludes by looking beyond 1952 to clarify the subsequent impact on later developments.

At the core of debates were the merits of shifting the basis of Irish social security to one in which social insurance would be the predominant mode of provision. The focus on the merits of social insurance is only explicable by understanding the influence of policy models from outside Ireland. Most obviously, the publication of the Beveridge Report was enormously influential, as it was elsewhere in the world. But policy-makers were influenced by wider models too. In particular, they had access to, and indeed commissioned, International Labour Organisation (ILO) reports on social security arrangements around the world. In this period, the ILO was committed to social insurance as the way forward in social security, as they had clarified in 1944 at their 26th session in Philadelphia. As we'll see, it is clear that key Irish policy-makers (particularly but not exclusively civil servants) felt strongly that 'the modern trend [was] towards an extension of insurance' (Department of Social Welfare, 1949: 10). The lure of social insurance, especially as formulated by Beveridge, has been incisively captured in Baldwin's (1994) analysis of the Beveridge mythology.

On a relatively simple level, part of the appeal of social insurance was the contributory principal on which it is based. As Baldwin notes, in general terms 'whether financing was assured through taxes or earmarked contributions was a bookkeeping distinction, or at best a question of which method seemed politically most astute' (1994: 45). But the notion of benefits received as of right on the basis of contributions made had a psychological and political appeal. Certainly, the lack of a means test is both administratively efficient, and avoids the necessity for penalising thrift. But more fundamentally, earned benefits could be said to safeguard the self-respect of recipients and to avoid 'the stigma of dependence' (p. 46). Thus, as was clear to Irish policy makers, social insurance might be said to have advantages of 'a moral and psychological character' (Department of Social Welfare, 1949: 11). In this sense, social insurance had an appeal beyond the left, as it seemed to promise the ability to provide state-supported protection against key risks, while continuing to endorse the values of self-reliance and independence.

On their own though, these factors would not be sufficient to account for the striking appeal of the Beveridge plan. Thus Baldwin argues that the mythological aspects of the Beveridgean social insurance scheme owe their origins to the 'universal' approach which he claimed to take; his scheme promised complete coverage against all risks for all people (1994: 40–5). Insurance, generally, is a collective pooling of risk through contributions to a fund from which individuals are reimbursed for harm suffered (Schmid et al., 1992: 59). However, social insurance can be differentiated from private insurance schemes in a number of ways. A fundamental difference is that it generally involves 'a pooling of risk without differentiating contributions according to exposure to risk' (Erskine and Clasen, 1997: 241). Alongside this, social insurance schemes are usually compulsory; compulsion is necessary in order to avoid the problem of adverse selection. Adverse selection implies the greater likelihood of 'bad risks' – those who feel more vulnerable, perhaps due to ill health or insecure employment – voluntarily opting to enter social insurance schemes.

Collective pooling of risks can be seen to combine solidarity (between the young and the old, the working and the currently unemployed) with redistribution. In general, the redistributive element arises from the fact that, though all may be united in the same scheme, not all are, in fact, equally at risk of the contingencies for which social insurance offers protection. All may contribute, but some, by virtue of greater risk-proneness, benefit more than others. As noted above, the 1911 National Insurance Act had initially been limited to certain categories of workers. While extended over time, social insurance was by and large limited to workers with broadly similar risks. But in the Beveridge scheme, all would be included –relatively secure civil servants along with insecure manual workers, whose likelihood of claiming benefits was obviously higher. 'Beveridge in this way heralded the fulfilment of the solidaristic potential of social insurance. The quarantining of certain groups within their own risk pools, the excusing of the wealthy and fortunate from sharing burdens with the harder pressed: these characteristics of the old style of social insurance were now to be superseded' (Baldwin, 1994: 44). That this interpretation of the Beveridgean model is flawed, as Baldwin notes, is perhaps less important than the fact that there was a widespread perception that comprehensiveness and solidarity were linked. For contemporaries, the Beveridge scheme was enticing in that it seemed to balance both collectivism and individualism, and thus it had an appeal which to some extent transcended the divisions of left and right (Baldwin, 1994).

Baldwin, however, points us to a problem which would loom large in Irish debates. The vision of extending the contributory system to encompass virtually all citizens (beyond an irreducible minimum) was predicated on the ability of all to become contributors. However, thus conceptualised, 'the insurance principle presupposes a fundamental degree of homogeneity within its target population' (p. 47). The extent to which the Irish population was sufficiently homogenous was problematic, and this would be one of the major issues with which policy-makers would grapple. Moreover, while solidaristic principles were attractive to some, to others the prospect of coercing 'the wealthy and fortunate' into a common redistributive risk pool was not in fact desirable. Thus both the structure of the Irish economy and the way in which class interests were expressed in Ireland are fundamental to understanding the debates about social security which culminated in the 1952 Act. However, while this is clear in retrospect, it took time for these issues to become apparent to policy-makers of the period, and to understand this, we need to consider the long-drawn-out nature of the policy process in this case study. It is useful to think of the policy-process as constituting three main phases: an initial agenda-setting period during and after the war under Fianna Fáil, a more-focused approach on details under the inter-party government between 1948 and 1951, and a period where a final synthesis was arrived at by Fianna Fáil.

The chronology of reform

The question of reforming social security and, in particular, of con-
solidating existing schemes into a unified social insurance scheme on
British lines, was begun under the Fianna Fáil government, which
had been in power from 1932 and was to lose power only in 1948.
As the end of the war came into view, this government increasingly
saw itself as facing demands for social service reform. Indigenous
pressures for reform had been building for some time, but these were
hugely increased by the publication of the Beveridge Report.
Initially, social security was not clearly distinguished as a separate
policy area, and the issues involved in choosing between different
forms of social security provision were embedded in a wide-ranging
process of social service reform generally. Debates about the
administrative structures of social security are particularly important
in this phase, partially because administrative reform generally was
to the fore in the period. Additionally, however, a very public
controversy erupted between the Minister for Local Government and
Public Health, Seán MacEntee, and the Bishop of Clonfert, Bishop
Dignan. Dignan, who was at that time a leading figure in the area of
social services, had suggested reforms that were based on vocationalist ideas, which if adopted would have had major implications for
administering social security. The conflict and its eventual resolution
under the next government are extremely revealing of the nature of
Church–state relations in the period. In particular, the episode raises
question marks about long-established perceptions about the role of
the Church in the social policy sphere, and helps to clarify some of
the factors which make the Irish welfare state difficult to locate in
comparative typologies.

The terms of the debate were set by this government in a number
of fundamental ways as the process of administrative reform developed. Thus, one of the key legacies of this period is the creation of
the Departments of Health and Social Welfare in 1947, which marks
the recognition that social security was a discrete policy field.
Contemporaneously with this division was the appreciation that a
central question in the field of social security concerned the problems
involved in the coordination of the diverse, fragmented income
maintenance schemes which were in existence at this point. As this
awareness emerged, so too did a recognition that the nature of Irish
society presented certain problems if the goal was to be a comprehensive and coordinated scheme of social insurance. A central

problem identified in the period was that of reconciling the interests of urban and rural Ireland.

However, it was the inter-party government which took power in 1948 under the leadership of John A. Costello which tackled the substantive details and brought proposed legislation into the public sphere. The ten points of policy agreed to in the formation of the coalition had included a commitment to the introduction 'of a comprehensive social security plan to provide insurance against old age, illness, blindness, widowhood, unemployment, etc.' (McCullagh, 1998: 37). Labour leader and Minister for Social Welfare William Norton outlined his plans for reform in the 1949 White Paper, *Social Security*, and made important moves towards the unification and coordination of diverse schemes by centralising the administration of all social insurance schemes under the Minister for Social Welfare. But although legislation was introduced to give effect to these plans in 1950, the government collapsed before this could be enacted. Although this government had agreed in principle on a social security scheme, in practice a range of issues surrounding the implications of redistributive risk-pooling proved to be intensely divisive within a government which encompassed very different ideological perspectives. In both the White Paper, and the subsequent legislation, Norton was forced to make compromises which moved the scheme substantially away from the universalism of the Beveridge scheme. These decisions – many of which would be carried over into later legislation – would have long-term distributive consequences for the Irish welfare state. They point us to the importance of understanding both the agrarian context of policy-making in the period, and the way in which the interests of different classes are expressed in the Irish party system.

By the time the inter-party government collapsed, the policy-process had thus moved a considerable distance from the early tentative considerations of the emergency period. Administrative issues had been resolved, problem areas identified, and a clear policy template awaited the incoming Fianna Fáil government. Thus the 1952 Social Welfare Act was implemented very speedily, becoming law in June of 1952, within a year of Fianna Fáil's return to power. One of the most interesting features of the Act is the way in which it differs from the proposals which William Norton had made in 1949. Because many of these differences are small – for example, differences in contribution and benefit levels – they have often been neglected in relation to the undoubted similarities between the two schemes. However, as discussed above, in social security small details often have large effects, and the differences between the two schemes, and in particular, how these outcomes were arrived at across the three governments concerned, tells us a great deal about the way in which distributional conflicts have been resolved in Ireland. These issues are discussed thematically rather than chronologically in this book: thus Chapters 2 and 3 focus on administrative issues and look in particular at the role of the Catholic Church. Chapters 4 and 5 focus on the agrarian dimension of policy making in social security, and Chapter 6 examines debates about solidarity and re-distribution in relation to specific categories of workers. Chapter 7 provides an epilogue which traces the continuing relevance of the debates explored in the book across the succeeding decades.

Conclusion

While the Beveridge plan was extremely influential in providing a springboard from which all policy-makers discussed their plans, the outcome was a distorted and truncated version of Beveridge. Although clearly influenced by developments in Britain, there were important differences between it and the Beveridge scheme as ultimately applied. Most notably, the self-employed and higher-paid workers were excluded from the scheme. This was to have long-lasting effects, since social insurance was not extended to higher-paid workers until 1974 and to the self-employed until 1988. In tandem with the extension and development of social-assistance schemes, this would have important consequences for the redistributive character of the Irish welfare state. Other differences to the British scheme existed, too. One of the best-known aspects of the UK scheme was flat-rate contributions and benefits: that is, everybody paid the same contributions and everybody received the same benefits. The Irish scheme did not go down the alternative 'corporatist' route of pay-related social insurance, but instead created a hybrid scheme where some paid lower contributions yet received the same benefits. Partially as a result, Irish social insurance is, as Cousins (1997) has pointed out, 'somewhat more diffuse than is generally recognised', with different schemes for private and public employees and – later – the self-employed, and several sub-categories for specific types of worker (Cousins, 1997: 231 and 233 fn. 24). The complexity of Irish social security in this sense has been pointed to by a number of authors (Daly and Yeates, 2003; McCashin, 2004) It is not, however, a corporatist insurance scheme; rather, it straddles the universalistic UK scheme and the more-differentiated Continental schemes. Many authors have drawn attention to the 'hybrid nature of Ireland's arrangements for providing social protection' (NESC, 2005: 35). In turn, the distinctiveness of social policy outcomes has posed problems for those interested in locating Ireland in contemporary typologies (O'Donnell, 1999). The hybridity of the social welfare system which emerged in the period means that it is a useful case-study for exploring wider debates about the nature of the Irish welfare state, and for considering some of the puzzling questions about the factors shaping distributive and redistributive outcomes in Ireland.

CHAPTER ONE

Theorising the Irish Welfare State

Introduction

The formidable problems facing any attempt to provide an over-view of Ireland's place in the field of welfare state theories springs from a fundamental asymmetry: there is, to be frank, rather too much comparative theory, and rather too little Irish theory. The territory of welfare state studies generally has been described as resembling 'a battlefield, with researchers sending waves of hypotheses across it, hoping to claim sovereignty for one theory or another' (Amenta, 1993: 752). The range and number of theoretical perspectives is so great that, as Uusitalo points out, 'there is no agreement even about how theories of the welfare state can be classified' (1984: 412). This bewildering diversity of approaches has also been observed by Baldwin:

> Explanations of the origins, rise and development of the welfare state abound. Scores of theories compete to explain why it exists at all, dozens of comparative analyses account for its variations, legions of narratives detail how individual examples contradict or confirm general hypotheses . . . Even the seasoned observer may be forgiven for feeling lost in this academic Babel of paradigms, models, interpretations, accounts. (1990: 36–7)

Moreover, as van Kersbergen notes: 'The range of research designs and methods is probably as wide as the theoretical approaches that can be distinguished' (1995: 8).

Lurking beneath this battlefield is the perennial problem of competing definitions of the welfare state itself, and very different conceptions of what the object of study is. As Veit-Wilson notes, 'much argument between authors might be explained by their apparent unawareness that they are pursuing disparate projects and doing so in incompatible discourses' (2000: 8). Hence, he identifies six separate projects: among other issues, researchers may be concerned with explaining how states came to be involved with welfare, they may want to evaluate how effectively states carry out their welfare functions, or they may wish to define and classify types of welfare states. Any attempt to review theories of the welfare state encounters the problem that there are, in effect, different 'welfare states' with which theories are concerned.

When we turn to Ireland, however, it is clear that one of the most distinctive aspects of welfare state theory in Ireland is its late emergence and relative underdevelopment. The paucity of research in the field of welfare state theory was first observed by McCashin (1982), and despite a growing body of research subsequently it remains true that 'the task of theorising Irish social policy is incomplete' (Fanning, 2004: 22). The relative dearth of theoretically oriented Irish accounts reflects both the small scale of the Irish academic community and the specific nature of the social policy field in Ireland (O'Sullivan, 2005). It is tempting to suggest, however, that an equally important reason for the underdeveloped condition of welfare state theory in Ireland is the late emergence of a developed welfare state.

State of the art surveys of welfare state theory generally agree that comparative theory was kick-started by the post-war growth of welfare expenditures across industrialised countries, otherwise known as the 'golden age' of the welfare state (Uusitalo, 1984; Amenta and Skocpol, 1986; Quadagno, 1987; Myles and Quadagno, 2002). This theorising could build on an existing base of substantial empirical research in the 'social administration' approach which had previously dominated, in the English language at any rate. However, although the roots of the Irish welfare state can be traced back to the 1838 Poor Relief (Ireland) Act, Ireland did not participate in the major expansionary stage of post-war development (Maguire, 1986). Consequently, the timing of welfare state development meant that much early work was primarily concerned with describing and assessing the effectiveness of newly expanded social services. While there is now an extensive and rapidly growing body of research on all aspects of the Irish welfare state, much of it is only tangentially concerned with the primary focus of this study, which is the applicability of theories of the welfare state to Ireland. Unfortunately, then, many insights from the international literature are still in the process of being explored, and in considering their applicability we frequently need to rely on elliptical glances from scholars whose real focus is elsewhere. 'In the absence of a distinct canon of theoretical works on Irish social policy it becomes necessary to draw upon the works of modern historians, sociologists, economists, geographers and political scientists to piece together the equivalent of the theoretical debates usual in larger societies with larger academic and intellectual communities' (Fanning, 2004: 7). Thus while we can identify broad schools of thought on the welfare state in the comparative literature, it is only sometimes possible to find a matching example in the Irish literature.[1]

One of the most useful ways into considering theoretically oriented work on the Irish welfare state is to note that, as is the case with the wider comparative literature, the field of welfare state studies in Ireland is multi-disciplinary, and is intimately related to wider social science concerns. A fundamental debate within Irish social science generally has been the extent to which Ireland's social, political and economic history has been 'atypical', with consequent problems for locating Ireland in a comparative or theoretical context. The level of specificity has varied from the problems of locating the Irish party system in standard typologies to attempting to define the type of society Ireland is (Mair, 1987; Peillon, 1994; Goldthorpe, 1992, *inter alia*). Given that Ireland has presented comparison problems in the fields of economics, politics and sociology in particular, it should be no surprise that much recent welfare state theory has also focused on the issue. This debate crystallised around Cousins' (1997) suggestion that Ireland sat very uneasily in the influential worlds of welfare identified by Esping-Andersen (1990).[2] Cousins (1997) identified Ireland's colonial and post-colonial status, the importance of agriculture, the impact of being a dependent and peripheral country, the role of the state and the centrality of Catholicism as factors which have had an impact on the development of the Irish welfare state, and which are not well dealt with in the welfare state literature generally.

While it would be an exaggeration to say that debate has raged around the topic subsequently, there has certainly been a continuing discussion in the literature about the essential comparability of the Irish welfare state (Lewis, 1992; O'Donnell, 1999; O'Connor, 2003; Adshead and Millar, 2004; O'Sullivan, 2004; Payne and McCashin, 2005). The last decade has seen a growing range of studies, from diverse disciplines and using widely varying methodologies, with a specific focus on issues of similarity and difference. Leaving aside the findings of quantitative cross-national studies, and focusing only on 'indigenous' accounts, we can identify two broadly oppositional strands in relation to the location of Ireland in comparative typologies. The first stresses issues relating to *difference* when it comes to classifying Ireland, and tends to focus our attention on hybridity, heterogeneity, atypical development and divergence (Cousins, 1997; O'Donnell, 1999; O'Sullivan, 2004). The second strand, on the other hand, focuses on *similarities* and implicitly or explicitly points to coherency, comparability and convergence (McLaughlin, 1993; O'Connor, 2003; Adshead and Millar, 2004). I consider both approaches in more detail below, but a central point to note is that this concern with the tensions around similarities and differences in welfare states is by no means unique to Ireland. In O'Connor's (1988) words, a key question for theorists of the welfare state concerns whether *convergence or divergence* is the central trend in welfare development. This provides us with a useful theme around which we can consider the previous few decades of research both internationally and in Ireland.

Both convergence and divergence have been conceptualised in varying ways, responding both to what might be called paradigm shifts within wider social science which change the focus of contemporary concerns, and to methodological advances which provide new lenses through which to examine these shifting concerns. Hence, at different times, different processes, actors and outcomes have been prioritised. So, for example, the first wave of welfare theorists tended to address convergence as resulting from a 'logic of industrialisation', while for many contemporary theorists, convergence may be said to arise from a 'logic of globalisation'. Nevertheless, an exploration of the tensions between an underlying idea of 'the' welfare state and the existence of a variety of actual 'welfare states' underlies many studies in the field.

This chapter explores the evolution of these concerns with similarity and difference by focusing on three, main theoretical approaches: the (functionalist) logic of industrialism, political theories and institutionalist theories. The central conclusion is that conventional theories all have something to offer as explanations of Irish developments, but only if considered as complementary rather than exclusive, and if their core insights are stretched and adapted to suit Irish outcomes. This chapter suggests that the tensions around convergence and divergence which form much of the substance of the comparative literature are particularly visible in debates around the historical determinants of the Irish welfare state, and the nature of contemporary outcomes. It concludes by arguing that the current 'state-of-the art' in both the comparative and indigenous literature suggests that theoretically informed studies of specific policy areas seem to offer the most promise in addressing current concerns within the field.

Focusing on convergence: the logic of industrialism

For the first generation of scholars interested in the welfare state as a cross-national phenomenon, the seemingly inexorable growth of social expenditure across the industrialised world suggested that there was a functional link between industrialisation and social welfare (Myles and Quadagno, 2002). There was, in other words, a 'logic of industrialism' which explained why states, as they industrialised, would devote increasing resources to welfare functions of varying kinds (Kerr et al. 1973; Wilensky, 1975). As Myles and Quadagno note, there are strong and weak versions of the thesis, but the 'implicit claim of the strong version is that nations with comparable levels of economic development would converge at similar levels of welfare state development' (2002: 37). Hence the logic of industrialism is generally described as a functionalist theory, resting as it does on assumptions that 'public policy is the product of large, impersonal, economic forces' (ibid).[3] This assumption has been much questioned, and indeed van Kersbergen points out that a relatively wide recognition of the inadequacies of functionalist theories meant that, by the 1980s, they were 'virtually dead' (2001: 91). This is almost certainly true of the 'strong' version of industrialism, but the perception that the emergence of the phenomenon known as the welfare state is inexplicably intertwined with long-term economic processes remains valid. In fact, it might be said that broadly functionalist theories were resurrected and dusted off in the globalisation theses of the 1990 (van Kersbergen, 2001).

The logic of industrialism is thus of much more than historical interest. Many of its central tenets are convincing and persuasive, the methodological approaches it spawned continue to generate dynamic insights, and the critical debate about its utility was the birthplace of what we call welfare state theory. In any account of any welfare state, we would need to pay homage to the theory, but we might need to do so only at a cursory level. In an account of Irish welfare state development, however, we need to do much more than this. For reasons explored in more detail below, it is impossible to apply contemporary theories of the welfare state to Ireland without engaging in a critical analysis of the logic of industrialism, and its legacies for contemporary understandings of welfare states. Very briefly, this is because distinctive paths to industrialisation and modernisation in Ireland have left legacies which continue to influence the contemporary welfare state, and moreover, which create a range of problems for those who wish to use the insights generated by the comparative literature. As a late-industrialising European nation, Ireland's experiences have been seen to be particularly useful in exploring the theory of industrialism generally. There is, consequently, an extremely large body of work that attempts to understand the Irish case (Wickham, 1983; Kennedy, 1989; O'Hearn, 1989, 1995, 1998; O'Malley, 1985, 1989, *inter alia*). Underlying much of this work is a concern with the extent to which the Irish experience of industrialisation supports the theory's claims to convergence, or the extent to which the Irish experience is divergent, implying some flaw in the theory of industrialism itself. Before considering these debates in the context of welfare state theory, we need first to sketch out the main terms of the industrialism thesis itself.

The logic of industrialism as applied to welfare states emerged from a wider social science paradigm which argued that the processes of industrialisation had wide-ranging social and economic impacts which were essentially similar across all societies (Kerr et al., 1973) The general terms of the debate were sketched out by the path-breaking work of Kerr et al., first published in 1960. This argued that there was a logic to the process of industrialisation which was inexorable and universal:

> the logic of industrialism prevails eventually, and such similarities as it decrees will penetrate the outermost points of its universal sphere of influence. Each industrialised society is more like every other industrialised society – however great the difference among them may be – than any industrial society is like any pre-industrial society. (Kerr et al., 1973: 56)

The 'logic of industrialism', as conceptualised by Kerr et al., had a much wider remit than social policy. However, attempts to empirically validate this theory led to research that looked at a range of public policies to assess the impact of 'industrialisation' on policy outcomes. Cutright (1965) and Wilensky (1975) are usually cited in tandem as among the earliest expressions of the 'logic of industrialism' as applied specifically to welfare states, rather than as wider theories of societal development generally. Their primary finding has been taken to be that economic rather than political factors lie behind the development of the welfare state. Wilensky's assertion – that 'economic growth and its demographic and bureaucratic outcomes are the root cause of the general emergence of the welfare state' – must be one of the most cited quotes in the history of welfare state theory (1975: xiii). In addition, these studies were influential in shaping the development of cross-national quantitative research utilising various measures of welfare effort. Their work has thus left a number of profound legacies, in terms both of conclusions and of methodology.

From its roots in Kerr et al.'s (1973) interpretation of the nature of industrial societies, this theoretical approach has broadened and developed, and been applied with increasing sophistication and complexity in an attempt to explain the origins of welfare states. One key development has been that industrialisation has at times been subsumed into a broader account of the link between *modernisation* and welfare states. The best-known account of this is probably Flora and Alber's (1981). 'The concept of modernization has largely replaced the traditional concept of development as well as superseded more specific concepts such as industrialization and democratization' (Flora and Alber, 1981: 38). The logic of modernisation has been described as 'a politicised version of the industrialism thesis' (Pierson, 1991: 21). Politics, in this sense, is less the clash of organised interests and more the wider process of democratisation, which acts in tandem with industrialisation to create a need for social policies to meet the demands of modern industrial societies. Flora and Alber (1981) focused on the chronological development of social insurance, arguing that the timing and development of social insurance is related to variations in socio-economic development, political mobilisation of the working class and constitutional development. Although their work incorporates variation they are generally seen as stressing convergence, given the implicit 'progressive-evolutionary' logic in their approach (Pierson, 1991: 21). Countries may be 'late' or 'early', but the process is one which all societies will ultimately undergo in some manner. Hence, Flora and Heidenheimer describe the welfare state as 'a more or less conscious or reactive response to long-term processes and basic developmental problems' (1981: 22).

Industrialisation and the Irish welfare state

As noted above, the general theory of industrialism has been the focus of sustained attention by Irish social scientists, and in the process, some have paused to assess the extent to which welfare state development in Ireland is explicable by a logic of industrialism (O'Connell and Rottman, 1992). The proposition that the emergence of welfare states is essentially a response to the 'logic of industrialism' seems superficially attractive in the Irish case. On the surface, welfare expansion and economic expansion seem to be closely related, with the major period of welfare state expansion following closely on the heels of the late industrialisation process from the 1960s on. One of the most extensive surveys of Irish welfare development is Maguire's (1986) contribution to *Growth to Limits*, a comparative project that stresses the impact of industrialisation and modernisation on welfare development in Europe. She remarks: 'There can be little doubt that the marked acceleration in economic growth rates since the beginning of the 1960s has been a crucial factor in the development of the Irish welfare state' (1986: 328). She identifies two factors that partially explain this, both of which have echoes in the 'logic of industrialisation' literature. These are the increase in resources created by economic expansion, and the creation of new pressures and needs generated by industrialisation.

Late industrialisation and late welfare development, therefore, seem intimately related and provide grist for those who see convergence as the central theme in welfare studies. However, as McCashin notes, 'to attribute the emergence of a rapidly-developing welfare sector solely to economic growth is to posit too mechanistic a link between the economy and the welfare services' (1982: 203). Indeed, Maguire points out that the overlap between phases of economic growth and phases of social-expenditure growth has not been perfect, and suggests that economic factors could provide only a partial explanation (1986: 331). O'Connell and Rottman broadly agree arguing that 'the theory of industrialism does not fare well in Ireland' (1992: 238). In general, it is fair to say that the Irish case raises, in microcosm, problems which the theory had encountered in explaining welfare state development generally. In addition however, the specific nature of Irish welfare state development points to a set of concerns with standard theoretical perspectives which will run through our consideration of welfare state theory generally. The most explicit attention to the applicability of logic of industrialism to the Irish welfare state remains O'Connell and Rottman's (1992) account.

Their analysis was not concerned with assessing a particular policy area, but looked at the entire package of activities which collectively can be considered as 'the welfare state'. Hence they focused on broad sets of state policies, programmes and activities designed to alter market outcomes: policies affecting the range of positions in the labour market, policies affecting recruitment to those positions, and policies that redistribute income to offset market-generated inequalities. Their conclusion is that, while on the surface, 'social citizenship' has expanded in Ireland, this expansion has been nominal rather than real, and has left privilege essentially undisturbed. 'What has evolved is a pay-related welfare state in which minimal levels of universal entitlement to income and services are supplemented by market-based resources' (p. 206).

The claim about the kind of welfare state which has emerged in Ireland is central to the reasons underlying their rejection of industrialism as an inadequate explanatory account. To a large extent, the theory fails because the expansion of social rights in Ireland has been nominal rather than real, and because of 'the failure, thereof, of advancing industrialism and expanding social citizenship to create a more open, achievement-oriented society' (p. 238).[4] Both implicitly and explicitly their account rests on comparisons between Ireland and other welfare states, in particular 'universal' welfare states of the Scandinavian kind (pp. 223–4). Their account implicitly suggests that the theory of industrialism might help explain expansion in welfare effort (by generating an increased surplus to underpin this) but cannot explain why Ireland should have one particular type of outcome rather than another.[5]

On one level, this strongly echoes the critiques of the thesis of industrialism in the wider comparative literature. The initial flowering of post-war welfare states had, perhaps naturally, focused attention on similarities among states; yet, as quantitative cross-national survey techniques became more sophisticated, and as a wider variety of measures of welfare effort were drawn upon, it became clear that there were important qualitative differences between national welfare states. The inability of the logic of industrialism to account for this cross-national variation stimulated the growth of alternative approaches, discussed below. It is worth pausing to consider why the logic of industrialism struggled to explain cross-national diversity. Largely, it was because of the key concepts on which the perspective rested.

The wider manifestation of modernisation theory – which saw all societies as being on a common trajectory of development, with some societies merely 'behind' others but engaged in a process of catching up – collapsed under a weight of evidence which suggested that the processes of industrialisation and modernisation which 'core' countries had followed was proving impossible for 'less-developed' countries to follow. The predictive ability of the theory lacked clout. Likewise, in its manifestation as welfare state theory, it faced similar problems. At the core lies a generalised weakness of structural/ functional accounts. Commenting on the liberal theory of industrialism, Goldthorpe remarked:

> the theory derives its explanatory potential from the notion of the functional exigencies of an industrial society. But it has, then, the problem, like all functionalist theories, of showing why the courses of action that are actually pursued by individuals and collectivities – or at least their outcomes – *should be* ones consistent with the exigencies that are specified. (Goldthorpe, 1992: 422, emphasis in original)

That is, the theory paid little attention to the processes by which the 'demands' of industrial societies were translated into outcomes; outcomes were assumed to be an automatic effect, 'called forth' in some unspecified way by very broad processes. The link between an apparently objective need and a particular response was inadequately conceptualised and theorised. In a similar vein, van Kersbergen notes that functional theories took 'little or no account of the causal mechanisms producing functional responses' (2001: 90). As O'Connell and Rottman note, 'from the standpoint of the logic of industrialism, the role of the state is determined by socioeconomic forces' (1992: 238). Although the process of industrialisation is an important element in the expansion of the Irish welfare state from the 1960s on, outcomes cannot be explained as emerging from impersonal abstract processes. Instead their account suggested that distributional outcomes reflected the ways in which an interventionist state sought to manage social and economic change, implying that the state was 'an independent rather than a dependent variable' (ibid.).

The perspective that the state in Ireland is fundamentally important to understanding distributional outcomes has become almost a truism and a range of analogous accounts have sought to understand and explain these by understanding the dynamics of the Irish state (Breen et al., 1990; Ó Riain and O'Connell, 2000; NESC, 2005). In an important sense, this focus on the state derives from the very factors which make the logic of industrialism particularly problematic in the Irish case. The problem lies with the fact that to a large extent 'modernization theories rest on a crude dichotomy between 'traditional' and 'modern' societies' (Cleary, 2003: 91).

A central problem occurs when the concepts of industrialisation and of modernisation are treated as essentially one process (Goldthorpe, 1992).[6] Contrary to most conceptualisations, it is possible that modernisation may precede industrialisation (Wrigley, 1972; Goldthorpe, 1992). Convergence theory has rightly drawn attention to the importance of profound changes in how societies may be organised, including, for example, shifts in the balance between agricultural and industrial employment, urbanisation, changing family forms, extensions of the franchise and a variety of developments in how governmental power is organised. These, however, are neither universal nor inexorable in their timing, they may take a variety of forms and, moreover, may not occur in combination with one another. This point becomes clear if we consider the long-term evolution of the Irish welfare state.

Inheriting welfare: the legacies of colonialism

Although the 1960s, and in particular the 1970s, mark a major expansion in welfare expenditure, it is debatable whether we can argue that the Irish welfare state 'began' in this period. In fact, considering what the logic of industrialism might say about earlier developments is helpful both in highlighting problems with the general theory and in drawing our attention to why Ireland has been so difficult to either explain or classify. The extent to which it can be said that the welfare state 'began' at some fixed, identifiable point in time is debatable. Nevertheless, it has become conventional to consider the introduction of social insurance in the 1880s as marking an important transition. The transition is measured both quantitatively (in terms of rising social expenditure) and qualitatively (in terms of emerging social citizenship) (Flora and Heidenheimer, 1981; Pierson, 1991). The logic of industrialism perspective has most commonly been applied to explain this transition from poor-law provision to provision 'as of right'. From this narrow perspective, Ireland's welfare experiences can in fact appear mainstream.

As in other states, welfare provision in Ireland has its roots in poor-law legislation (see Appendix I). As elsewhere, early legislation reflected a desire to distinguish between the deserving and the undeserving poor, was localised in character and contained strong punitive elements (Burke, 1987; Pierson, 1991; Goodin and Mitchell, 2000). The roots of contemporary welfare provision in a variety of fields can be traced back to these early beginnings. Similar points can be made about the introduction of later legislation around the period described as the 'birth' of the welfare state. If the introduction of insurance is used to mark the birth of the welfare state, Ireland appears in the mainstream of European welfare development. Workman's compensation in 1897 and health and unemployment insurance in the 1911 National Insurance Act reflected broad European trends (Flora and Alber, 1981). But within this lurks a paradox, which is that the roots of the Irish welfare state pre-date (Irish) industrialisation. It is this (among other factors) that has led Cousins (1997) to argue that any understanding of Irish welfare history must encompass its history of colonialisation. We cannot understand the Irish welfare state solely by looking at Irish conditions, but must look, too, at the factors which led the British state to make the transition from the Poor Law in the early twentieth century. I do not look at these factors here, but few would dispute that the impact of the Industrial Revolution and its attendant social and economic changes is central to our understanding of the origins of social insurance. In this sense, aspects of the Irish welfare state *are* explained by a logic of industrialism – insofar as the theory explains developments in the (then) wider UK. Long before the delayed industrialisation of the country – due to its colonial status – Ireland had an embryonic income-maintenance system predicated on an employment experience created by the process of industrialisation.

A second characteristic of colonialism that mattered in Ireland was that legislation (designed for British industrial conditions) was either applied differently in Ireland or, over time, was shaped by the different Irish social and economic conditions. The early period of the Irish welfare state has been described as reflecting 'colonial paternalism'. Ireland 'was treated differently and less favourably than any other part of the Kingdom, being more like a colony than an integral part of the Union' (Kiely, 1999: 1). The new English Poor Law of 1834 was not extended automatically to Ireland, but followed a long period of debate over the extent to which English solutions were relevant to Irish problems (Burke, 1987). In the event, these solutions proved inadequate given the scale of Irish poverty, exacerbated by the Famine, forcing some abandonment of the all-or-nothing principle in 1847. The growth of a dispensary system providing medical relief to the poor outside the walls also reflected adaptation to Irish conditions. The roots of income support as expressed in the 1847 Poor Relief Extension Act, and the existence of a dispensary system, reflected, then, both the factors which gave birth to the Poor Law in the wider UK *and* indigenous factors which forced adaptation (Burke, 1987). These interactions shaped later developments: for example, as we'll see in more detail later, the 1911 National Insurance Act was not applied in its entirety to Ireland because of the combined impact of the Irish Parliamentary Party and the Church, and the existence of a dispensary system (Barrington, 1987).

We can draw together what have been quite diverse points and point to the single biggest problem with the theory of industrialism for the Irish case, which is that its central suppositions are problematic in the Irish case. As Goldthorpe remarks: 'The underlying assumption of the theory is that pre-industrial society is "traditional" society' (1992: 416). As I discussed above, implicit in many accounts of the impact of industrialisation is a perception that modernisation is a synonym for industrialisation. This perception, however, is undermined by the Irish case. As many theorists have noted, the Irish state played a central role in the industrialisation process in Ireland, and implicit in this analysis is the existence of a developed, modern state *prior* to industrialisation. As Goldthorpe discusses, many of the key aspects of a modern society were in place long before the industrialisation of the 1960s. Ireland had a modern state apparatus and financial system, mass literacy, a market-oriented agricultural sector and a long history of electoral participation in evolving democratic political institutions (Goldthorpe, 1992). The problem with the application of the logic of industrialisation to the Irish case is that the central assumptions of the thesis cannot be applied to a state whose welfare history is shaped by an industrialisation process it did not, in fact experience independently until much later, and whose journey from a 'traditional' to a 'modern' society has been by routes not on the map of comparative theory. The Irish case, then, demonstrates the well-accepted problems functionalist perspectives face when accounting for divergent outcomes, but perhaps, even more importantly, is clearly at odds with the basic preconditions of the theory itself.

One of the central reasons why functionalist accounts have been poor at explaining variation is that they are reliant on processes that are less standard and generalisable than is usually recognised. Flora was clear about the origins of welfare states: 'The modern welfare state is a European invention – in the same way as the nation state, mass democracy, and industrial capitalism. It was born as an answer to problems created by capitalist industrialization; it was driven by the democratic class struggle; and it followed in the footsteps of the nation state' (Flora, 1986: xxi). It is obvious that this creates problems in any attempt to apply welfare state theory outside of Europe. However, it also overstates the extent to which the creation of the nation state, capitalist industrialisation and the democratic class struggle have taken the same form even *within* Europe, as the Irish case demonstrates.

We might, then, wish to turn to theories that have stressed differences rather than similarities in our quest for an understanding of the determinants of welfare development in Ireland. Pre-eminent among these have been theories which have argued that while underlying processes such as industrialisation may be important, we need to understand how their outcomes have been shaped by political actions. Industrialisation helps explain the emergence of social insurance across a range of countries (including, as we have seen, Ireland) – but does not explain the profound variations in these schemes. So, for example, Bismarck and Lloyd George are united by social-policy initiatives featuring social insurance, but divided by administrative details that inaugurated two quite different welfare regimes. Hence Britain and Germany developed in very different ways over the long-term (Clasen, 1994). These differences might be said to owe their origins to the very different constitutional, social and economic context in which policy innovation was located. In Esping-Andersen's terms, the 'class coalitions' in which welfare state regimes were founded explains their past evolution and future prospects (1990: 33). Again, the impact of colonialisation affects how we might approach a consideration of the role of politics in Ireland. If, for example, we consider the period of the 'birth' of the welfare state, we can see that we need to look at the intersection of two political systems. On the one hand, the well-examined politics of the liberal conversion to social reform and, on the other hand, the emerging politics of a very different society, where the social issues that had shaped the birth of modern electoral politics were the relationship between Ireland and the UK, between Catholics and Protestant, and between tenants and farmers (Coakley, 1999: 11). In the next section, I pick up and examine some of these political factors in more detail.

Explaining divergence: 'politics matters'

What might be termed 'first generation' theories of the welfare state left enduring legacies which continue to shape contemporary research, and there is general acceptance that the broad processes of democratisation and industrialisation are central to our understanding of the emergence and development of welfare states. However, as noted above, the increasing scale of research together with methodological innovations clarified the extent of cross-national variation in welfare states, and underlined the shortcomings of the logic of industrialism. It became increasingly clear that there were alternative paths through shared processes, and a growing understanding that outcomes were not automatic, but reflected political processes of varying kinds. There was, in effect, a realisation that 'politics matters' in shaping welfare states (Castles, 1982).

Beginning as a debate with the 'logic of industrialism' this thesis initially sought to counter the view that welfare outcomes were largely automatic, arguing that they clearly reflected political processes which varied across states. Hence it may be true that modern industrial societies generated new needs, but the process by which these needs were translated into policy outcomes involved actors, and it is the cross-national variation in the political capacities of these actors which is central to understanding variation in welfare states. An ever-growing body of research has led to a broad consensus that politics has mattered, but equally there has been a growing realisation that 'not all politics mattered in the same way' (van Kersbergen and Becker, 2002: 193). The gradual maturation of our understanding of how exactly politics might influence welfare outcomes is important, not least because there is a perception that politics has been relatively unimportant in Ireland. As this section discusses in some detail, however, while there are many problems in applying political perspectives to the Irish case, the latter conclusion holds true only if we use a narrow conception of how politics has mattered in shaping welfare outcomes. I begin by clarifying some of the problems with the application of standard theories before turning to argue that as elsewhere, politics has clearly mattered in shaping outcomes in Ireland.

Perhaps the central problem in applying the insights from standard perspectives is that the focus of politically oriented accounts has largely been on political parties, and in particular, on the partisan composition of government. Welfare state theory has stressed that parties matter because, as Castles comments, they have diverse ideological leanings which – through their control of government – have been translated into diverse patterns of policy implementation (1982: 26). Very briefly, the first wave of theorists in the 'politics matters' perspective stressed the centrality of social democratic parties, 'equated with whatever locally constitutes the left' (Esping-Andersen and van Kersbergen, 1992: 189). A large number of mostly quantitative studies 'supported the conclusion that major differences in welfare state spending and entitlements among the capitalist democracies could be explained by the relative success of left parties, particularly Social Democratic parties' (Myles and Quadagno, 2002: 38). The 'social democratic thesis' was gradually broadened to include considerations of the extent to which parties were aligned with strong trade union movements, but the partisan composition of government remained to the forefront of concern.[7]

This narrow focus on parties of the left was gradually broadened to consider other political parties. One of the earliest qualifications was Castles' (1978) contribution which argued that the weakness of the right was central. This view was strengthened by comparative historical research that pointed out that many welfare reforms – most famously, Bismarck's social-insurance innovations – had conservative roots. Arising out of this, religion – or more specifically, Christian democracy – has been posited as important. This thesis is most associated with van Kersbergen (1995), but from quite early on, researchers suggested that religion might be a factor (Stephens, 1979; Wilensky, 1981; Castles 1982). However, it was probably not until Esping-Andersen's (1990) account that it began to be seen as a well-recognised independent variable in its own right. Castles (1994) and van Kersbergen (1995) have helped to clarify the essential argument that Catholicism or Christian democracy can in some ways act as a functional equivalent to social democracy.[8]

The problems with applying the insights from these perspectives to Ireland will be immediately clear to those familiar with the literature on the Irish party system. The parties on which the comparative literature has focused are broadly those identified by Lipset and Rokkan (1967) in their influential account of the development of European party systems. Their work stressed the stability of European 'party families', and accounts for this by seeing them as the product of four great cleavages: a centre–periphery cleavage, a Church–state cleavage, an urban–rural cleavage and a class cleavage. It is the interaction of these core divisions that has created the European party systems, laying down patterns of political organisation that persist, to a greater or less degree, to the present. Comparative welfare state theory has focused on these party families, though all four have not attracted equal attention. However, commenting on the application of comparative theory on party systems to the Irish case, Mair remarked: 'At worst, Ireland is ignored by the comparative literature. At best, it is accorded to a residual category where few of the conventionally accepted theories apply' (1987: 7–8). This presents particular problems for the application of the quantitative cross-national welfare state literature, where the operationalisation of 'partisan control of government' has at times been incongruous in the Irish case.

The social-democratic perspective has one key advantage in terms of its applicability to Ireland – it is relatively easy to identify the central party of the left. However, the 'striking electoral debility of class-based, left-wing parties' (Mair, 1992: 385) together with a fragmented trade union movement have been seen to set Ireland apart from other European countries. But it is when we come to the 'right' of the divide that we really encounter problems in locating Irish parties in comparative typologies. The right is generally considered to include two main kinds of parties: Christian democratic parties, on the one hand, or secular conservative parties, on the other (Gallagher, Laver and Mair, 2001). Both Fianna Fáil and Fine Gael sit uneasily in these categories; Fine Gael is not clearly Christian democratic, nor is Fianna Fáil clearly secular conservative, since both stem from very different origins than either of these two types. We can see the problems for theories of the welfare state if we turn to consider Castles' (1982) comments on classifying parties in support of his thesis that parties of the right have a negative impact on public expenditure. His thesis requires identification of the single, strongest party of the right. This, he claims, presents problems only when the right of the political spectrum is occupied by both a sizeable secular party and a party of Christian democratic persuasion. On the whole, his thesis would prefer only secular parties of the right, since Christian-democratic parties attract strong, cross-class support. The problems should be obvious, then, in the Irish case. In his analysis, Fine Gael is classified as the 'major party of the right' and Fianna Fáil as an 'other governing party'. He does not grapple with the problems involved in this categorisation, which are, perhaps, relatively unimportant for his thesis given Ireland's size and peripherality. But in terms of applying his thesis to Ireland, there are enormous problems in considering whether Irish parties are comparable with parties of the right as conceptualised by his thesis, or indeed, if they are comparable with Christian democratic parties, as conceptualised by other theorists. Thus even when Ireland *is* included in cross-national surveys, the results are not always meaningful.

Moreover, when we consider the party system as a whole, and the pattern of government alteration in particular, we can see why few have pursued explanations which assign a primary role to Irish parties as shapers of welfare state outcomes. During the main period of welfare state expansion in Ireland, the partisan composition of government seems intuitively unrewarding as an explanatory independent variable. As Mair has convincingly argued, we see in this period the emergence of a pattern of competition based on 'two broad coalitions of diverse social groups, two large catch-all electorates which are more or less indistinguishable from one another in terms of class, region or whatever' (Mair, 1987: 40). Since Irish political parties have generally been seen as lacking the 'social bases' that have provided parties in other countries with distinctive stances on social policy, we should not be surprised that few have given them more than cursory attention, and have largely dismissed them as key actors.[9] Hence Curry, for example, remarks: 'While party political ideology may have influenced the shape of social service provision in other countries, its impact in Ireland has not been significant' (2003: 9). Other authors have broadly concurred.

Perhaps the most extensive consideration of the role of parties in shaping welfare outcomes is that of Maguire (1986). She begins by outlining what has been seen as one of the central features of Irish party politics – the absence of parties based on the social cleavages common to other countries, and the gradual emergence of a party system where alternative governments are similar in class terms. She does argue for a role for political factors, but it is not the ideological complexion of political parties which is central. Instead, it is the rise in the political salience of social policy which she sees as contributing to the expansion of welfare from the 1960s. The rise in the political salience of social policy in the period reflects changes in the 'terms of the major political opposition' in the post-war period. The central change is the emergence of the well-known pattern of 'Fianna Fáil against all the rest', identified by Mair (1987), the origins of which lie in the transition period with which this book is concerned. This pattern of competition has distinctive outcomes: 'The net effect of a Fine Gael/Labour Party coalition is to produce a government which is as heterogeneous in terms of its support base as is Fianna Fáil'

(Maguire, 1986: 333). This, she argues, leads to the expectation that government alternation should have little effect for the development of the welfare state. She examines different phases in the development of the welfare state from the Second World War on, primarily through the lens of expenditure, but also through the enactment of 'core' laws. She compares these phases with the composition of government, and concludes that neither in terms of expenditure nor in terms of legislative activity does party alternation in government play a very significant role in the development of the welfare state. She argues then that parties have mattered solely because of the rise in the political salience of social policy, through which electoral competition and 'counter bidding' contribute to explaining expenditure increases.

Only one account engages explicitly with welfare state theory as considered here, and that focuses rather narrowly on the social democratic perspective (O'Connell and Rottman, 1992). They argue that the post-war expansion of the welfare state cannot be explained by the social democratic thesis 'since the welfare state expanded in Ireland in spite of the weakness of left-wing political parties, and neither the timing of that expansion nor the nature of the new citizenship rights can be explained by reference to working class strength' (1992: 239). They conclude that 'there is no simple correspondence between political parties and welfare issues', but do suggest that electoral politics have played a role in welfare state expansion. In this they concur with Maguire (1986) that the increased saliency of welfare issues to party competition was important in explaining expansion.

The conclusion to be drawn from these accounts, perhaps, is that if politics is interpreted narrowly to mean the partisan composition of government, then politics has not mattered to any real extent in Ireland. Should we interpret politics more broadly to mean the effects of electoral competition, then we might say that party competition increased the pressures for welfare state expansion. Finally, embedded within O'Connell and Rottman's (1992) account and discussed at more length below, is the possibility that social class interests have played a role, but not via the standard route of competition for control of government. None of these accounts seems compatible with a comparative literature which largely concludes that 'the dominant political coloring of the incumbent government – social democratic, Christian democratic, or secular center and right – over the three or four decades after the war is the most important determinant of the kind of welfare state that a given country had in the early 1980s' (Huber and Stephens, 2001: 1). Hence, the Irish welfare state might thus be fairly definitively a 'counter factual' and politics, in one of its most fundamental incarnations at any rate, might be seen not to matter much at all. However, this conclusion seems unmerited if we consider both the role of parties in Ireland and the nature of comparative theory in rather more detail.

Politics and the Irish welfare state

Although this chapter has stressed the extent to which party politics seems to have mattered little in shaping welfare outcomes, it is clear that this does not apply when we consider the Irish welfare state in a longer historical timeframe, and look back before the expansionary period. This period has sometimes been seen as rather uneventful in social-policy terms, as Maguire notes: 'The period between the attainment of independence and the end of World War II saw few new developments in social policy. The existing institutions were taken over as they stood by the incoming regime and continued to operate in a relatively unchanged fashion for the following two decades. Social policy was low on the list of priorities of the newly independent state' (Maguire, 1986: 245). But for other authors, the 1930s were more important from both a social-policy perspective and a political-party perspective. Cousins is not alone in arguing that 'the lack of development of the social welfare system up to 1932 and the subsequent growth in the 1930s were linked to the differing political ideologies of the Cumann na nGaedheal and Fianna Fáil parties' (1995: 42). Dunphy (1995), Lee (1989) and Mair (1987) also stress the centrality of social policy to political strategies in the period.

In fact, the inter-war period is important for students of social policy for a variety of reasons. For one thing, it marks the emergence of an independent policy process. The characteristics taken on in this period were crucial in shaping later developments during more activist periods. As in earlier periods, we can see important differences between Irish experiences and those of other welfare states. In other (European) welfare states, most of the central characteristics of the political system were in place. In Ireland, however, this period marks both the foundation of the state and the establishment of a distinctive party system, though within the context of a longer electoral history. These often momentous events occurred, however, *after* the introductory stage of social insurance and other aspects of the Irish welfare state, and this accounts for some of the difficulties in categorising the Irish experience. Hence, from the perspective of 'institutions and practices', as well as from a 'politics matters' view, it is worth noting briefly some features which emerged from 1922 on.

Despite Maguire's comments above, the inter-war period was one where some administrative reform did occur, largely in the interests of greater efficiency (Barrington, 1987). The outcome was central-isation under the control of central government. The Ministers and Secretaries Act of 1924 established the doctrine of ministerial respon-sibility, with the establishment of the minister as a 'corporation sole'. As later chapters discuss, this was to have an important effect on the context of social-policy formation, with politicians acquiring and developing strong conventions shaping their policy preferences. The Department of Local Government and Public Health became, as the title suggests, the key department for health-related functions. Also, reform of local government and the Poor Law saw amalgamation and rationalisation. The extent to which this involved improving relief functions is debatable. Lee remarks acerbically that 'The government introduced Poor Law legislation in 1923 which substituted for what the Democratic Programme had called "the present odious, degrading and foreign poor law system", an odious, degrading and native system' (1989: 124). In terms of reform and innovation, then, con-servatism and fiscal liberalism has been said to be the central feature of social policy in the first decade of the new state (Cousins, 2005). A key question concerns the *source* of this conservatism. That is, what accounts for the undoubtedly conservative nature of social policy in the new state?

One answer is that the source lies in the nature of the state, rather than in political parties. O'Connell and Rottman suggest an important role for a 'post-colonial legacy' which can be seen in the policy stance of the state itself. 'The Department of Finance, which, following the Treasury model inherited from the British adminis-tration system played a dominant role in state policy formation for much of Ireland's post independence history, was opposed in prin-ciple to increases in state expenditure and taxes, and in particular to increased commitments to social welfare' (1992: 231). Undoubtedly, as Fanning (1978) clarifies, and as this book indicates, the Department of Finance has been a consistent opponent of public spending. But there is a major problem in assigning the state bureaucracy respon-sibility for the direction of social policy in the period. The problem is that the policy stance of the state shifted significantly with a change in the partisan composition of government in 1932. This raises the clear possibility that party politics, as much as inherited post-colonial legacies, played a role in shaping policy outcomes.

Although it seems clear that bureaucrats in the period had strong and distinctive conservative views on public expenditure, Cumann na nGaedheal itself shared much of this economic conservatism. Its adherence to classical liberal economics was not merely a 'colonial legacy', but was rooted in its understanding of the nature of Irish society. Mair (1987), commenting on Cumann na nGaedheal's conservatism, points out that its constituency tended to reflect its conservative bias, being strong in areas dominated by large, commercial farming interests. Both Barrington (1987) and Lee (1989) have suggested that the primacy of agriculture was a key factor in understanding why the focus of early reform was on economy and efficiency. Cumann na nGaedheal believed that economic development in Ireland would, of necessity, be based on the agricultural sector. Hence, farmers' costs had to be kept low, given the centrality of agriculture to the economy, and, consequently rates, which were seen to have an impact on farming costs, must be kept low too (Barrington, 1987: 99).

This view provided much of the rationale for the austerity of the first independent government, notorious among social-policy students and contemporaries for its decision to reduce the old-age pension as an economy measure. This broad ethos was applied to social policy in general, and also to the insurance system in particular. In 1924, for example, the government's contribution to the insurance fund was reduced. But while Cumann na nGaedheal was in the process of developing an economic policy based both on inherited ideas and on its appraisal of Irish conditions, an opposition was emerging which differed substantially on both of these perspectives. Fianna Fáil emerged in the late twenties and early thirties with an appeal to different support bases and, consequently, different socio-economic policies. It appealed to the less well-off – and this included the less well-off among the agricultural population as well as the urban working class. Its stance on social policy can be explained by its desire to appeal to this distinctive constituency in a way which differentiated it from Cumann na nGaedheal. Once in power, Fianna Fáil initiated welfare reforms designed to appeal to the constituency which had won it power (Dunphy 1995).

Hence, a number of income-maintenance schemes were inaugurated in the period – a sharp contrast with the retrenchment of its predecessors. As well as a wet-time insurance scheme in 1942 for workers in the building trade, a widows' and orphans' pension was introduced in 1935. This included both a contributory and a non-contributory scheme. Both were necessary because of the limited scope of the insurance scheme, with only 32 per cent of the male population of insurable age covered by social insurance (Commission on Social Welfare, 1986). Widespread unemployment in the 1930s, coupled with the narrow coverage of social insurance, meant that an unemployment assistance scheme was introduced in 1933. Housing was another central area of activity. In the field of social insurance, the main developments were again administrative. As outlined above, social insurance was shaped by British imperatives, with the outcome that friendly societies had a role in welfare provision. Consequently, friendly societies also played a role in Ireland, though they were far fewer in number because of the small size of the industrial workforce. By 1933, a variety of problems led to reform. Centrally, societies catering for higher-risk groups were encountering severe financial problems, while wealthier societies were able to offer groups enhanced benefits. By 1933, there were approximately 474,000 insured persons in the state, catered for by sixty-five approved societies with membership varying from fifty-five to over 100,000. The National Health Insurance Act 1933 allowed for the amalgamation of all these societies into the National Health Insurance Society (NHIS) over a three-year period (Barrington, 1987: 126). The Bishop of Clonfert, Dr John Dignan, became first chairman and was to be an important actor in the post-war-reform period.[10]

Hence, while it is true that in many respects 'the social services which existed at the end of World War II differed little in their essential characteristics from those of the early 1920s' (Maguire, 1986: 247), nevertheless the period was one where social policy clearly emerged as a major marker of party-political differences. The perspective that political parties were not major actors then clearly relates mainly to the expansionary period of the welfare state, following the emergence of a particular pattern of party competition, producing governments which are broadly similar in class terms. Since all parties were broadly positive to welfare, the partisan composition of government has been seen to be irrelevant for welfare expansion. However, it is not at all clear that a shared commitment to expanding social expenditure is a sufficient reason to ignore the role of parties.

At the core of the comparative theoretical perspectives that stress the importance of politics are arguments that parties matter not merely because they differ in terms of commitment to, or opposition to, public spending, but also because not all spending counts equally, and because the input of parties affects outcomes in ways which expenditure measures alone cannot capture (Esping-Andersen, 1990; van Kersbergen, 1995; Huber, Ragin and Stephens, 1993; Huber and Stephens, 2001). Hence, for example, while both social democracy and Christian democracy might have a positive effect on welfare state expenditure, they may vary substantially in the composition and impact of that expenditure, reflecting their different ideologies and constituencies. Among a variety of differences, it has been argued that Christian democracy has focused more on transfers and has a less redistributive impact, while public delivery and financing of services is central to social democracy, and this has a more redistributive outcome (Huber, Ragin and Stephens, 1993; van Kersbergen, 1995).

This insight points us to the importance of what has been termed the 'dependent variable problem' (Green-Pedersen, 2004). Debates about the nature and extent of welfare state retrenchment have clarified an already recognised problem, referred to in the introduction. This is that it is not always clear exactly what constitutes the welfare state, a point that becomes apparent when we attempt to evaluate competing explanatory frameworks. Hence, Esping-Andersen (1990) argued that expenditure levels, long relied on a key way of measuring welfare effort, were not on their own sufficient to distinguish between different kinds of welfare states.[11] The implication for this argument is that it is necessary to give greater attention to what might indicate the impact of parties, over and above levels of spending. Arguing that all Irish parties were 'pro-welfare' tells us little about what was envisioned by them in terms of degree of welfare and in terms of welfare for whom. Moreover, Irish parties may have been *united* in being pro-welfare, but *divided* by differing perceptions of what this implied in practice. So, for example, Mair has argued that beneath the consensus on welfarism, 'the language and ideology within which that commitment was expressed differed markedly across the political spectrum' (1987: 208). In particular, he argues that these differences lay in contrasting emphases on redistributive issues. We know from comparative studies that the way in which spending is structured can have profound differences for the quality of welfare experienced by citizens, in terms, for example, of whether it contributes to maintaining status differentials, or whether it contributes to greater equality. On this latter point, it is clear that increased expenditure has not necessarily led to more egalitarian outcomes in Ireland.

Hence Maguire's account argued that 'the re-distributive process operates unevenly from a social class perspective, treating the property owning classes in a relatively favourable fashion' (1986: 320). This perspective has been endorsed by many other authors. For example, both O'Connell and Rottman (1992) and Ó Riain and O'Connell (2000) point to the 'pay-related' and 'two-tiered' nature of the Irish welfare state. Although these latter accounts are clearly state-centred, both draw heavily and explicitly on political factors to explain these outcomes. Thus Ó Riain and O'Connell's account of the state's complementary developmental and distributive roles contains numerous references to politics, and to the specific kind of party system which exists in Ireland. 'Both the developmental and distributive strategies had their roots in the catch-all parties through which the state was embedded in society' (2000: 336–7). Likewise, O'Connell and Rottman stress that their account is one where 'political factors are subsumed within the state centred approach' (1992: 239). The class structure, its transformation, and the political organisation of class interests *have* in fact been drawn on to explain distinctive Irish welfare outcomes. Perhaps the central question then is less about whether politics has mattered, and more about whether it has mattered in ways which are captured by standard theoretical perspectives, or in ways which have mattered elsewhere.

A central argument of this book is that while Irish parties do not map precisely onto the party systems of the core literature, this does not mean that we cannot draw on that literature to enhance our understanding of Irish outcomes. While the ambiguous assumptions of comparative theory are problematic, recent more nuanced accounts of political influences are increasingly applicable. O'Connell and Rottman (1992) suggested that one of the distinctive aspects of how politics affected outcomes in Ireland is that the 'emergent welfare state was shaped to attract the support of the middle classes; it was not targeted at the working class, as it had been in other European countries from the 19th century onwards' (1992: 239). However, as noted above, the assumption that it is working class strength which is the primary variable, or that it is parties of the left which are the key actors, has been undermined by research pointing to the influence of right party strength (Castles, 1982) cross-class Christian democratic parties (van Kersbergen, 1995), and parties and movements of the self-employed and agrarians (Esping-Andersen, 1990; Baldwin, 1990).

Nowhere is this clearer than in the welfare-regime literature, and in particular in the original formulation by Esping-Andersen who argued that welfare-state construction depended on political coalition building, a process which involved both rural classes and the middle classes (1990: 29-31). Varying class coalitional strategies lead, in effect, to qualitatively different distributional outcomes. It does not stretch these insights to breaking point to suggest that the class coalitional strategies embedded in a catch-all party system may constitute an explanatory factor or independent variable helping to account for distinctive Irish outcomes. This is particularly the case since few now argue for monocausal explanations of welfare state expansion, or indeed, retrenchment (Allan and Scruggs, 2004: 497). Moreover, it might be argued that this perspective is in tune what was termed 'a new emphasis on essential comparability' which stressed that the policy stances and strategic behaviour of Irish parties were in line with those of parties in other countries (Mair, 1992: 383. See also Laver, 1992; Adshead, 2004).

What conclusion can we draw from this extended discussion? It is clear that, at certain periods, politics has mattered, but has done so in ways which have been little examined. The period covered by this book has been described as a pivotal one for understanding the dynamics of party politics, and it is also a period about which much has been written from a social-policy perspective, given the controversial nature of social policy in the period. But these two perspectives have rarely overlapped. To the extent that politics has been seen to matter from the perspective of social policy in this period, parties have fared very poorly relative to the attention given to other actors, such as the Church, other key interest groups, individuals and the central bureaucracy. What is missing is a sense of the *actual* way in which Irish political parties have conceptualised social policy and how they may have contributed to shaping policy outcomes, and this is discussed throughout the following chapters.

Although it is possible to argue that a close examination of the policy process reveals that politics has mattered in Ireland (albeit in a manner imperfectly captured by much theory), there is one central objection that may be launched against this thesis. This is that political interests may be shaped and constrained by the institutional context within which they are located. It has been argued that it is with the state, and its particular institutional configuration that we should be concerned, since, in the Irish case in particular but also in general, states must be considered to have their own interests to pursue.

A role for the state: the institutionalist critique

In her seminal introduction to *Bringing the State Back In*, Skocpol pointed to a contemporary upsurge of interest in the state: 'Whether as an object of investigation or as something invoked to explain outcomes of interest, the state as an actor or an institution has been highlighted in an extraordinary outpouring of studies by scholars of diverse theoretical proclivities from all of the major disciplines' (Skocpol, 1985: 3). Irish academics were not immune from this development. King's lament that there was 'little systematic study of the role of the state in the contemporary Irish political system' (1986: 81) swiftly became of historical interest only, as the state became a key focus of study across a range of disciplines. As discussed in more detail below, scholars from diverse fields have argued that distributional outcomes in Ireland have been shaped by the manner in which an activist state sought to initiate and manage social and economic change in the context of growing internationalisation (Breen et al., 1990; Peillon, 1996; O'Connell and Rottman, 1992; Ó Riain and O'Connell, 2000). Perhaps no other perspective from the international literature has been so extensively utilised to explain welfare outcomes in Ireland – possibly because of the perceived explanatory failure of other core accounts. I discuss these views in more detail below, but before doing so I locate them briefly in the context of the wider comparative literature.

Although the perspectives outlined in the previous two sections may be divided by whether the emphasis is on convergence or divergence, they have all focused on shared processes and patterns in search of generalisable theory transcending national boundaries. This concern with what has sometimes been termed 'grand theory' was assisted by methodological developments allowing for ever-more sophisticated measurements that appeared to allow these theories to be empirically validated (Amenta, 1993). Comparativists sought to cut through 'idiosyncratic, country specific categories' in search of broadly applicable concepts and variables (Thelen and Steinmo, 1992: 4). But despite the proliferation of cross-national studies, not all questions concerning difference were satisfactorily resolved. Continuing attempts to grapple with the tensions between convergence and divergence led to the emergence of theories that were said to 'emphasize the irregularities rather than the regularities of history and demonstrate the limits of universal causal models' (Immergut, 1998: 15).

This latter point is best illustrated by considering Skocpol's (1992, 1995) work on the US. Skocpol is a useful starting point, as both a leading scholar in the field, and as someone whose insights speak remarkably clearly to Irish concerns. American theorists, much like Irish theorists, had long struggled to locate the 'exceptional' US welfare state in the comparative literature. One of Skocpol's most incisive insights was that the problem lay less with the precise nature of its welfare state, and more with the assumptions of core theoretical perspectives. Perhaps the starting point was a perception that many of the broad processes taken for granted by standard theories of the welfare state simply did not apply to the USA, either in their focus on convergence or their explanations of variation. In particular, the paths to industrialisation and democratisation (combined in many theories into a grand process of modernisation) were highly distinctive in the USA, and were in many ways contrary to the basic assumptions of much welfare state theory (Weir et al., 1988; Amenta, 1998).

Skocpol argued that a central problem was that standard theories of the welfare state 'have been argued with certain state and party structures in mind, namely, centralized and bureaucratized states with parliamentary parties dedicated to pursuing policy programs in the name of entire classes or other broad, nation-spanning collectivities' (Skocpol, 1995: 19) The USA, however, had very distinctive patterns of state formation: hence, for example, mass electoral democratisation preceded state bureaucratisation in the USA in a way which did not occur in Europe (Skocpol, 1992). Summarising the work of Skocpol and other US authors, Béland and Hacker remark that: 'As a consequence, the US entered the 20th century with a relatively undeveloped, patronage-ridden national administrative state, non-programmatic political parties, and a fragmented constitutional structure that fostered a highly decentralised form of federalism – all of which have hindered the passage and expansion of national programmes of social insurance and assistance' (2004: 45). Dissatisfaction with grand theories based on taken-for-granted processes of industrialisation, democratisation and state formation was thus instrumental in the emergence of this perspective. American scholars were to the forefront of the field, but their insights were rapidly adopted by students of other countries. State-centred perspectives consequently began to look not merely at grand processes, or at organised interests, but at the distinctive institutional structures within which these were located (Thelen and Steinmo, 1992).

What then of Ireland? As noted above, the state has featured prominently in a number of accounts focusing on the distributional and other impacts of an activist developmental state. Allowing for differences of focus and interpretation, these have generally noted the distinctiveness of the Irish welfare state, variously described as 'pay-related', 'two-tiered' or 'three-tiered', and suggested that these outcomes can be traced back to the specific nature of the Irish state (Breen et al., 1990; O'Connell and Rottman, 1992; Ó Riain and O'Connell, 2000). Hence, Ó Riain and O'Connell point to the role of the state 'in inserting Ireland into international economic processes, reshaping both the economy and the welfare state in the process' (2000: 311). The outcome of the state's complementary roles in the developmental and distributional spheres has been 'growth with inequality'. While there has been some commitment to solidarity, largely expressed through the development of the social insurance system and the provision of basic levels of services, the way in which the public and private sector interact allows for market generated advantages to be used to supplement basic social citizenship rights. Perhaps the clearest example of this is the 'three-tiered' pension system which consists of a means-tested non-contributory pension, a more generous contributory pension, and a third tier composed of the combination of contributory state pension and private and occupational pensions. 'The contributory pension forms a floor for middle-class employees, who can combine a social insurance pension with occupational pension entitlements, private pensions and savings, all subsidised through tax expenditures, to achieve a more comfortable standard of living in old age' (p. 327). A core suggestion of these accounts is that state-driven development is one explanation of why 'the Irish welfare state expanded in so distinctive a manner and with consequences that proved to be so favourable to privilege' (O'Connell and Rottman, 1992: 206).

A key question obviously concerns why state-centred approaches might more usefully explain these outcomes than the logic of industrialism or politics centred accounts. O'Connell and Rottman suggest that the distinctiveness of the Irish case, which involves a combination of a 'dependent, peripheral and relatively less-developed economic structure with the liberal democratic political institutions of an advanced capitalist society' (1992: 230) puts the focus on the state as an actor: 'Both the logic of industrialism and social democratic approaches view the state as determined by, or responsive to, societal forces and interests. The state centred approach, in contrast, regards the state as an organisation with interests of its own to pursue' (p. 208). Thus, as noted above, the state must be treated as an independent variable (p. 238). Perhaps the most important general point to be taken from O'Connell and Rottman is the idea that Irish distinctiveness 'requires' that a priority be given to the structure and policies of the state itself. There are then parallels with the concerns of US scholars, in that state-centred perspectives seem rewarding in explaining outcomes in countries where patterns of state-formation, democratisation and modernisation diverge from those on which the core literature is predicated. A central concern, however, is whether an approach which might be said to prioritise national specificities can either draw from or contribute to a wider comparative literature.

From the state to institutions: narrowing the focus?

The Irish accounts cited above are probably best located in the context of state-centred perspectives for whom debates about degrees of autonomy and state effectiveness are central (Peillon, 1996). As noted above, their accounts of the role of the state (and of its ability for autonomous action) are qualified by reference to wider factors, such as its 'embeddedness in society through a particular form of catch-all politics and its flexible and adaptive character' (Ó Riain and O' Connell, 2000: 335). However, as Béland and Hacker (2004) remark, state-centred accounts in the comparative literature have 'evolved into a broader perspective in which state autonomy is less a central claim and a variety of arguments about the role of institutions and policy feedback effects (sometimes uneasily) coexist' (2004: 45). Initial, wide-ranging concerns with state capacities and autonomy have increasingly generated specific hypotheses about the impact of variations in state structures on social policy. The concept of 'the state' has accordingly been decomposed in a variety of ways, as theorists have chosen to focus on diverse but increasingly specific institutional configurations. In the process, the term state-centred has largely been replaced by the term institutionalist, a process which has brought greater clarity and enhanced comparability, but perhaps reflects reduced ambition.

In Breen et al.'s (1990) formulation, the state is 'a type of organisation', a defining characteristic of which is that only one such organisation can exist in a society at a given time:

> In practice, of course, we can identify a diversity of organisations as constituting 'the State'. These share a common purpose of governing, a monopoly on the use of coercion, and a form of administration based on an executive comprised of individuals who act in the capacity of office holders within carefully specified rules and regulations. The State is the structure that underlies and unites these agencies, offices and individuals, a structure that can be thought of as either a set of organising principles or of regulations. (1990: 12)

The idea that the state can be thought of as a set of organising principles or regulations is reminiscent of a common definition of institutions as the 'rules of the game'. But there is profound disagreement within the field as to what exactly counts as a rule – formal rules (presidential versus parliamentary systems) versus informal rules (shared social norms or culture) (Rothstein, 1996: 145). Skocpol (1995), for example, defines her key institutional parameters very broadly. Describing how 'state formation' has influenced US social provision, she describes this as including 'constitution making, involvement in wars, electoral democratization and bureaucratization – large-scale historical processes, in short, whose forms and timing have varied significantly across capitalist industrialising countries' (1995: 19). The attraction of such a broad definition of institutions is obvious – the pitfalls of an approach in which virtually anything appears to be an institution are likewise obvious. As Rothstein comments, 'if it means everything, then it means nothing' (1996: 145).

Consequently, theorists are increasingly tending to focus on narrower 'intermediate level institutions'. Hence Thelen and Steinmo, for example, include 'the rules of electoral competition, the structure of party systems, the relations among various branches of government, and the structure and organisation of economic actors like trade unions' (1992: 2). While Guy Peters et al. remark that this may still be 'so inclusive that the approach becomes difficult to falsify' (2005: 1286) this narrower perspective has generated useful insights which do seem to be generalisable in some key respects, as the following example illustrates.

At the heart of institutionalist perspectives is the idea that, for a variety of reasons, different institutional configurations generate different outcomes (Maioni, 1997). For example, one focus has been on how interest groups have been shaped by their institutional context which may create incentives for groups to organise, may shape preferences in particular directions, or make some types of action easier than others (Immergut, 1992; Pierson, 1993; Skocpol, 1995, *inter alia*. Hence, Immergut focused on the differing political institutions of Switzerland, France and the UK to explain why medical interests varied in their ability to shape outcomes. She argued that 'social demands must be channelled through political institutions if they are to have an impact on political decisions', and suggested that these institutions can provide incentives, opportunities or constraints (Immergut, 1992: 19). She suggested that, rather than thinking of veto *groups* (Heclo, 1974), it is more useful to think of veto *points* in particular systems. This approach has become an important component of theories attempting to explain retrenchment: certain structural legacies are said to make retrenchment either more or less feasible (Pierson, 1996). Subsequently, various measures of constitutional structures and/or veto points have been incorporated into the comparative cross-national literature with some explanatory success (Huber, Ragin and Stephens, 1993; Huber and Stephens, 2001; Schmidt, 2002).

In terms of the usefulness of the institutionalist perspective to the Irish situation, it is helpful to consider the application of institutionalist perspectives in two main ways. The first is in terms of the general idea of institutions as sets of formal and informal rules or as the institutional context within which policy is made, as outlined above. The second approach is in terms of ideas usually considered under the headings of policy feedback and path dependence. Effectively, these concepts suggest that decisions about institutions and policies made in the past shape later decisions, and also that 'policies themselves must be seen as politically consequential structures' (Pierson, 1993: 624). Thus 'once a path is taken then it can become "locked in" as all the relevant actors adjust their strategies to accommodate the prevailing pattern' (Thelen, 1999: 385). While the precise implications of this are the subject of intense debate, there is a broad acceptance of Heclo's early insight that that 'the content of a policy can itself be a crucial independent factor in producing effects on the policy-making process' (Heclo, 1974: 5), and of the argument that political actors are constrained to varying degrees by historical legacies. Although differentiating the two perspectives within institutionalism this sharply is in some ways an artificial distinction, it is analytically useful in considering its usefulness to Ireland. I begin by making some points about the 'rules of the game' in the Irish context, which are then examined in more detail in later chapters.

All states vary in their institutional structure to some extent. Hence the policy process must be seen as being located in a particular institutional framework that varies from state to state, which may shape the policy preferences of actors in various ways and, hence, affect policy outcomes (Steinmo, 1989).While this institutional framework varies, political scientists and others with an interest in political institutions have nevertheless tried to generalise about 'packages' of institutional frameworks in a manner reminiscent of regime theory in welfare studies (Rothstein, 1996). It has been suggested that Irish institutions are a hybrid, or mixture, of models (Gallagher, 1999). One of the basic distinctions within parliamentary systems has been between a consensus model and a majoritarian (Westminster) model. The key features of a majoritarian model are 'single-party and bare-majority cabinets, no effective separation of power between government and parliament, unbalanced bicameralism, a two-party system, a plurality electoral system, unitary and centralised government, and the absence of a written constitution' (p. 178). The key features of a consensus model, on the other hand, are 'government by grand coalition, a genuine separation of powers between government and parliament, balanced bicameralism, a multi-party system, a proportional representation electoral system, and a written constitution' (p. 178). It can be seen that Ireland has features of both models: it has obviously been strongly influenced by the Westminster model, but has key features of the consensus model, too. In fact, the post-war period with which this book is concerned is one that sees institutional development on a number of important levels; in particular, by seeing the emergence of coalition government in what had, until then, been a majoritarian system. This, in turn, fundamentally influenced the shape of the party system in the direction we have already looked at. As the following chapters clarify, the institutional context of Irish politics has structured outcomes in a variety of ways, in particular, by mediating the way in which class interests were expressed politically, but also by shaping the policy preferences of policy-makers. These ideas are explored, in particular, in Chapters 3 and 6.

The second area around which institutionalist ideas are organised is that concerning ideas of policy feedbacks and path dependency. The extent to which this aspect of institutionalist thinking has influenced Irish researchers is limited. There are a variety of accounts that, while not consciously institutionalist, clearly echo institutionalist concerns. The idea that earlier choices shape later ones is to some extent intuitive. Hence, as early as 1969, Ó Cinnéide, commenting on the home-assistance scheme, remarked: 'The various features of the present service can be traced back in unbroken lines to administrative and legislative decisions made over a period of a century and a half' (p. 307). Since the late 1990s however, accounts of the welfare state have emerged which draw explicitly on the institutionalist literature. Healy's (1998) account, from the perspective of sociological institutionalism, is a very broad overview, and pays little heed to specific outcomes, but began the process of integrating comparative insights. Millar's (2003) application of diverse institutionalist perspectives to a case-study of the mother-and-child scheme usefully points to the value of including a consideration of inherited policy legacies, the structure of the political system and the wider political culture in understanding outcomes. However, an article length study which combines an overview of the mother-and-child scheme, with a description and application of the three 'new institutionalisms' is clearly limited in its ability to provide detailed analysis. Adshead and Millar (2004) apply the concept of path dependence to the Irish health sector in support of their claim that Ireland belongs in the Catholic corporatist regime, and this general argument is examined in some detail in chapter three. The latter two accounts suggest that institutionalist insights are attractive to Irish researchers., but the perspective has not yet received much critical analysis.

It is worth drawing together briefly why statist/institutionalist perspectives seem to be promising in explaining Irish outcomes, before pointing to some now acknowledged weaknesses. A central reason for their attractiveness is that, as has been discussed, institutionalist perspectives are, almost by definition, well targeted at understanding national specificities. Whether in relation to very broad processes of state formation, or to the more narrow understandings of intermediate level institutions, institutionalist perspectives emphasising the 'irregularities' of history appear particularly attractive to the Irish case. The discussion in this chapter has pointed to a variety of features which frequently conspire to present Ireland as a counterfactual: the distinctiveness of the modernisation process, the hybridity of political institutions, the peculiarities of the party system, and running through all these, the experiences of colonialisation within a broadly European context. Institutionalist perspectives, and perhaps particularly the case-study-oriented historical institutionalist variant, easily incorporate these as no more than the specific institutional configuration within which the policy process is located. The further application of institutionalism, however, is likely to point to both limitations and unresolved issues.

The most common criticism made about historical institutionalism 'is that although it is well suited for explaining the persistence of policies, it is much less capable of explaining change in those same policies' (Guy Peters et al., 2005: 1288). In this sense, the perspective risks becoming effectively a functionalist one (Guy Peters et al., 2005; Hogan, 2005). One problem concerns insufficient definitional rigour around key concepts such as path dependence, critical juncture, sequencing and so on (Pierson, 2004; Hogan, 2005; Guy Peters et al., 2005). Thus there is no 'set of universally applicable criteria' defining what counts as a critical juncture, for example (Hogan, 2005: 274). Identifying whether significant change has occurred – as opposed say, to incremental change or indeed persistence – is thus to a large extent a matter of the researcher's subjective interpretation. This partially reflects the largely qualitative methodology of historical institutionalism (Guy Peters et al., 2005: 1286–7).

More fundamentally, perhaps, is the risk that institutionalist perspectives have perhaps 'abandoned the ambiguity of a larger question for the certainty of a smaller and less important one' (Baldwin, 1990: 47). This problem has become more visible in the transition from state-centred to intuitionalist perspectives. If we turn our attention briefly back to state-centred accounts of the Irish welfare state, it is clear that broadly political factors were subsumed or otherwise harnessed into these accounts. As described above, the nature of the class structure and its transformation, and the mediation of these interests by a particular type of party system, were incorporated as central factors constraining or motivating state action. This raises questions about definitions of the state perhaps – for example, whether action by government should be considered action by the state, or action by party politicians and thus by political actors, and about whether this distinction is important. More fundamentally though, it points to the continuing importance of society-oriented accounts, and to the possibility that as institutionalist perspectives have narrowed the focus of attention on precise types of institutional structures, and on policies as key objects of studies, they may have de-emphasised the role of politics. Guy Peters et al. (2005) suggest that 'most scholars working in this approach, especially those focusing upon the state, overemphasise the importance of civil servants and bureaucrats in policymaking processes, belittling excessively the continuing (and on occasions elemental) significance of politicians as creative actors' (2005: 1283). More fundamentally, Gilbert and Howe suggest that it is possible that statist or institutional perspectives 'oversimplify societal forces and ignore class conflict within and beyond the state' (1991: 205). The intermediate-level focus of institutionalists, and their stress on venues or mediating structures may lead to relatively banal understandings of outcomes (Guy Peters et al., 2005). This may be a particular risk for scholars of the Irish welfare state, since the acknowledged centrality of state led action combined with a party system lacking clear ideological contours can easily conspire to de-emphasise macro-level concepts such as class.

Conclusion

On the surface, the debates explored in this chapter may seem somewhat abstract and esoteric, particularly when explored, as here, through a historical case-study of what may seem like a relatively obscure piece of legislation. However, although this book is a detailed case-study of one policy area, and is thus clearly both nationally and historically specific, nevertheless its underlying concerns are comparative and contemporary. The questions raised have a clear relevance to our understanding of the contemporary welfare state, and to its future potentialities. The most recent road-map for welfare in Ireland calls for the creation of a 'developmental welfare state' (NESC, 2003, 2005). NESC's account of the potentialities for the future clearly draws heavily on the theoretical literature referred to above, in particular, their description of the hybrid Irish welfare state, which 'resists easy classification' (2005: 140): 'The more mature welfare states of other European countries have more defined ideological contours than the Irish welfare state for historical reasons' (ibid). An obvious question concerns what these historical reasons are, and this, in effect, is the key concern of this book.

However, the discussion of the welfare state literature in Ireland has pointed to a number of problems in attempting to understand the determinants of the Irish welfare state. Although the arguments above pointed to some explanatory potential in each of the perspectives outlined, none was entirely satisfactory. We could, on the one hand, stress similarities in the Irish experience: broad economic processes have left their mark, competing social groups have struggled to have their interests expressed, and have been constrained by the institutional structure in which they have been located. To some extent, standard welfare theory captures all this – even if no *one* theory can combine them. On the other hand, we could lay our stress on differences: the path to industrialisation and modernisation escapes theory, the party system struggles to find a home in comparative theory, and there are distinctive aspects to the structure of the Irish state. It seems likely that it is precisely here, where the disjuncture between standard accounts and Irish experiences is most visible, that we might find answers to the contested question of the nature of the Irish welfare state.

An obvious question though is whether in fact there *are* any puzzling aspects to the Irish welfare state. The argument that there are questions to be answered rests mostly on the perception that there are particular difficulties in locating the Irish welfare state in existing typologies, a perception which as noted above has become embedded in the contemporary policy process (NESC, 2003, 2005). However, it may well be the case that Ireland is either not puzzling at all, or at any rate, no more puzzling than any other state. Certainly, there is one dimension of the Irish welfare state on which it might be said that there is a broad consensus in terms of comparability. This is that gender has been a core principle structuring outcomes across a range of policy sectors, and that consequently the Irish welfare state is a prime exemplar of a 'strong' male breadwinner model (Lewis, 1992). There is general agreement that this has been particularly visible in social security policy, at least until the very recent past (Yeates, 1997; Cook and McCashin, 1997; Cousins, 1995, 2003; McCashin 2004). As Yeates has argued, 'gender inequality has been an organising concept of the system from the foundation of the social welfare system in the nineteenth-century to the present day' (Yeates, 1997: 145). I consider some specific aspects of these arguments very briefly in chapter two, but the focus of this book is on approaches to comparability on which there is more division, viewed through the lens of the three theoretical perspectives outlined above, and the gender dimensions of the policy process in social security are therefore not further explored here.

As the introduction noted, while some scholars have stressed hybridity and heterogeneity, others have concluded that classification is relatively straightforward. Indeed, Adshead and Millar have argued trenchantly that 'the persistent presentation of "Ireland as the counter factual" in comparative work is damaging to Irish policy studies and analysis' (2004: 2). Certainly, Ireland has been assigned with varying degrees of confidence to *either* the liberal/Anglo-Saxon world, *or* the Catholic corporatist world.

On the one hand, inheritances from the colonial period seem likely to explain liberal outcomes, and this is perhaps the 'most usual conclusion' (NESC, 2005: 139). Hence O'Connor has argued that 'In terms of the core elements of stratification and decommodification . . . and the relationships among state, market and family in the provision of services, the conclusion of this analysis is that the Irish welfare state fits the liberal cluster and this has been strengthened rather than weakened throughout its EU membership and recent economic choices' (2003: 399). Some support for this thesis is provided by Payne and McCashin's analysis of data on welfare legitimacy which argues that 'it is possible that a liberal-individualist element has taken root in Irish public life' (2005: 16). Thus we might discern a strong 'neo-liberal' dimension to the contemporary policy process which builds on historical and institutionalised patterns of provision. However, other authors have argued that the (social partnership) policy process might in fact be seen as broadly corporatist, springing to some extent from the acknowledged centrality of the Catholic Church in Ireland (Daly and Yeates, 2003). For some then, Catholicism rather than liberalism is the primary influence, and Ireland might best be thought of as a 'Catholic corporatist' welfare state (McLaughlin, 1993, 2001; Adshead and Millar, 2004).

The conflict between these perspectives might be resolved quite simply: the Irish welfare state, for historical reasons, reflects both influences, and which element we stress depends very much on where exactly we look. 'Part of the difficulty in interpreting the nature of the Irish welfare state lies in the historical trajectory of each area of policy that collectively made up the welfare state in the post-independence period. Different areas had very different influences and pathways' (O'Sullivan, 2004: 326). This book endorses that argument, and as we'll see, the policy process in the area of social security indicates a very different trajectory than that in other policy areas. We can extrapolate from O'Sullivan's (2004) insight, and suggest that if other welfare states have 'more defined ideological contours' (NESC, 2005: 140) this may be because they have more coherency across policy areas. In other words, the historical trajectories of each policy area are perhaps more similar in other countries than they are in Ireland, explaining the difficulties in classification. This may help to clarify some of the puzzles underlying Irish welfare development, and gives us a much clearer idea of the roots of divergent Irish experiences. Yet, at the risk of circularity, it must be noted that this variation across policy areas may be less divergent than it seems.

Similar arguments have been made to damn the entire worlds of welfare project by Kasza, who points to the fact that 'the various welfare policies in one country typically have different histories from one another' (Kasza, 2002: 274). Policy making involves different sets of policy actors in different fields, is a cumulative and incremental process, and is open to being influenced by foreign models. These points taken together imply that 'few national welfare systems are likely to exhibit the internal consistency necessary to validate the regime concept' (2002: 271). The regularity with which Ireland is an outlier in cross-national studies might indicate that Ireland lacks internal consistency to a greater degree than elsewhere, but is by no means unusual in exhibiting variation across policy fields. Ireland's divergence may thus be more a matter of degree than of kind. It seems unlikely that Kasza's critique will fatally undermine the regime approach. Bambra, for example, concludes that while some aspects of his argument have utility, 'it is unnecessary to wholeheartedly reject the entire regimes concept' (2004: 209). It does seem though that an awareness of distinctive paths in different policy areas must be embedded in any consideration of regime types. Kasza's conclusion that future research might more profitably focus on particular policy fields which would provide 'fewer variables and more cases' (2002: 284) is certainly relevant to Ireland. It is clear that unresolved questions about convergence and divergence require much more nuanced accounts of specific policy areas, and more explicit attention to the precise variables on which claims are made (O'Sullivan, 2004). The Irish welfare state as a whole can be understood only in so far as we have a clear understanding of its various parts, and the following chapters are intended to contribute to this aim.

We can bring to an examination of the particular policy field of social security questions which have been generated by the comparative and indigenous literature about the determinants of the Irish welfare state. Among these questions are those relating to the impact of politics, and in particular the impact of political parties said to have no or weak social bases. One reason why parties have traditionally been accorded a relatively unimportant role is the emergence of a pattern of governments which are broadly cross-class in their support bases, with the result that partisan control of government has been seen as neutral for the welfare state. Yet it is likely that cross-class governments produce outcomes that are, in themselves, highly distinctive. One possible outcome may be that ideological coherency across policy areas is reduced, and that, conversely, the interests of interest groups (which vary across sectors) may play a stronger role. The catch-all nature of the Irish party system, often used to negate a political perspective, might, in itself, be a factor shaping particular policy outcomes. Moreover, Irish parties do have some social bases, which have varied over time (Mair, 1987, 1992; Sinnott, 1995). The weakness of the left in the Irish party system, coupled with the problems of locating Ireland in comparative party typologies, has perhaps deflected attention from how social interests are actually expressed in the party system. I argue in Chapters 4 and 5 that the structure of agrarian interests in Irish politics has been under-estimated as an important social force and, in Chapter 6, that the nature of the party system mediated the representation of class and, consequently, had an impact on distributional outcomes.

A final question about the role of politics concerns timing. For reasons outlined above, most accounts of the Irish welfare state have been concerned with accounting for the shift in policy from the 1960s on, yet the explanations for the absence of a strong social-democratic party and the existence of a party system with distinctive social bases long pre-dates these events. If welfare development is viewed as a long, evolutionary process, then we need to put the period of expansion and development more clearly into a historical context. Questions of continuity raise issues about the factors shaping social policy before the emergence of an activist state and the extent to which these factors continued to shape policy even after the 1960s. Some of these continuities, in terms of party politics as well as legislative inheritances, are obscured by a focus on the period of change in the 1960s. For example, we have seen that social policy was a central feature in the emergence of the Irish party system in the 1920s and 1930s. We have also seen that, by the 1960s, a pattern of competition based around cross-class governments, all broadly pro-welfare, had emerged. We might, then, wish to know rather more about the transition between these two periods, particularly since the period is one of intensive and often controversial activism in social policy. In terms of the impact of political parties, the impact of a particular pattern of party competition deserves closer attention.

Questions about continuity and change point to the unanswered questions about the impact of policy legacies and the effects of institutional structures at the heart of the state. As outlined above, a strong case has been made for a central role for the state in shaping welfare outcomes, but it is not always clear if we should be focusing on the autonomous actions of bureaucrats, on the role of elected governments, on the state as a set of organising principles, or on some combination of these. I turn in the following chapter to a closer consideration of these issues, using questions about the impact of Catholicism on the structure of social insurance to consider both the role of institutional legacies on shaping outcomes, and the range of arguments about the role of religion in influencing outcomes in Ireland and elsewhere.

CHAPTER TWO

'Something is Missing': Catholicism, Corporatism and Social Security in Ireland

Introduction

> Social security, some years ago not more than a slogan, the
> expression of an idea, has with this war come to mean in the
> minds of men in all countries a wide-visioned constructive
> programme – a promise to the peoples of support in their
> struggle to live, a promise of a new order in society in which
> men will be freed from the fear of want and the spectral anxiety
> of poverty, a promise to the unborn generations of a better land
> in which the dragons of prolonged and mass unemployment,
> preventible sickness, unnecessary hunger, inadequate shelter,
> dependent and servile old age, will be as unfamiliar as the
> dragons of our fairy tales are now to us.[1]

Those who have some familiarity with the history of welfare state
theory might locate this quote in the context of early rather
Anglocentric accounts, which saw the Second World War as the key
explanatory factor underlying the emergence of the 'golden age' of
the welfare state. These early explanations focused on 'the consequences of the Second World War – its expansion of the powers and
competence of government, the generation of new forms of collective
provision and, above all, the broadly shared experience of austerity
and mutual mortal danger generating a high degree of citizen
solidarity in favour of radical reform' (Pierson, 1991: 125). The
trauma of war was thus the wider context through which we could
understand the astonishing impact of the Beveridge Report, the
surprise bestseller which underwrote the cradle to grave post-war
welfare state in the UK.

There is then some poignancy in noting that its author, writing with such optimism in January of 1944, was in fact the secretary of the National Health Insurance Society (NHIS) established by the Fianna Fáil government in 1933. Within the year, he would be embroiled, along with the Chairman of the NHIS, Bishop John Dignan of Clonfert, in a querulous dispute with the Minister for Local Government and Public Health, Sean MacEntee. The Bishop's chairmanship of the society would not survive the clash. Nor, in the long run, would the NHIS itself. It would be abolished in 1950, as part and parcel of the series of measures involved in bringing the 1952 Social Welfare Act to fruition. This Act, moreover, could hardly be said to reflect 'a wide-visioned constructive programme', and has instead come to symbolise the limits to reform in post-war Ireland. It provided for 'a truncated version of social insurance' (McCashin, 2004: 39) which abjured the universalism of the Beveridge scheme, and ensured that means-tested assistance would continue to be one of the central planks of the Irish welfare system.

As this and the next chapter discuss in some detail, standard explanations for the outcomes above have extrapolated from events in the sphere of health to suggest that the Catholic Church was a central actor in frustrating reform, retarding expansion, and shaping the nature of outcomes in the post-war Irish welfare state. 'Attempts during the 1940's and 1950's to copy the advances being undertaken by other countries in health and social welfare provisions were met by sufficiently strong opposition from the Catholic Church to frighten politicians into headlong retreat' (Breen et al., 1990: 30). The hierarchy argued that its opposition to the proposals for reform under the inter-party government – the so-called Mother and Child Scheme[2] – were based on Catholic social thinking, and politicians of every hue responded to the expressed opposition of the Church by stressing their adherence to the teaching of the Church (Whyte, 1980). At the height of the Mother and Child Scheme, for example, the Taoiseach wrote to the Archbishop informing him of the government's decision to withdraw the scheme: 'that decision expresses the complete willingness of the Government to defer to the judgement so given by the hierarchy that the particular scheme in question is opposed to Catholic social teaching' (quoted in Whyte, 1980: 232).

In the field of social security however, the perhaps surprising reality was that the Catholic hierarchy was on the whole indifferent. Far from frightening politicians into retreat, the only active member of the hierarchy in the field was decisively defeated by a trenchant and not even remotely deferential political response. The puzzle presented by the startlingly different policy processes in health and social security is deepened if we add a comparative context. As Chapter 1 noted, comparative political accounts have suggested that religion is an important factor underlying cross-national variation in welfare states. Nowhere is this more visible than in the field of social security, where a range of theorists have noted distinctive administrative structures and different financing arrangements for income maintenance systems in countries where Catholicism has been influential (Esping-Andersen, 1990; Huber, Ragin and Stephens, 1993; Huber and Stephens, 2001). Yet the Irish social security system, viewed comparatively, shows little indication of a Catholic influence. In his survey of Irish social security, Korpi noted: 'When I compare the institutional structures of Irish social insurance programmes with those in Europe, it strikes me that something is missing. What one might have expected to find in a country with such a strong Catholic Church are the classical corporatist arrangements in the institutions of social insurance programmes' (1992: 18). As will become apparent, those corporatist arrangements, strongly associated with Catholicism elsewhere, are absent in Ireland.

It is clear that these outcomes cannot be explained by an approach which seeks to theorise the entire welfare state as a unified body utilising mono-causal explanations. As Green-Pedersen and Haverland have argued, 'the expansion literature rarely paid much attention to dynamics within particular policy sectors' (2002: 47). The previous chapter noted, however, that different policy sectors frequently have different histories (Kasza, 2002) and O'Sullivan (2004) has suggested that it is the considerable variation in the historical trajectories of the different policy areas which accounts for much of the debate surrounding Ireland's location in various typologies. A clearer understanding of the precise policy process in the social security field thus helps us to understand both divergences *within* the Irish welfare state, and divergences *across* the different welfare regimes.

The specific area of social security raises its own questions, separate from those of other fields. Hence, a central issue in the field of income maintenance is the extent to which it fosters (or does not foster) redistribution and equality. We might reasonably expect these issues to be more visible when we discuss cash transfers, even though distributive questions are certainly embedded in other policy areas also. Questions about who pays and who benefits from social security arrangements in Ireland are at the heart of this book, but I consider these questions in later chapters. Instead I begin here with issues which may seem rather less fundamental, with questions of administrative control and organisation. These are less immediately enticing than the pounds, shillings and pence of overt and visible redistribution. But it is in the area of administration and control that we see most clearly the answers to the puzzles about the nature of Church–state relations in the field of social security. To clarify precisely why this is so, we need to consider what we know about the role of religion in shaping patterns of provision both in Ireland, and elsewhere.

Catholicism, Christian democracy and welfare states

There is little doubt that the Catholic Church in Ireland has generally been seen as particularly influential relative to the Church in other countries – though there is debate over whether Ireland is, or was, a 'theocratic' state (Whyte, 1980; Keogh, 1996). Certainly, the Church has been in a uniquely powerful position in Irish society and cannot be thought of as merely one among a number of pressure groups. Its influence is due to a number of factors. Religious homogeneity is one: in 1926, shortly after independence, there were 2,751,269 Catholics in what is now the Republic and a mere 220,723 non-Catholics (Keogh, 1996: 103). The Church had a well-developed infrastructure and through the nineteenth century had become embedded in the provision of a range of social services, especially in the fields of health and education. It has also been suggested that the Church's influence owes much to the new state's desire to achieve legitimacy in the aftermath of civil war (pp. 102–4).

> Possessing a strong popular base, exercising a profound ideological influence over the leaders of the new Irish State, and speaking as one voice through the National Conference of Bishops, the Catholic Church was traditionally in a position to mobilise its resources to protect its interests. This position lasted virtually unchallenged until the 1960's. (Keogh, 1996: 94)

In some senses the period under discussion might be seen as the apogee of Catholic influence, marking the high point before the long decline and fall of the next half century. The Fianna Fáil government which took power in 1938, and which was to both lay the foundations for and bring to fruition the 1952 Act, had, previously, copper-fastened the 'special position' of the Church in the 1937 Constitution. Yet delineating the precise nature of the Church–state relationship is far from easy – thus the very meaning of these constitutional provisions on religion and whether they are best understood as reflecting religious or political imperatives has been variously interpreted (Whyte, 1971, 1980; Keogh, 1988, 1996; Kennedy, 1998; Bartlett, 2002). These problems become even clearer when we consider the comparative literature on religion and welfare states, which points to very different modes of influence, and very different social policy outcomes in other European countries.

The perspective that Catholicism is an important factor in shaping welfare states lies in the growing realisation, explored in Chapter 1, that 'there might be different aspects of welfare effort, both among countries with high effort and those with low effort, and that these different aspects might have different causes' (Huber, Ragin and Stephens, 1993: 712). Initially, researchers identified social democracy as the key political factor underlying variation between welfare regimes, though there were early suggestions that religion might also be a factor (Stephens, 1979). Esping-Andersen (1990) considerably expanded the range of historical and political factors seen to influence outcomes in identifying three separate 'worlds of welfare', among them a conservative Catholic world. This conservative world reflects a number of intertwined influences: feudalism, etatism and corporatism. A unifying theme, though, is that 'traditional status relations must be retained for the sake of social integration' (p. 58). These ideas were, to some extent, implicit in Catholic social teaching as expressed in the papal encyclicals *Rerum Novarum* (1891) and *Quadragesimo Anno* (1931), which will be discussed in more detail below. A key insight, therefore, is that welfare regimes might be influenced by Catholic social thought.

Esping-Andersen's insights have generated an enormous range of theorising around the idea of worlds of welfare, and one strand of this debate has focused on the influence of religion on welfare states. Perhaps the most influential contribution has been van Kersbergen's (1995) study of 'social capitalism'. His work is, in many ways, a deliberate corrective to the dominance of the social-democratic thesis. He argues that even those who are explicitly arguing for alternative conceptions (such as Esping-Andersen, 1990; Baldwin, 1990) nevertheless think in terms of a social-democratic paradigm that sees the 'natural' expression of wage labour as being social democracy.

> In other words, labour has autonomous social policy needs which
> would normally lead to social democratic power mobilisation
> concentrated around the goals of solidarity, equality and univer-
> salism, unless those demands are 'filtered' and 'interpreted' (and
> implicitly assumed to be 'distorted') by other movements,
> notably Christian democracy. (van Kersbergen, 1995: 26)

Van Kersbergen suggests that wage-earners are not necessarily social
democrats by nature and that it may be useful to consider a Christian
rather than social democratisation of capitalism. His central conclusion is that 'Christian democracy is a distinctive political phenomenon
that – despite variations – nourishes a distinctive welfare state regime'
(p. 231). From an Irish perspective, his thesis presents problems highlighted in chapter one. These problems concern the extent to which any
Irish political party can legitimately be considered 'Christian democratic' and, indeed, van Kersbergen himself points to this problem in
relation to Ireland (p. 50 fn).[3] If it is difficult to clearly identify any
party as Christian democratic, then it may be difficult to extend his
insights to Ireland. Alternative approaches, however, may be more
relevant.

Castles (1994) expanded the debate by questioning whether the
idea of a Catholic world of welfare 'travels': he considered its
application to southern Europe, as expressed in welfare expenditure,
family policy and labour-market outcomes, and concluded that there
is a distinctive Catholic family of nations in policy-outcome terms. In
the process, however, he raised a central issue. He criticised the use of
Christian democratic parties as the 'operational definition of membership of the Catholic family of nations' (p. 23). This is because it
'denies the power of the Church in predominantly Catholic countries,
such as France and Ireland, to influence politicians of all parties
through its role as an elite pressure group and as a force shaping the
demands of the electorate at the mass level' (p. 24). Castles suggests
that countries with 'a predominantly Catholic population' should
be seen as being potentially part of a Catholic family of nations.
However, while he includes Ireland in order to make the point that
the use of Christian democracy underestimates the power of the
Church in some predominantly Catholic countries, he then, in a
detailed footnote, suggests that it may be 'that the Irish case cannot
properly be subsumed as part of an argument that explicit Catholic
doctrines of subsidiarity lead to higher transfer expenditure' (p. 37
fn).[4]

A number of authors have criticised Castles' suggestion that Catholicism should be substituted for Christian democracy as the key independent variable (Therborn, 1994; Schmid, 1996; van Kersbergen, 1995). Some of the criticisms of Castles are relatively straight-forward: for example, Schmid (1996) and Therborn (1994) both object to his classification of Greece as Catholic. On a similar note, questions arise where there is a mix of denominations. But the key issue is perhaps that of the operationalisation of religion: what exactly should be measured to define the independent variable? It is clear, I think, that this is an important issue if we wish to consider how Catholicism may have influenced the Irish welfare state. Van Kersbergen (1995) makes the point that using numbers of Catholics in a population as the criterion presents problems: for one thing, states vary enormously in terms of what percentage of 'nominal' Catholics are actually 'practising' Catholics. A related point is that there is also cross-national variation in the extent to, and method by, which the Church influences policy outcomes. Hence, 'it matters considerably for the political direction of political Catholicism how Church–state relations are defined and to what extent the social movements are integrated into the party' (van Kersbergen, 1995: 51).

In a similar vein, Schmid suggests that

> it would make more sense to consider separately the proportion of denominationally-tied citizens, the strength of the Churches (operationalized by funds and personnel), of Christian Democratic parties (by votes and membership), of Christian Democratic trade unions (by membership), of denominational charity organisations (by funds and personnel) and to use all these figures as indices in a statistical analysis. (1996: 104)

It is, perhaps, not surprising that this approach has so far not generated quantitative studies, and that most work has opted to focus on cabinet shares of Christian democratic parties instead (Huber, Ragin and Stephens, 1993; Huber and Stephens, 2001); that is, Christian democracy is relatively easily defined and measured, and admirably suited to quantitative cross-national studies, where it can easily be contrasted with cabinet shares of social democratic parties to determine if there are contrasting outcomes. Catholicism is a more nebulous concept, and difficult to conceptualise and measure. Much of the discussion in this chapter, however, indicates that equating Catholicism with Christian democracy is obviously a problematic approach from an Irish perspective. Daly has stressed this latter problem, noting that 'when scholars have sought to uncover the relationship between religion and social policy, Christian Democracy has hogged the attention' (1999:106). She rightly draws attention to the fact that to conflate the two movements is reductionist, that it obscures the multi-dimensional character of Christian democracy, and that it ties us rather too narrowly to a focus on 'political parties as the fathers of social policy' (ibid.). Thus a central problem with comparative theory is the narrow focus on Christian democracy as the central way in which a religious impact has been conceptualised, and this is clearly at the core of our concerns here.

At the same time, theories stressing Christian democracy are not, therefore, irrelevant, and do have the capability of providing us with some important insights. It is clear that it is difficult to disentangle ideas about Catholicism from ideas about Christian democracy. 'The "little" tradition of social Catholicism has provided the Christian democratic movements of Western Europe with a distinctive social theory of capitalism, a common core that all movements share' (van Kersbergen, 1995: 230). However, the impact of Christian democracy is, to some extent, contingent upon the structuring of power relations and coalitions within the political system, leading to divergent outcomes across political contexts (p. 178). It is certainly problematic to consider Christian democracy as a straightforward operationalisation of Catholicism, since it reflects certain strands of Catholicism and not others, and since, as a political movement centred on electoral politics, its character is also shaped by nationally specific factors. Nevertheless, with these caveats in mind, research on Christian democracy provides a valuable starting point for considering the Irish case. This is because there is general agreement that Catholicism is by far the most important factor shaping the character and social policy aims of Christian democracy, and there is growing evidence that, despite variations, there is a common core of policy outcomes that can be linked to Christian democratic incumbency. In other words, current research on Christian democracy offers us a starting point by indicating what we might expect to see if Catholic social teaching has influenced welfare outcomes.

As chapter one discussed, quantitative studies based on cabinet shares of Christian democratic parties have corroborated van Kersbergen's (1995) insights. Huber, Ragin and Stephens found 'contrasting effects of Christian democracy and social democracy on transfer payments, social benefits expenditure, and total government revenue' (1993: 711). Welfare states influenced by Christian democratic parties place 'a greater reliance on transfer payments, a deemphasis of the provision of subsidised goods and services, and weak active labour market policies' (p. 740). One of their core insights is that some of the apparently contradictory findings in quantitative studies can be explained by recognising that social democracy and Christian democracy have qualitatively different outcomes. Hence, Wilensky (1981) concluded that Christian democracy was a key force, based on his use of ILO (International Labour Organisation) measures of social security benefits expenditure, while Cameron (1978) and Stephens (1979) used total revenue and concluded that social democracy was more important (p. 743). 'The commitment of social democracy to the correction of inequalities created by the market finds its reflection in an expanded public sector; the commitment of Christian democracy to a protection of the position in the labour market acquired by individuals and families from such adversities as sickness and old age is reflected in large transfer payments' (p. 740). These outcomes can be clearly traced to Catholic social thinking on the role of the state, the family and the individual.

Fairly specific claims for the influence of Christian democracy and/or Catholic corporatism have also been made for the structure of social insurance. Esping-Andersen sees social insurance in the conservative Catholic world as being influenced by both etatism and corporatism. Etatism has influenced, in particular, the tradition of endowing civil servants with 'extraordinarily lavish welfare provisions' (Esping-Andersen, 1990: 59). Corporatism, particularly as expressed in the papal encyclicals *Rerum Novarum* (1891) and *Quadragesimo Anno* (1931), led also to a focus on status maintenance.

> Either because of state recognition of particular status privileges, or because organized groups refused to be part of a more status-inclusive legislation, there emerged the tradition of constructing a myriad of status-differentiated social-insurance schemes – each with its peculiar rules, finances, and benefit structure; each tailored to exhibit its clientele's relative status position. (Esping-Andersen, 1990: 60)

Van Kersbergen (1995) also argues that a bipartite or tripartite structure in the control of social-security schemes is related to Christian democratic strength. Huber, Ragin and Stephens suggest similar effects. 'The typical Christian-democratic welfare state . . . is segmented, and it tends to reproduce social inequalities, not reduce them. Different occupational groups have different insurance schemes, with different contribution requirements and different benefits' (1993: 740). Castles (1994) also identifies the corporatist social insurance systems common in southern European as being suggestive of those countries' membership of a Catholic family of nations.[5]

Hence, in a Catholic welfare state, we might expect to see classical corporatist arrangements in the administration of social insurance. These generally involve occupationally distinct social insurance schemes with tripartite participation by employers, employees and the state in the governing of social insurance systems (Korpi, 1992: 18). This may also be linked to a particular pattern of financing social security expenditure, with more focus on insurance contributions than on direct taxation (Castles, 1994; Wilensky, 1981). Moreover, benefits tend to be income related. As I have suggested above, however, these features are largely absent in Ireland (Korpi, 1992).

The administration of social insurance in Ireland is centralised in the Department of Social and Family Affairs (formerly the Department of Social Welfare). Benefits are flat-rate, and hence an important point is that they lack the 'status-maintaining' impact of corporatist schemes and both contributions and benefits tend to be lower than in other EU states.[6] Historically, social insurance has not been the dominant transfer method, and has accounted for a smaller segment of social-welfare expenditure than is the case in many other EU countries. At the end of the twentieth century only 42 per cent of social-welfare expenditure was financed by social insurance, compared to approximately two-thirds in Germany, France and Belgium, and Ireland was second only to the UK in having the lowest combined employee–employer contribution rate (Department of Social Welfare, 1996). The share of social insurance in social welfare expenditure had risen to 46 per cent by 2003, a figure that rose to 55 per cent if child benefit was excluded (Department of Social Welfare, 2005: 3). Despite the recent rise in social insurance coverage, the social security system in Ireland still seems, in many important respects, to belong to what has been variously described as a liberal, or English-speaking, family which has a greater tendency to rely on means-tested 'assistance' schemes, with few universal benefits, and a greater tendency to finance from general revenue (Esping-Andersen, 1990; Castles, 1994).[7] Thus a recent account of comparative social expenditure points to the 'relatively marginal role of social insurance', and in particular to the flat-rate benefits capped at a low level, which it suggested was 'one of the main contributory factors behind the weak attachment of middle-and high-income earners to the social protection system in Ireland' (Timonen, 2005: 27).

The reliance on means-tested benefit figures heavily in Daly's (1999) account of the relationship between Catholicism and social policy in Germany and Ireland. In considering the relationship between Catholic dogma and social policy, she argues that a key element is a particular aspect of social policies: how they treat the family and interfamilial relations. Her comparison of Germany and Ireland concludes that Germany was 'the more obviously social Catholic welfare state whereas the influence of Catholicism on social policy in Ireland defies easy classification' (1999: 108). This conclusion is counter-intuitive, given that there is general agreement that the 1952 Act consolidated 'a social welfare system which was built around the notion of family headed by a male breadwinner' (Cousins, 2003: 195).

One solution to this apparent inconsistency is that the male breadwinner mode of provision in social security can be ascribed to policy legacies and policy diffusion from the UK. Thus McCashin (2004) argues that the 'male breadwinner assumption was at the core of the post-war Beveridge system that was constructed in the UK' (2004: 131). It is an assumption which can also be traced back through earlier social security provisions from the Poor Law on (Yeates, 1997; McCashin 2004). Thus Lewis (1992) describes the UK, as well as Ireland, as a 'strong' male breadwinner model. The gendered provisions of the 1952 Act are undoubtedly congruent with Catholic social teaching, and clearly reinforced a prevailing ideology visible in many legal and constitutional provisions (McCashin, 2004). They do not, however, necessarily owe their origins to the influence of Catholicism, and thus Daly's (1999) arguments do not automatically conflict with the perception that a male breadwinner model is clearly visible in Irish social security provisions.

Having said that, her general argument *is* that in many respects there is a stronger male breadwinner aspect to the German transfer system, which owes its origins to the centrality of social insurance. Hence women have traditionally had little or no independent access to benefits if they did not engage in paid work. In Ireland, on the other hand, women are considerably more likely to have a personal entitlement to benefit, and thus, in effect, greater autonomy. Moreover, state provision as a consequence, interfered in the private sphere of the family to a greater extent than in Germany.[8] As she notes, this feature does not spring from a greater commitment to gender equality, but from the specific way in which the social security system has evolved. The key feature she identifies here is the 'fact that each of the classic income risks is covered not just through social insurance but also through social assistance' (pp. 115–16).[9] Her analysis extended beyond income transfers and included a consideration of how these interacted with service provision to effect families and particular sets of family relations. Her conclusion was that German policies sought 'to protect and support the traditional family with children in a manner which promotes its continued autonomy and functioning. The Irish welfare state is informed by no such clear vision. Its attitude to the family is at best half-hearted, at worst inconsistent and contradictory' (p. 127). Her account, in effect, points to the absence of a sustained and coherent 'social Catholic' vision of the family underpinning provision in the specific areas she examined. As she herself notes, her analysis differs from other scholars in the field in some important respects, but it is one which is highly compatible with wider interpretations which have seen no discernible Catholic influence on Irish social security.

In considering this puzzling absence, one suggestion is that the Catholic Church in Ireland was simply not interested in the sphere of social security. Hence Fahey points to the fact that while attention has focused on the role of the Church in the Mother and Child Scheme, 'less attention has been given to the broad welcome (or at least acceptance) which it simultaneously accorded the 1952 Social Welfare Act' (1998a: 420 fn). Peillon (1996) also noted the 'general indifference' of the Church in relation to the Act. Ó Cinnéide too has argued that that 'while Catholic experts and self-appointed spokespersons played a role in it, the bishops or the Church played no role, issued no official statements, and said nothing about it' (1999: 29). He concludes that the view that the Church played a dominant role in social welfare is 'not substantiated' (ibid.). This is a clear but ultimately incomplete answer to the puzzle we are considering here, since an immediate question is *why* it was indifferent, given its activism in health, and given the fact that Catholicism in other countries strongly influenced the policy sector.

Daly (1999) provides us with a useful starting point for considering these ambiguities. Her account is in line with the institutionalist perspectives outlined in chapter one, in that she stresses the national specificities of the institutional configurations, broadly interpreted, within which the Catholic Church is located. The specifics of her argument are considered in more detail below, but might be broadly taken as suggesting that we need to consider the 'particular historical and institutional contexts' of the Catholic Church to understand divergences in its impact on social policy (1999: 125). Before turning to a detailed consideration of the debates about social security in Ireland, we need to sketch out the broad terms of this context, and I conclude this chapter by considering first, the specific nature of Catholic social thought in Ireland, and secondly, the context of social policy reform with which this would engage.

Catholic social thinking in Ireland: 'sui generis'?

As we've seen, those who have argued that the Church in Ireland has played a role in influencing social policy compatible with that in the comparative literature have looked to the nature of Catholic social teaching as a guide to understanding both motivations and outcomes. In doing so, they follow in the footsteps of Whyte (1971, 1980) who located the battle over health policy in post-war Ireland in the context of opposing philosophies of government, those of a bureaucratic state and a vocationalist church respectively. Subsequently, various authors explain Catholic activism by reference to an interlocking set of beliefs, variously termed vocationalist or corporatist, or to the doctrine of subsidiarity (McLaughlin, 1993, 2001; Adshead and Millar, 2004). Certainly, it is clear that Catholic social thought had, at least potentially, implications for the development of social security in Ireland.

By the 1940s, Catholic social teaching seems to have become well entrenched in Ireland (Whyte, 1980). As elsewhere, the papal encyclicals *Rerum Novarum* (1891) and *Quadragesimo Anno* (1931) were influential in shaping a distinctive attitude to social policy. The central doctrine was that of subsidiarity – that the state should not take upon itself what could be left to 'lesser and subordinate' organisations (Whyte, 1980: 67). Side by side with this was the doctrine of vocationalism. This sought to counter what was seen as excessive state centralisation by devolving authority for various issues to vocationally organised bodies – that is, to organisations based on people's vocations, or occupations. In addition, of course, Catholic social teaching accorded a primary position to the family and to the position of fathers as providers. The emergence of a Catholic social movement was influential in leading to the establishment of the

Commission on Vocational Organisation in 1939 to examine the practicality of developing vocational organisation in Ireland. The commission presented a 300,000-word report in 1943 that recommended vocational organisation as an alternative to bureaucracy, which it criticised heavily. It was also critical of politicians. In return, the report was received negatively by both civil servants and the government of the day (Lee, 1979; O'Leary, 2000).

It is clear that state run welfare schemes had, potentially, far-reaching implications. The comments of Rev. E.J. Hegarty (1950) on the 1949 White Paper are clear about this. He argued that 'comprehensive State Welfare Schemes are opposed generally to moral, legal, social and economic principles, and are utterly discredited by experience and history' (Hegarty, 1950: 1). Governments, he comments, were not instituted by God to take over the work of families in providing for the members, but to safeguard their function which 'is inviolable and prior . . . to any State power' (p. 2).

> From this principle the arguments for the unity and indissolubility of marriage derive; so if the State can take over these duties of the family, there is no compelling reason against polygamy or divorce! In fact, you might well ask: why ought people to bother with any form of marriage at all, if the State will care for them 'from the cradle to the grave' by maternity benefits, children's allowances, public housing, free education, free medical attention, vouchers for food and clothing and fuel, free dole for the idle, finally a life-pension, a grant at death, and pensions for widows and orphans? There is much sober truth in the paradox that we have as much right to free love as to free spectacles. (pp. 2–3)

As the introduction to this chapter commented, the hierarchy drew heavily on Catholic social thought, as outlined briefly above, to justify its opposition to developments in health. It is thus not surprising then that many, if not most, analyses have prioritised Catholic social thought as a central factor explaining delayed welfare state development in Ireland. 'Until the 1960's Catholic teaching largely determined the nature of Irish social policies. Strict adherence to the subsidiarity principle ensured that the austere state had a limited welfare role' (McLaughlin, 1993: 232). McLaughlin (2001) has subsequently argued that even after the role of the state in welfare provision shifted following the modernisation strategy adopted from

1958 on, 'the core principles of Catholic corporatism determined the manner in which state welfare was delivered and this had a considerable impact on the outcome of this increased expenditure' (ibid.). Daly and Yeates, while distinguishing between 'social' Catholicism and 'traditionalist' Catholicism, argue that: 'As well as subsidiarity, the Irish Catholic Church was also insistent on the principle of vocational organisation. It therefore advocated traditions of voluntarism and charity and was opposed to state intervention. Holding fast to those principles, the Catholic Church acted as a brake on the development of state welfare in Ireland' (2003: 88). Even Daly who as we've seen has questioned the impact of Catholicism in some respects, argues that the Church 'emphasised the principles of vocational organisation and subsidiarity' and was consequently 'vehemently opposed to state intervention' (1999: 121–2). Most recently, Adshead and Millar's (2004) application of Esping-Andersen's typology to Ireland concluded that Catholic corporatist values have left an enduring legacy for the organisation of contemporary health-care in Ireland. The argument that Church action in social policy in the period was motivated by a commitment to the twin doctrines of subsidiarity and vocationalism, and that the contemporary welfare state can be understood by reference to the legacies of corporatist forms of organisation is thus a standard and widely shared perspective up to the present day.

However, once we consider the specific historical and institutional context of the Irish Catholic Church, it becomes clear that the evolution of and nature of Catholic social thinking in Ireland does not accord with this standard perception, as O'Leary's (2000) definitive study of vocationalism has clarified. As the next chapter discusses in some detail, these differences are crucial to understanding the absence of corporatist outcomes in Ireland. To clarify this point, it is first necessary to look in more detail at the concept of corporatism, and at the nature of its association with Catholicism. A closer examination of the concept of corporatism leads to the conclusion that its origins are historically and spatially specific to continental Europe between around 1870 and 1940 in particular. The term corporatism is one which is widely used, but which has a number of distinct usages. Hence, Catholic corporatism may be distinguished from neo-corporatism or liberal-corporatism, or from what is sometimes termed authoritarian corporatism (Williamson, 1985, 1989). While common threads unite all these usages, nevertheless, they differ substantially in their theoretical concerns. The specific association between Catholicism and corporatism has long roots. For many authors, the French Revolution and the divisions between Church and state that arose from this are central to understanding the long-term genesis of the emergence of corporatism as a key component of Catholic social and political thought. Having said this, it is the nineteenth century and the response to the disappearance of the *ancien régime* and the rise of industrial capitalism that lies at the core of corporatism. *Rerum Novarum* and *Quadragesimo Anno* were concerned with responding to the linked problems of the rise of liberal capitalism and the associated breakdown of the 'organic community' seen to lie at the heart of medieval society, and with countering the threat posed by the socialist response to the class conflicts generated by the rise of industrialised societies (Williamson, 1989: 2).

In addition, the legacy of medieval patterns of organisation find their expression in corporatism in forms of association arising from a long history of worker organisation in guilds. 'Corporatism has always been a major conservative alternative to etatism. It springs from the tradition of the estates, guilds, monopolies and corporations that organised social and economic life in the medieval economy' (Esping-Andersen, 1990: 60). Hence, as Esping-Andersen argues, corporative social welfare emerged as the state built on existing patterns of organisation in Germany, Austria, France and Italy in particular. Corporatism, he argues, is most strongly associated with late-industrialising, continental-European countries, where 'status distinction, hierarchy and privilege' have been unusually strong, and in which Catholicism was also influential in social reform (1990: 61). Thus particular patterns of Church–state relations, of industrialisation and of class mobilisation underlie the emergence of Catholic social teaching in late nineteenth-century Europe.

A number of authors have argued that a widespread interest in Catholic social thought took hold rather later in Ireland than in other European countries (Whyte, 1980; Daly, 1999; O'Leary, 2000). The growth of an influential Catholic social movement in many parts of the European continent between 1880–1920 in particular was not replicated here, and Catholic social thinking remained weak until the 1930s (Whyte, 1980). Reviewing nineteenth- century developments O'Driscoll remarks: 'Whereas other continental Catholics built up extensive and often elaborate intellectual frameworks for the Christian organisation of their societies, Irish Catholics did not' (O'Driscoll, 2000: 121). Part of the reason for this was that conditions in Ireland 'were conducive neither to the necessary indigenous development of a social Catholic vision of society nor to its realization in practice' (Daly, 1999: 127). Thus Whyte has argued that '*Quadragesimo Anno* had been written with the experience of industrialised nations on the continent primarily in mind' (1980: 106). O'Leary (2000) suggests that there were a variety of interlocking reasons why social Catholicism was not influential in Ireland in the formative period between the end of the nineteenth century and independence. First, the associated processes of industrialisation and urbanisation were not at an advanced stage. Hence, 'the church pursued its mission in a socio-economic environment which did not threaten its position and [*Rerum Novarum*] had no significant impact on the country' (p. 21). There were also other important differences: Germany, France, Belgium and Holland were not preoccupied with a struggle for national independence; they were not bound up with a social problem comparable with the land question; they had not suffered the suppression of the Penal Laws and did not have to put similar effort into reconstructing basic institutions (p. 21).

The Irish Catholic Church then had, historically, a very different relationship to Catholic social thinking even before independence. Post-independence, its experiences would continue to be highly distinctive, and this would nurture a particularly Irish response to the ideas of corporatism and vocationalism in Ireland. Thus O'Leary (2000) has overturned the consensus on the nature of the Church's attachment to vocationalism in the period. His work suggests that the traditional picture of an ardently vocationalist Church opposed by a largely supine state, a perspective heavily based on events in the Mother and Child Scheme, may be profoundly misleading. One of the central reasons why we do not see corporatist structures in social security is that the specific experiences of Irish Catholicism differed very considerably from that of continental European Catholicism, and these differences would structure the nature of its response to proposals for reform in social security. However, its responses cannot be understood without reference to the specific nature of the Irish state, and I conclude this chapter by outlining the wider context of state proposals for social policy reform in the period.

From social services to social welfare: the context of reform

When we turn to consider the policy context as the war began, it is clear that our contemporary understanding of social policy as comprising separate and distinct policy areas was only beginning to emerge. As Cousins notes, 'the social welfare system as we know it today simply did not exist in the 1930s' (1999: 36). At that time, a variety of different bodies and departments operated the various income-maintenance schemes: unemployment insurance as well as workmen's compensation were under the control of the Department of Industry and Commerce, unemployment assistance and children's allowances were administered by the Department of Industry and Commerce and the Revenue Commissioners, health insurance was administered by the NHIS (under the aegis of the Department of Local Government and Public Health), and old-age pensions and blind pensions by the Revenue Commissioners and the Department of Local Government and Public Health. Thus the health and unemployment insurance schemes were administratively separate, 'each with its own insurance cards, insurance stamps, indexes and individual records' (Farley, 1964: 130. See Appendix I). This reflected the incremental nature of policy development, where independent governments had essentially built on top of schemes inherited from the colonial period.

A central part of the reform process aimed at coordinating this extremely diverse body of 'social services', which encompassed other policy areas too, and this involved substantial administrative reorganisation and innovation. Embedded in this process was the gradual creation of a separate social welfare system and health system, each with its own department. Barrington (1987) and Cousins (2003) have detailed the interlinked process of social policy development in health and social welfare, respectively, and both draw attention to the 'rush of proposals' for reform in the period (Barrington, 1987: 165). For our purposes here, a key factor was that there was a gradual but ever growing demand for the coordination of the various income maintenance schemes, alongside demands for improved social services generally.

A key event was the appointment of Seán MacEntee as Minister for Local Government and Public Health in 1942. His department was to be the fulcrum on which debates about social-service reform revolved and, following administrative reform, was to be the genesis of the Department of Social Welfare that emerged in 1947, and which would subsequently propose a comprehensive social insurance scheme culminating in the 1952 Act. MacEntee is an enigmatic figure, lecturing simultaneously on the evils of Beveridgeism while supervising a Department that proposed 'probably the most radical document ever produced on the Irish health services . . . [offering] . . . the goal of a free national health service for all who wished to avail of it' (Barrington, 1987: 165). As well as being 'a little bit vain', he has been described as 'an elegant little man, always beautifully turned out, with most courteous manners, a bon viveur, a cultured intellectual and charming' (Deeny, 1989: 156–7). Perhaps his most salient characteristic was that he was 'completely political' (p. 157). Moreover, it is clear that he had a 'belligerent political style' (Feeney, 2001: 66). The processes of reform involved a range of questions which were broadly administrative, but also inherently political, ranging from intra-departmental disputes about where different kinds of social services rightly belonged, through to much wider questions about nature of ministerial authority in the Irish political system. The nature of Church–state interaction in the field of social security in the period during and immediately after the war needs to be contextualised by appreciating that it occurred in the context of very wide-ranging processes of reform, in which the Minister for Local Government and Public Health was active on a number of fronts simultaneously.

Although the question of coordinating social and health services had been mooted as early as 1937 by the NHIS little real progress was made for some years (Cousins, 2003). Successive movements within government to establish a committee to discuss this coordination were proposed but failed to progress from 1937 through to the early years of the war (ibid.: Ch. 6). One relatively substantial reform was that there was change in the financial structure of the NHIS with the National Health Insurance Act, 1942, which shifted the financing method from a funded to a pay-as-you-go basis. The debate on the bill indicated the existence, amongst Labour in particular, of a growing desire to improve social services. The committee stage of the Health Insurance bill was debated on the same day that the Labour leader, William Norton, had tabled a question enquiring as to whether the Taoiseach would consider the establishment of a Department of Social Welfare. The Taoiseach had replied that this would not necessarily result in any economy or efficiency.[10] Later in the day, on the debate on the NHIS bill, Norton lamented the limited scope of the bill, and stressed that the question of national health and national health insurance could only be dealt with by 'the inauguration of a comprehensive scheme which will provide adequate cash benefits, medical surgical, convalescent home, optical, dental, T.B. treatment and every other type of medical attention which is needed to keep the insured person in a state of good health'.[11] A fellow Labour deputy, James Hickey, pointed to 'the necessity for having a unified social insurance scheme, covering all . . . forms of insurance' and for these to operated by one state department.[12] In the same month, the ICTU had met with the Parliamentary Secretary of the department, Dr Ward, to seek a single Ministry of Social Services (Cousins, 2003). Labour's James Hickey returned to the theme in June:

> Anybody who reviews the social services in this country for the past ten or 15 years must realise also that there is great need for some kind of co-ordinated social insurance scheme which would include national health insurance, unemployment insurance, unemployment assistance, old age pensions, widows' and orphans' pensions, hospital and medical treatment, and I would also include workmen's compensation. They are all forms of social insurance. In bringing in a unified scheme of that kind I think we should also include the well-paid workers as well as the poorly-paid workers. Some scheme of that kind would be worth having.[13]

Hickey suggested that the New Zealand schemes might be studied in this regard. However, it was the publication of the Beveridge Report in Britain in December of that year which really focused attention on what would be generally termed 'social service' reform. As a memo in the Department of Local Government and Public Health (dating from 1944) remarked:

> The publication in England of the Beveridge report, of the British Government's White Paper on social insurance, and on the Comprehensive Medical Service have undoubtedly awakened interest and expectation of similar developments in this country. The Trades Union Congress has asked that the government should give early and favourable attention to a proposal that all the social services should be unified; there is a motion on the order paper to the same effect; the Plan has received much publicity and has attracted comment and approval. The government may decide to make this question the subject of examination.[14]

It was not surprising that the publication of the Beveridge Report was viewed as an electoral issue by Fianna Fáil. Hugo Flinn, Parliamentary Secretary to the Minister for Finance, remarked that the Beveridge report could be a godsend for the Labour Party and, properly worked, worth quite a few seats (quoted in Feeney, 2001: 65). As the war progressed, there were clear reasons for Fianna Fáil to consider electoral issues. Ireland was one of only two countries to hold elections during the conflict (O'Leary, 1979). Ireland had entered the war with a Fianna Fáil government in a strong position, having won its fourth successive election in 1938, and having succeeded in carrying out major constitutional change in 1937. In fact, however, 1938 marked its peak in electoral terms: the 51.9 per cent it won at this election would not be repeated. The 'emergency' witnessed the stirrings of discontent in the emergence of Clann na Talmhan, whose first election outing was in 1943, where it won a dramatic 11.3 per cent of the vote. Fianna Fáil, campaigning under the slogan, 'Don't change horses when crossing the stream', lost its majority in this election (O'Leary, 1979: 35). Thus, de Valera relied on the Clann na Talmhan vote for him as Taoiseach. Labour had gained ten seats, but the period subsequently witnessed the explosion of simmering tensions in the Labour movement, and in January 1944 the ITGWU disaffiliated from the Labour party, and a second rival party – National Labour – and a rival congress emerged.

The signs – most visible in the emergence of Clann na Talmhan – that Fianna Fáil might encounter increased opposition in the post war period are perhaps apparent only retrospectively, since the 1944 election returned Fianna Fáil with an overall majority, while all the other parties performed worse than in 1943 (O'Leary, 1979). Labour was in disarray and Fine Gael seemed to be in unstoppable decline. As Fianna Fail took its sixth successive general election there are grounds for Whyte's suggestion that perhaps 'hubris had set in' (Whyte, 1980: 113). Nevertheless, it is clear that they recognised that the post-war period would witness increased demands for social services. Hence in December of 1943 the Taoiseach's department wrote to Finance, requesting information on expenditure of social services: 'It is very clear, I think, that social services will figure largely in coming discussions about post-war reconstruction, etc. and there are bound to be repeated requests from various quarters for information as to what is our expenditure on such services both absolutely and in relation to our total annual expenditure and our national income.'[15] Finance did not reply until May 1944. In the course of doing so, the department took the opportunity to consider what exactly was meant by social-service reform in some detail, pointing out that defining expenditure on social services was rather more difficult than might be expected, since there was no clear definition of what precisely they were.[16] Given that there was no clear separation of social policy fields, the following few years witnessed health and social welfare being discussed in tandem under the general term of 'social services'. Not until 1946 would the term 'social welfare' be definitively adopted to cover income maintenance services, with the legislation for the establishment of the Department of Social Welfare passing in that year (Cousins, 2003).

That health reforms would be one central plank in the development of post-war social services was indicated by the delegation of some responsibilities in the Department of Local Government and Public Health to the Parliamentary Secretary Dr. Ward. Under the aegis of Dr Ward, the department had begun the process of reforming health. Hence towards the end of 1944, a departmental committee had been set up to examine the public medical services. The subsequent *Report of the Departmental Committee on Health Services* would be an important step towards the later Mother and Child controversy (Barrington, 1987). In addition, an alternative medical plan had been in existence since April, and in December of 1944 the medical association produced a second. Both of these were concerned, to varying degrees, with defending the turf of the medical profession from what it suspected might emerge from the Department of Local Government and Public Health.

At the same time, the department was also increasingly embroiled in debates about the administrative structures of social services generally, and income maintenance in particular. As we've seen, Labour had been calling for a coordinated scheme since 1942, and the question had been raised at various times within government since 1937. In February of 1945, an interdepartmental committee was established to consider the advisability of assigning social services to a single ministry. That MacEntee had an immediate interest is indicated by his memorandum submitted the following day arguing that this was contrary to the Taoiseach's Dáil statement that a single ministry would necessarily achieve efficiencies (Cousins, 2003: 139) Should it be established, he argued that his department should have two members. When a committee was subsequently established, and ultimately recommended the establishment of a new department to deal with income maintenance services, the representatives of Local Government and Public Health submitted a minority report, arguing generally that health insurance belonged, along with public health matters, in that department (Cousins, 2003: 140). Debate about this

issue continued throughout 1945, and one author has suggested that
in the debate about departmental re-organisation, MacEntee would
fight to extend his departmental remit in a process described as a
'territorial war' (Feeney, 2001: 67).

It is also worth noting that the Department of Local Government
and Public Health, in addition to considering reform of social
services, also spearheaded a process of reform of local government
which involved the 'appointment of county managers in 1942, the
reduction in the size of county councils by a third and the introduction of new codes of procedure governing the activities of local
authorities' (Barrington, 1987: 140). The process attracted much
adverse criticism, and the department 'came under increasing criticism
in the Dáil for its dictatorial methods, unhelpfulness and slowness to
reach decisions' (p.141). Hence the call for coordinated social
insurance by James Hickey (above) had included a suggestion 'that it
is not possible for any one Minister to deal efficiently with all these
departments of local government and public health and that there is a
very definite need for a second Minister to deal with social services as
apart from local government'.[17] Labour's Jim Everett had also
suggested removing some responsibilities from the department:

> In my opinion the Department of Local Government is too big
> for one Minister. I think there should be two Ministers, one to
> administer the affairs of public boards and the other public
> health and social services, including, of course, the Widows' and
> Orphans' Pensions Act, national health insurance, tuberculosis
> and other such schemes. If the work were divided in that
> manner it would provide ample scope for two Ministers, and the
> administration, generally, would be more efficient.[18]

Thus, in the period under discussion, the Department of Local
Government and Public Health was at the centre of very wide-
ranging debates about reforming social services. It was a period when
administrative structures in social security in particular were to the
fore, as the processes of delineating 'social welfare' as a separate
policy field were just beginning. It could be argued, with some
justification, that this period of administrative innovation and wide-
ranging policy debate offered a window of opportunity for those who
might have wished for the future direction of policy to be one which
was congruent with vocationalist thought. In fact, the opposite was
to be the case.

Conclusion

From shortly before the Second World War began in Ireland, there was growing pressure, accelerating as the end of the war approached, for the co-ordination and improvement of social services, culminating in the establishment of a Department of Social Welfare in 1947. This department would begin work on coordinating the diverse income maintenance schemes almost immediately, although nothing would emerge into the public domain until the inter-party government took office. The debates which began then about the precise details of how this should be achieved will be the subject of a number of later chapters. However, to understand precisely why developments in income maintenance would not go down a corporatist path, we need first to look in some detail at events which began in October of 1944, shortly before the inter-departmental committee to consider a new department was established, and just as the processes of detailed consideration of social security began. In that month, the Bishop of Clonfert, John Dignan, published his plan for reforming health, which had a strong vocationalist ethos, and which led to a dispute with MacEntee which lasted just under a year. It began with MacEntee's outraged response to the newspaper coverage given to the plan in October 1944, and culminated in the decision to replace Dignan with a civil servant when his term of office expired in August 1945. The so-called 'Dignan affair' has attracted attention from a number of scholars, who have, however, differed somewhat in their analyses. Briefly, some have stressed the centralising and authoritarian tendencies of MacEntee, others the aggressive and uncompromising vocationalist ardour of Dignan (Whyte, 1980; Riordan, 2000). The episode is little more than a footnote to the story of the evolution of Irish social security, but it is fundamental in terms of understanding Church-state relations in the social policy field, and the following chapter examines it in some detail.

Throughout the course of the dispute, MacEntee would operate within a particular institutional configuration in which he held firm views on the nature of ministerial authority, and these would be fundamental in shaping his response to suggestions that income maintenance ought to be governed by vocationalist structures. An important background to the dispute is that both Church and state were located within a distinct set of inherited policies, and operated within a particular institutional framework of formal and informal rules which constituted the political system. As the next chapter discusses, it is the interaction of these two institutional settings – welfare state institutions and political institutions – which explains the absence of a Catholic influence on social security outcomes. Political institutions encompass both the formal rules governing the political system, and also the informal rules governing the relationship between church and state, and structuring the sets of beliefs which policy-makers held about modes of government. As we'll see, these were an inhospitable environment for the vocationalist ideas put forward by Dignan. Moreover, in terms of welfare state institutions, policy legacies – in particular those emanating from the 1911 National Insurance Act – also militated against corporatist structures. Consequently, the events described in the following chapter make it clear that corporatism is a much misused term in relation to the Irish welfare state. While Catholicism has certainly been influential, corporatism has not.

CHAPTER THREE

A Situation Rather Disturbed? Vocationalism and the state in Ireland

Introduction

One of the most fundamental factors setting Ireland apart from countries in the conservative corporatist world of welfare is the administrative structures of its social security system, lacking as it does bi-partite or tri-partite structures of governance. These administrative structures, which work to keep the state at a distance, have been said to be 'reinforced by the principle of subsidiarity' (Daly, 2001: 82). A central move which ensured that there would not be similar structures in Ireland was the decision to abolish the NHIS, described as 'the nearest approach to Vocational Organisation' in Ireland (Dignan, 1945: 31). The decision to abolish the NHIS in 1950 was taken as a step towards the coordination of the income maintenance system, and thus it needs to be considered in relation to the wider influences which shaped both this system, and the policy process within which reform was debated. Two influences in particular were crucial – the policy legacies of social insurance schemes which pre-dated independence, and an adherence to a 'Westminster style' of government that conflicted with Irish interpretations of 'subsidiarity'.

The extended process of reform outlined in the previous chapter occurred within the context of already existing welfare state institutions, and long established patterns of provision which date from the colonial period. Many authors, not necessarily explicitly institutionalist, have attributed a central explanatory function to these inheritances in understanding contemporary patterns of provision. Hence Kaim-Caudle stressed the close historical ties between Ireland and the UK in explaining Irish social security outcomes:

In spite of political antagonism against Britain in certain circles in the Republic, in spite of a very different economic structure and in spite of a much lower level of income, Irish legislation in social and economic matters has been more influenced by happenings in Britain than by those in any other country. This is especially true in the field of social insurance. (Kaim-Caudle, 1967: 39–40)

This link was also part of the reason for Castles' (1994) exclusion of Ireland from the Catholic 'family of nations' in social security, discussed in the previous chapter. He remarks that 'the shaping of the Irish social security system owes much to the legacy of English rule in the formative period of welfare formation (which is, of course, an assertion that Ireland was once a member of a quite different family of nations)' (1994: 37). Castles (1994), in effect, is suggesting that the absence of a Catholic influence on social security outcomes in Ireland reflects the centrality of policy legacies. By this analysis, the Irish case seems to offer support to institutionalist arguments for the importance of policy legacies and lends credence to the core concept of 'path dependence'.

However, it is clear that path dependence is unsatisfactory as a complete explanation. For one thing, although the Irish system bears a close resemblance to the UK system, it also differs from it in some important respects. As Daly and Yeates (2003) suggest, the 'common origins' of the two systems do not preclude movement in different directions subsequently. Inherited legacies have certainly contributed to some outcomes, and have militated against others, but the Irish social security system has also been subject to indigenous pressures and influences. In terms of explaining the absence of a Catholic influence, it is profoundly counter-intuitive to argue that policy legacies in social security were sufficiently strong to outweigh the influences of a Church generally acknowledged to wield considerable power in other social policy spheres. To fully understand outcomes, we need to add an understanding of the network of formal and informal rules which structured Church–state relations in the period. Nevertheless, inherited welfare state institutions are fundamental and I start by considering these. I begin with the 1911 National Insurance Act, which as we've seen, introduced contributory unemployment and sickness benefits to insured workers – the key provisions of the Act are outlined in Appendix I. As I discuss below, although the Act was applied across the then UK, there were some differences in how it operated in Ireland.

The role of policy legacies

The 1911 National Insurance Act has, to some extent, acquired an importance over and above its actual provisions, in that it is one of a cluster of legislative initiatives deemed to signal the shift from the poor-law period to the development of social insurance, thus signalling the birth of the welfare state (Rimlinger, 1971; Flora and Heidenheimer, 1981). The inauguration of social insurance combines two measures of welfare stateness; increasing social expenditure and institutional innovation (Flora and Heidenheimer, 1981). Famously, the UK was influenced by the earlier German example in the 1880s, yet the two schemes differed considerably in terms of the influences that shaped them and, consequently, the form they took. Rimlinger (1971), for example, argues that Germany, as a late industrialiser, developed its insurance model in terms of the patriarchal tradition of the absolutist state. On the other hand, the British model was a late adaptation to industrialisation, which had occurred under the influence of the liberal tradition.

Thus the Act reflected the legacies of British experiences, and friendly societies were a core part of the scheme. Friendly societies had been central in providing protection against some risks for the large class of industrial workers, and there were approximately six million members of around 2,500 societies at the time (Barrington, 1987). These societies had, in fact, initially been hostile to state schemes. Although the model for the plan was the trade-union and friendly-society schemes, it provoked trade-union hostility at the greater risk-pooling involved by the inclusion of unorganised workers (Heclo, 1974). The TUC (Trades Union Congress) had called for non-union workers to be excluded. The state contribution to the scheme 'prevented the more regularly employed workman from having to bear the extra cost of bringing along his high-unemployment-risk brethren in the same public insurance program' (pp. 86–7). The scheme was thus financed on a tripartite basis and was administered by those organisations that had already been involved in the administration of sickness benefit.

The 1911 Act was extended to Ireland, though in a slightly amended form. In terms of unemployment, the Act applied to Ireland in essentially the same form as in the UK (see Appendix I). As in the UK, benefits and contributions were flat-rate and the scheme was financed by contributions from employees, employers and the state (Kaim-Caudle, 1967; Commission on Social Welfare, 1986). The

much smaller number of friendly societies existing in Ireland pointed
to the large differences that existed between the two countries – it has
been estimated that only around 40,000 people were members of
friendly societies in Ireland. Two main reasons accounted for the lack
of friendly societies in Ireland. The first was that the industrial
working class was small, and concentrated largely in Dublin and
Belfast. The second was that some of the functions friendly societies
fulfilled were met by the existence of a dispensary system providing
free health care in Ireland. The Irish Poor Law had diverged from
the British Poor Law, largely under the impetus of the Famine.
Consequently, Ireland during this period had a 'free' medical service
based on a network of dispensary doctors operating under the aegis
of the Poor Law Boards of Guardians (Burke, 1987). Therefore,
different arrangements for the operation of insurance had to be made
for Ireland. In Ireland, the Act was supervised by the Irish Insurance
Commissioners. The Act allowed that trade unions could become
'approved societies', accounting for a large rise in trade-union membership in Ireland, especially for the ITGWU (Irish Transport and
General Workers' Union) (Keogh, 1994). By April 1913, 700,000
persons were insured (Barrington, 1987: 68).

A key area of difference concerned medical benefit. The Act allowed
for a compulsory health-insurance scheme for virtually all manual
workers and for lower-paid, non-manual workers, administered by
non-profit-making Approved Societies. However, medical benefit
(coverage for treatment by a doctor and prescriptions), which was
included in the provisions for elsewhere in the UK, was excluded for
Ireland. The exclusion of medical benefit reflected pressures from the
Catholic Church and the medical profession in Ireland, which in turn
reflected profound social and economic differences between the two
countries. In broad terms, Ireland was a largely agricultural nation
with a small, industrial working class. This had a number of effects,
as already noted; Ireland lacked the extensive system of friendly
societies on which the UK system was based, and a much smaller
group would be covered by the scheme since there were relatively few
employees. Arising partially from these differences, earlier social
policy developments differed in Ireland.

Although the Church opposed the 1911 National Insurance Act, it
is worth stressing that its opposition was not based on doctrines of
Catholic social thought, such as 'subsidiarity', but, rather, on the
grounds that the bill was unsuited to Irish conditions. As the previous
chapter noted, Irish Catholicism was slow to develop an interest in

social policy, and ideas current in other European countries were weakly developed in Ireland. Likewise, the context within which Catholicism was operating was also quite different – the pressures which industrialisation threw up in many European countries were absent here. Hence, the clergy's arguments have been said to reflect its 'predominantly rural and capitalist eyes and [to come] from the standpoint of the farmer and small trader' (Barrington, 1987: 50). Other authors have noted the extent to which the preferences of the Church were synonymous with those of farmers. Lee has described the clergy in this period as 'strong farmers in cassocks, [who] largely voiced the concern of their most influential constituents, whose values they instinctively shared and universalised as "Christian"' (1989: 159). Bartlett (2002), in considering the extent of religiosity in independent Ireland, suggests an argument for seeing this as reflecting 'the cultural dominance of the main socio-economic class – the strong farmers – from whom the clergy were disproportionately drawn and whose values were hegemonic in Irish society' (2002: 251). Likewise, Daly suggests that 'the Catholic church in Ireland and its associated social movement idealized a society based on family property, small businesses, and farms' (1999: 121).

The Church's influence in 1911, then, must be placed in the context of the wider social structure – notably, a society in which a system of 'peasant proprietorship' had been created following a series of land Acts through the nineteenth and early twentieth centuries. This social structure owes its roots to the nationalist struggles of the nineteenth century, and Catholicism in Ireland in this period and later was shaped by these struggles. Secondly, while the Church was influential in having medical benefit excluded, the bulk of the Act was, in fact, applied to Ireland, shaping a model of social insurance along UK lines. This has been said to reflect the political skill of Irish politicians (in Westminster) in preserving most of the benefits of the bill for the Irish working class, and to indicate that 'the situation was not a simple one of clerical command and obedience by politicians' (Barrington, 1987: 64).

The birth of social insurance in Ireland, then, occurred during the period generally seen as the birth of the welfare state across Europe. However, many of the arguments that have been put forward to account for this did not, in fact, apply to Ireland (see, for example, Flora and Alber, 1981). The roots of the 1911 Act lay in the growth of an industrial working class in the UK, which was beginning to assert its electoral muscle; but Ireland, in this period, was a predominantly rural, agricultural country, dominated by owner-occupiers, and with a proportionally tiny, urban working class. It is true that this was a period of labour organisation and unrest, in which we see the foundation of the ITGWU (organising unskilled workers), an embryonic Labour Party in 1912 and the great Lockout of 1913. But, nevertheless, conditions differed profoundly from those in the UK or, indeed, Germany, the other path-breaking social insurance nation in this period. As noted above, the extension of social insurance, rather than reflecting the strength of trade unionism, contributed to increasing the numbers of Irish trade unionists in what might be seen as reverse causality. The concerns of continental European Catholicism in this period were very different and, consequently, the factors shaping the institutional structures of social insurance in the period differed considerably also.

Independence in Ireland was initially to see little development of the social insurance system. A contributory and non-contributory widows' and orphans' pension was introduced in 1935. This had been preceded by a committee of inquiry, which makes it clear that elements of Catholic social teaching had begun to influence the terms in which public policy was spoken of. Importantly, it is clear that contributory schemes are seen as being in line with Catholic social thought. Contributory schemes, as contrasted with non-contributory schemes, apparently strengthened individual responsibility and gave the state a lesser role than in schemes funded entirely from general revenue: 'The payment of direct contributions by the insured can be justified on the responsibility of the insured themselves in the occurrence of risk, the necessity for considering their self-respect, the desirability of encouraging thrift, on their right to share in the administration and in effecting economy in its working.'[1] Hence, contributory schemes appeared to be congruent with the doctrine of subsidiarity. In the Dáil debate on the scheme, the Minister for Local Government and Public Health, S.T. O'Kelly, quoted the report approvingly:

> It may not be out of place here to refer to the implication of schemes where the burden of social protection is borne by the general resources of the whole community. In looking to the State alone for protection against all the contingencies of life, the tendency is to weaken personal and family responsibility and to strengthen correspondingly the conception of the overriding authority and responsibility of an abstract State. It is necessary

to state that, in this country at any rate, such a tendency is not in accord with the type of social philosophy predominantly held.[2]

As Chapter 1 outlined, the mid-1930s saw some institutional changes to the Irish social insurance scheme. Among other reforms, the 1933 National Health Insurance Act instituted a committee of management for the new society. This consisted of a chairman, three trustees and three employers' representatives appointed by the Minister for Local Government and Public Health, and eight representatives of insured persons. Three of these were nominated by the Irish Trade Union Congress (ITUC) and five were nominated under a delegate system by local authorities (Riordan, 2000). In 1936, the Bishop of Clonfert, Dr Dignan, became chairman of this organisation. Post-war debates, then, took place in the context of already existing schemes of social insurance, and the adoption of corporatism would have involved a sharp turn away from existing practice. This point was explicitly made by policy-makers in a memo on reform in anticipation of the creation of a separate Department of Social Welfare, and in the 1949 White Paper, *Social Security*.

These sources make it clear that there was a broad awareness that variable rates of contribution and benefit was the method generally adopted in all countries except Britain, New Zealand and some of the Swiss cantons. However, it was felt that this was essentially due to what we would now call institutional legacies present in these countries, but not in Ireland. The point is made very clearly in the White Paper:

> It is seldom realised that the administrative background which makes variable rates feasible in European countries is not present in Ireland. On the Continent, administration is generally through a number of bodies or societies organised on an occupational or regional basis and the principle of varying rates was in operation before the State intervened. In most cases the State has done no more than to make insurance compulsory, to prescribe minimum requirements and, as a corollary, to grant subsidies, the principle of varying rates being carried into succeeding developments of compulsory insurance. It would be no easy matter to establish, *ab initio*, a suitable administrative mechanism in this country. (Department of Social Welfare, 1949: 18)

The previous creation of the NHIS, too, was cited as an obstacle to bringing in vocational-type schemes. The assumption that the NHIS was vocational was incorrect, a point made in the *Report of the Departmental Committee on Health Services*: 'The replacing at the end of 1933 of the network of approved societies by a single unified society covering the whole country was not a development but an abandonment of vocational organisation in the sphere of social insurance.'[3]

A central factor, then, which dictated the emergence of a social insurance system which was not corporatist was the legacy of schemes whose origins lay in *British* experiences. The Church's input in this crucial period was influential but not central. To the extent that it was influential, its input was not shaped by the doctrines of subsidiarity – which have been seen as crucial in shaping corporatist schemes in other countries – so much as by its specific location in a colonial and agricultural country. Having said this, it is possible that the comments on vocationalism cited above were influenced less by a genuine view that administrative legacies dictated avoiding corporatism, and more by personal animosity on the part of both bureaucrats and politicians. This is because the Dignan scheme, and the hostility to bureaucrats shown in the *Commission on Vocational Organisation Report*, are key parts of the post-war evolution of social insurance.

The emergence of Dignan Plan: Irish corporatism?

As noted previously, the bishop of Clonfert, Dr Dignan, had been appointed as chairman of the National Health Insurance Society in 1936. Although, previously, Dignan had not appeared to have a strong interest in social issues, this appointment 'gave him a practical knowledge of the workings of the social services which made him the Hierarchy's leading authority on the subject' (Whyte, 1971: 74). In 1944, Dr Dignan published a paper entitled *Social Security: Outlines of a Scheme of National Health Insurance*. The scheme was, in fact, concerned with the reform of social services generally, rather than merely health insurance. For Dignan, as for many others in this period, a central problem with Irish social services was that they retained the stamp of the Poor Law in many respects. Commenting on the public-assistance system, Dignan remarked: 'The system is tainted at its root and it reeks now, as it did when introduced, of destitution, pauperism, and degradation' (1945: 12).[4]

Dignan recommended sweeping reforms of social services. His proposals are clearly influenced by the Beveridge plan, in that they envisioned a wide extension of social insurance as a response to the problems of poverty and destitution in Ireland. But the plan diverged from the Beveridge scheme in a number of essentials. First, it was self-consciously based on Catholic social thinking in many respects. It begins, for example: 'As Ireland is a Christian and Catholic country, our Social Services ought to be Christian, that is, the spirit and teaching of Christ must be their life and their soul' (p. 7). Hence, he argued that it was the family, and not the individual, which deserved prior place in planning a social-security scheme. Within the family, there was an obligation on the father to maintain his family. 'Care must be taken in any scheme of Social Services claiming to be Christian not to attempt to relieve him of this obligation to support his family: all we should do is assist him so that he can better meet his family and social obligations' (pp. 8–9).

More specifically, while the plan proposed the unification and co-ordination of social services 'to remove redundancies, duplication, overlapping and other anomalies', it nevertheless attempted also to decentralise them. This was to be achieved by placing social services under an autonomous governing body that would be 'the Committee of Management of an improved and greatly expanded National Health Insurance Society' (p. 10). As noted in the introduction, Dignan saw this as the nearest thing to vocational organisation in Ireland. Hence, the doctrine of subsidiarity could be combined with aspects of Beveridgeism to provide an Irish solution to the problem of poverty.

There is, too, a second interesting feature of the Dignan plan, which is that it was influenced by wider European models of social insurance. Dignan broke with the flat-rate UK model and suggested, instead, earnings-related contributions and benefits. One author has commented that this vision of an autonomous social insurance scheme, organised vocationally and based on earnings-related benefit, was closely related to the Continental pattern (Kaim-Caudle, 1967). To some extent, then, the Dignan plan may be seen as a proposal for 'Irish corporatism'. Many aspects of the Dignan plan have been seen to function well in other European countries, and as the previous chapter suggested, the fact that this proposal appeared at a time of widespread administrative reorganisation and social service reform theoretically gave it some chance of being adopted.

The best-known account of the clash between MacEntee and Dignan is probably that of Whyte (1980), who suggests the emergence, by the mid-1940s, of a conflict between different 'philosophies of government'. The vocationalist perspective has been outlined in the previous chapter. The contrasting position, which Whyte labels 'bureaucratic', 'defended the centralisation of authority in government departments' (Whyte, 1980: 117). In accounting for the 'virulence' with which MacEntee responded to the Dignan report, he stresses Fianna Fáil's succession of six general-election victories and the possibility of 'hubris', as well as questioning the role of the civil service. But he lays pre-eminent stress on the doctrine of ministerial responsibility and its hold on government and the civil service generally. Although Whyte has a number of criticisms to make of the Dignan report, and comments on its intellectual shortcomings, he nevertheless sees it and the vocational organisation report as 'sincere attempts by public-spirited men to grapple with what they believed to be important issues' (p. 106). The intellectual shortcomings of their opponents 'were, if anything, worse' (p. 117).

More recently, Riordan (2000) offers a differing perspective. She suggests that 'Dignan and MacEntee were engaged in a real, no less than a philosophical, power-struggle' (p. 45). She points to earlier confrontations between the Department of Local Government and Public Health and the NHIS, and lays stress on the manner of publication of the Dignan report. 'Dignan's actions were, and were intended to be, aggressive and uncompromising' (p. 61). She lays stress, too, on 'Dignan's combination of right-wing Catholic ideology with a broad popular appeal', and the tendency of the vocationalist movement to 'foster a climate of contempt for the existing parliamentary forms'. Overall, her research 'suggests that Dignan's was a particularly "belligerent expression" of vocationalism and that MacEntee's response should be regarded in this light' (p. 45). As she suggests, the method of publication of the Dignan report certainly raises some questions about his motivations.

On 18 October 1944, Dignan's proposals for reform were published in the national press. The following day, a letter from MacEntee's secretary followed, questioning reports that a scheme had in fact been submitted. 'If by a scheme for the extension of social services is meant a proposal substantially worked out in detail, supported by factual argument and embodying estimates of the expenditure involved and concrete proposals for defraying the cost, the Minister can categorically state that no such scheme has been submitted to him.' O'Leary, drawing on an interview in the 1990s with MacEntee's secretary, Tom Barrington, suggests that this was a crucial factor: 'This lack of courtesy and tact was one of the main reasons for MacEntee's negative response. The minister, much renowned for his vanity, was incensed when he learnt of the Dignan plan through the newspapers' (2000: 111). While he would still have rejected the report, O'Leary argues that he would have done so in a more conciliatory manner. Certainly, he made clear his objections to the manner of publication.

The extent to which MacEntee took events personally cannot be doubted when one examines the material in his papers. Briefly, his department began the task of critically dissecting the scheme, and also undertook a process of investigation into the background to the publication of the report, a process characterised by hostility to the Committee of Management. He corresponded with the Minister for the Department for Posts and Telegraphs, criticising the coverage of the scheme on the radio and questioning the source of that coverage, which he suspected emanated from Hendersen.[5] He drafted and on occasion sent a number of hostile letters to Dignan. In addition, he wrote two extremely long speeches outlining in detail his account of the manner of publication and his justification for opposition. He pressed forward with legislation to strengthen the powers of the minister in relation to the NHIS, he attempted to place civil servants on the Committee of Management and, of course, he did not reappoint Dignan when his term was up, but replaced him with a civil servant, an act which can only be seen as a calculated insult given the hostility to the bureaucracy shown in the report of the Vocational Commission.

On 21 October, following the newspaper reports of the Dignan plan, the secretary of the Department of Local Government and Public Health, J. Hurson, wrote to the committee.[6] The minister, he said, had directed him to refer to the 'grave issues raised by the manner of publication', central among them being newspaper reports that the committee had been considering the propositions over the past ten years. The letter refers to sections of the National Health Insurance Act 1933, arguing that this prescribes unambiguously that the business of the society is to transact health-insurance business and that the society is definitely prohibited by statute from transacting any business other than health-insurance business:

> Notwithstanding this, however, it is to be apprehended from the reports in the newspapers that over a period of 10 years the Committee of Management has taken upon itself, without reference to the Minister, to consider, adopt and publish propositions for a 'fundamental change in the nature, the administration and the quality of our Health Services' involving, inter alia, the

creation of a special Ministry for Social Services, the establishment of a new and autonomous body to supersede and replace
in regard to *all* health services the Minister for Local
Government and Public Health and all existing authorities
concerned therewith, and the repeal of such comprehensive
measures of reform as the Public Assistance Act 1939.

The letter says that the minister, therefore, must ask the committee
why propositions which would affect the powers of the minister
himself, as well as of other members of the government and, indeed,
the constitutional position of the government as a whole, had been
adopted and published without securing his approval. 'On this point
the Minister feels it right to say that he has knowledge of the fact
that, while the Committee withheld from him all information as to
what it was doing in this regard, it referred its proposals, under
secrecy, to certain organisations for their views and approval.'

Hendersen replies with an account of events that disputes this
interpretation. According to his letter, the following was the series of
events leading to the Dignan plan and the subsequent controversy.[7]
At a committee meeting on 18 August 1943, Dignan referred to the
need for looking ahead and planning for the future of national health
insurance. 'No-one, he said, was satisfied that the scope of the present
scheme was adequate and there was need for maintaining a wider
conception of the Society's possibilities in the future. After discussion
the Secretary, at the request of the Committee, agreed to consider and
prepare proposals for a suitable scheme.' In April 1944, Dignan
called on the Parliamentary Secretary 'and, in the course of a general
conversation, informally mentioned the proposals for an extension of
National Health Insurance and promised to send the Parliamentary
Secretary a copy when the final proposals were ready.' The matter
was raised at a number of committee meetings in May, June and July
of 1944 and, on 21 June, the Secretary's memorandum was left over
for consideration at the next meeting. On 19 July, 'His Lordship the
Chairman stated the paper "Re-Planning National Health Insurance"
would be re-drafted by him and it was hoped to have a copy in the
hands of the members at the next meeting.' On 22 July 1944, the
Secretary, by direction of the Chairman, sent a letter to the
Parliamentary Secretary and enclosed a complete synopsis of proposals that were subsequently embodied in the paper read by the
chairman. The Parliamentary Secretary acknowledged receipt on 24
July. On 23 August and 20 September, the Chairman outlined his

proposals: 'At the committee meeting on 11th October 1944, His Lordship the Chairman formally read the paper and stated he accepted full responsibility for it and, if published, it would go out as a Paper read by him to the Committee.' On 14 October 1944, the secretary sent a complete copy of the paper, with a covering letter, by hand to the Parliamentary Secretary. On 17 October, the Secretary gave copies of the paper to the newspapers.

Riordan suggests that 'What is clear is that a decision was taken to by-pass official channels and put the plan directly before the public' (2000: 53), and this was almost certainly MacEntee's view. Two items in his private papers are suggestive of his access to private information that may have confirmed him in this view. One is a copy of a draft of the scheme circulated to the committee on 17 August 1944, presumably in advance of the meeting on 23 August referred to above.[8] This was headed 'Private and Strictly Confidential'. The letter itself states: 'it is particularly requested that you will regard it as extremely confidential and not to be shown to or discussed with anyone outside the Committee of Management prior to the meeting.' (At the same time, however, the letter remarks that the proposals are 'to be put before the Minister'.) Henderson's reply to Hurson on this point is slightly evasive. He remarks that Dignan had told the committee that the proposals were his own, and that he took sole responsibility for them. 'He said that in view of the fact that his proposals were his own the question of members of the committee consulting their various bodies did not arise. The Committee is not concerned with whatever communication, if any, His Lordship the Chairman may have had, at any time, with any outside person or organisation.'[9]

The other items were copies of two letters, whose appearance in MacEntee's papers is interesting. One is from Dignan to Dr Collis, dated 23 October 1944, just after Dignan read his paper, and also after MacEntee wrote to the committee. This almost certainly was Dr W.R.F. Collis, who had the year previously published a survey of the Irish health services, suggesting their unification under an autonomous board (Whyte, 1980). Dignan writes:

> My Outline-Scheme got too good a press and the reaction will set in shortly and the pendulum will swing as far in the opposite direction. What does it matter? The publicity the Outline received and the interest it seems to have aroused will compel the Government to make some move in the matter. That's what

counts. By the way I acknowledge my indebtedness to you for some of the points in the Outline.

I shall be very pleased to join with the medical profession and do my utmost to get the government to move. I shall not allow myself to be led into a wrangle with the doctors: I suggest, however, that the doctors should concentrate on the points of agreement rather than emphasise the points on which they disagree with me.

If Dr Shanley thinks it well to have a talk with me I shall be very pleased to meet him (and others) to produce a co-ordinated scheme. So keen am I on having something done that I am prepared to go to Dublin on any day that suits him . . . [10]

The second letter is signed 'Bob' (Dr Collis' first name was Robert). The addressee's name is missing, but is probably Dr Shanley. It begins:

I enclose letter from our friend the Bishop. He sent me a copy like he sent you of the National Health report and I replied to him saying that there were very considerable similarities between his report and the one we were bringing out, but that the question of control was fundamental and one which might cause very considerable difference of opinion and perhaps wreck the whole thing. Now the importance of the National Health plan, leaving out control for the moment, is that they hope to be able to produce a financial scheme which would make medicine self-supporting as it were. That is absolutely fundamental because otherwise whatever arrangements are made we come back to the dead hand of the Department of Finance which will ultimately control our destinies. Looking at the thing from the objective point of view one is faced with three main plans at the moment – ours, the Government's and the National Health Insurance, together with to a certain extent the Vocational Commission's report as well and it seems to me that our policy should be to combine as far as possible with the Vocational people, both of whom are really in the same direction as us.

Now whether you consider the present time a good one to meet the Bishop is another matter. I would say personally that if we could have a talk with him privately it might be a very useful thing. The point is where could such a meeting take place. I would be honoured to have you to supper here, but if it got around that such a meeting had taken place it might not help and at the same time obviously one would not want to meet in public or at the National Health Association or the Irish Medical Association. The thing is so important it might be worth getting a private room in the Hibernian or somewhere like that where one could just have a cordial discussion.[11]

A central question concerns how these letters found their way into MacEntee's hands. One possible answer is that the second letter was addressed to Dr Shanley, president of the Irish Medical Association (IMA) from 1942 to 1944. Dr Shanley was an influential member of Fianna Fáil and on good terms both with MacEntee and Ward (Barrington, 1987: 153). He himself had put forward proposals for reform, which had not been accepted by an IMA committee set up to consider the reorganisation of the medical service, and which he had published in the association's *Journal* in the previous April. His plan, interestingly, had 'recommended the appointment of a Minister for Health assisted by a medical council, which would have wide executive powers over the services and be subject only to the overriding control of the Minister in matters of major policy' (Ibid: 153). It is worth noting here that in the inter-departmental proposals for administrative reorganisation which would begin in February 1945 (discussed in the previous chapter) MacEntee would argue for the creation of a Minister for Health with an expanded role. Given uncertainty as to the origins of the letters, this point must remain speculative to some extent. But there are grounds for arguing that MacEntee suspected collusion between Dignan and the doctors, but could not explicitly raise the issue in public because of the nature of his source. This would help account for his spleen – which had initially been stimulated because of the manner of publication of the report.

However, in understanding the role of the Catholic Church, Dignan's motives are also central. This is a harder area on which to speculate, as the documentary evidence is much slighter. However, there are good grounds for arguing that Dignan was not representative of the hierarchy as a whole, and that this explains the ease with which MacEntee was able to dismiss what were, on the surface, deeply held doctrines of Catholic social teaching.

'Things that were better left undone': vocationalism and the Irish Catholic Church

Although, as the previous chapter described, most accounts of the Irish welfare state stress the impact of Catholic social thought, recent scholarship suggests that these long-established understandings need to be reconsidered, and that our views of the motivational springs of Church action may also need rethinking. O'Leary's (2000) study of vocationalism overturns the consensus on the extent of the Church's attachment to vocationalism in the period. He suggests that, for much of the hierarchy, vocationalism was a concept to which they paid public lip-service but which, in private, was seen as disruptive to the structure and operation of the Church in Ireland in general, and to their relations with governments in particular. 'In public they eulogised *Quadragesimo Anno* without reservation. In practise they either opposed or failed to support vocationalist schemes' (O'Leary, 2000: 52). His analysis of vocationalism concluded that it did not command widespread and sustained popular support, and that moreover, the concept lacked vigorous support from the hierarchy. Among other aspects of vocationalism, he looked in detail at attempts in the 1930s to form a vocational council of education. His analysis of the attitudes of key members of the hierarchy on the issue of vocationalism in education, including those of Dr John Charles McQuaid – then chairman of the Catholic Headmasters' Association but by the 1940s, Archbishop of Dublin – led him to conclude that they were essentially opposed to and, indeed, even deliberately under-mined, initiatives towards vocationalism. On the one hand, they were largely satisfied with departmental handling of education. On the other, they feared that 'the proposed council would also diminish the authority of the Irish Catholic Hierarchy over the educational system' (O'Leary, 2000: 50). In general, O'Leary notes that 'Matters of personal morality remained their dominant concern. They made no serious attempt to stimulate an interest in the social encyclicals and they were opposed to any radical changes that might disturb the harmonious relationship between church and state' (p. 55). Their opposition, however, was of necessity secretive, since they could not oppose papal encyclicals in public. One outcome was that some loyal Catholics were unaware that the hierarchy was hostile to such a proposal (p. 53).

Other research sustains the argument that the rhetoric of many loyal Catholics in the period was at odds with thinking of the hierarchy, and moreover, that members of the political elite were aware of this disjuncture. Delaney's (2001) analysis of the *Marie Duce* movement, which campaigned to replace the reference to the 'special position' of the Catholic Church in the constitution with a recognition of it as the 'one true Church' points to the marginal position of more radical elements in the Catholic social movement. O'Driscoll's (2000) account of social Catholicism and fiscal policy in independent Ireland likewise suggests that many who were amongst the most active in the movement were not always in line with the thinking of their superiors. Thus he remarks that 'the pursuit of vocationalism was in stark contrast to the conservative stance of the Irish hierarchy' and suggests that the 'development of popular political Catholicism could only serve to undermine the power of the bishops' (p. 130). To an extent, all three accounts point both to the heterogeneity of the Catholic social movement, and to the disjuncture between the thinking of many of its adherents and that of the wider Catholic Church.

It is interesting then to note that Dignan did not inform Archbishop McQuaid of his intentions to publish a scheme for reform of social services, especially given that McQuaid has been described as a 'control freak' (Cooney, 1999: 196–9). On 21 October, just after publication of the scheme in the press, and on the same day that MacEntee wrote to remonstrate with the committee, Dignan wrote to McQuaid:

> It occurs to me that I should send you a copy of the Paper I read last week to the Committee of Management of the National Health Insurance Society, and I do so because our Daily Press i.e. the Dublin Press made such a feature of it.
>
> I had not the remotest idea it would receive such a favourable reception from the Press and the public. Generally; did I think of or expect this publicity, you would have been the first to receive a copy. You will please excuse my apparent want of courtesy in not sending you a copy before this.
>
> I am fully aware of the many defects and shortcomings of the Paper, and I know when its implications are examined many 'vested interests' will be up in arms against many of the proposals. It will do some good however, and if it does I am more than rewarded for my trouble in writing it. You need not trouble to answer this.[12]

As I discuss in more detail below, the fragmentary documentary evidence that exists suggests that McQuaid was remarkably sanguine about the very public and bitter conflict between a bishop and a minister. In March 1945, as the tensions between Dignan and MacEntee mounted, Dignan apparently wrote to McQuaid. Only McQuaid's reply is available. It seems that Dignan had asked his

advice on a number of points, among them the desirability of accepting an invitation (or invitations) to speak in public.[13] McQuaid's
reply indicates no major concern about the affair:

> Your Lordship will kindly understand that, as far as I am con-
> cerned, a lecture by a Bishop in Dublin will always be welcome.
> In this case, however, all that I can find out confirms my hesita-
> tion about the wisdom of lecturing just now. An Rioghacht is a
> slight body. The U.C.D. Medical Society is not much less slight.
> And a Bishop's dignity may not easily fit in with such surround-
> ings . . . I find the situation rather disturbed by Mr MacEntee
> and Mr Lemass. I believe it would be well to allow a certain
> interval of time to elapse.[14]

Dignan replies on 24 March: 'I now fear I should not have replied to
Mr MacEntee at all and should have continued to bear his outburst
in silence. People are often forced through good intentions – in this
case truth and justice, to do things that were better left undone.'[15]
Despite this, Dignan issued a letter to the press on 27 March which
re-ignited the public controversy between the two, and which led
MacEntee to draft (but not send) a series of harshly worded letters
asking him to resign. It led, too, to a series of cabinet meetings on
curtailing the power of the NHIS (Riordan, 2000).

An unanswered question concerns whether Dignan, as a member
of the hierarchy, was aware that other members were, in fact, not
ardent vocationalists. It is far from clear that Dignan himself was a
fundamentalist on the issue of Catholic social teaching. O'Leary
remarks that the vocationalist movement was not monolithic and
included extremes of right and left, and as noted O'Driscoll (2000)
has also pointed to the heterogeneity of the movement. The left wing,
O'Leary argues, 'tended to anticipate the practices of modern social
democracy' (2000: 44). Among those on the left, he includes Dignan.
There are some indications in his personal papers that he was not
always in line with the thinking of the majority of the hierarchy. For
example, he has annotated (a draft?) of the hierarchy's letter to the
Taoiseach on the Mother and Child Scheme critically and quite
extensively. On the well-known argument that the state 'may not
deprive 90 per cent of parents of their rights because of 10 per cent
necessitous or negligent parents', Dignan writes: 'or because of the
high fees of doctors?'. He comments elsewhere on concerns about
doctors giving advice on sex relations, chastity and marriage: 'Don't

local medical officers advise at present? Who is to give advice? Teach our medical doctors and students Catholic doctrine in these matters'.[16]

Stronger comments occur in handwritten notes that seem to be a draft of a letter intended to be read to the bishops at a crucial meeting on 4 April.[17] What can be made out is that Dignan comments that he writes because, some months ago, two doctors asked his advice on whether the bishops had condemned the Mother and Child Scheme. He was approached, he says, because of his contacts with the medical profession due to work with the NHIS.

> I knew I could give them no answer for the present – I now wish their Lordships to agree with me that we have not as yet condemned the scheme . . . I myself hold very strongly there is absolutely nothing in the scheme opposed to Catholic teaching . . . There are other Bishops I am sure who agree with me: I know one or two.

He continues: 'We have not formally condemned it. I think that is an undoubted fact. Even if a majority is in favour of condemning it, it must be remembered that no majority can bind the whole body in a matter of faith and morals.'[18] Horgan (2000) also refers to Dignan's apparent support for the scheme, and cites interview material suggesting that Dignan was not necessarily representative of opinion amongst the hierarchy (p. 134).

It is difficult, then, to locate Dignan between the interpretations of Whyte (1980) and Riordan (2000). On the one hand, Dignan, perhaps because of his position within the NHIS, seems to have been committed to vocationalism and to have been 'out of step' with the hierarchy on this. This supports Riordan's interpretation, but not Whyte's, who has tended to see vocationalism as a widely held doctrine. However, it is difficult to see him as representing right-wing, fundamentalist Catholicism, as Riordan suggests, given his support for the Mother and Child Scheme. His reaction to the 1949 White Paper, which I discuss below, underlines this. However, for the time being, the key point to be brought out is that it is far from clear that the Irish Catholic hierarchy were genuinely vocationalist in its approach to social issues. Part of the reason that MacEntee was able to dismiss Dignan relatively easily was, perhaps, simply that Dignan was not representative of the thinking of the hierarchy in that he had a genuine commitment to, and interest in, social (as opposed to moral) thought.

In considering the conflicts between these different accounts of the scheme, a central issue concerns the extent to which 'a real, no less than a philosophical, power-struggle' took place (Riordan, 2000: 45). It is clear, I think, that there was certainly a philosophical power struggle between vocationalism and accepted modes of governance in Ireland. It seems, too, to have been real for the two protagonists, though it is easier to get a sense of MacEntee's genuine outrage and commitment than Dignan's. The extent to which vocationalism actually posed a real threat, however, is very debatable. The philosophical battle, however, was genuine, and it is to this that I now turn.

Vocationalism: an attack on ministerial prerogatives?

The arguments made so far are not, on their own, a sufficient explanation of the failure of corporatism in Ireland. I have suggested that the historical evolution of social insurance in Ireland occurred in a very different historical situation than that of continental European countries. The pressures which gave rise to corporatist structures elsewhere were not in place in Ireland and, consequently, the institutional structures of social insurance reflected British legacies and influences. I have also suggested that MacEntee's response needs to be placed in the context of an ongoing process of reform, where he was, perhaps, engaged in 'empire-building' (Feeney, 2001: 63) and resented the plan as a personal attack, a perspective which his vanity may have exacerbated And I have further suggested that Dignan was not, in any case, representative of the hierarchy as a whole, and might in some ways be seen as a 'loose cannon' among a hierarchy without a notable interest in social issues. It is not clear, though, that these arguments collectively account for the response of the government of the day to the *Report of the Commission on Vocational Organisation*, or to the Dignan plan, in particular, which has been described as 'unreasonably hostile' (Barrington, 1987: 151). There is, I think, one final issue, which is perhaps the most fundamental reason why vocationalism was not destined to take hold in Ireland.

This is an expansion of Whyte's (1980) argument that by the mid-1940s, a rift between two philosophies of government had emerged in Ireland. As is clear by now, I am dubious about the extent to which vocationalism can be said to genuinely represent the position of the Church. Nevertheless, it is clear that vocationalism was 'harshly critical of the British system of parliamentary democracy' (O'Leary, 2000: 43). The *Commission on Vocational Organisation Report* was equally critical of the civil service as being inefficient and undemocratic

(p. 103). In return, 'civil servants challenged, sometimes to the point of ridiculing, the findings of the commission' (p. 127). Apart from a natural resentment at the criticism they had received, it is also clear that policy-makers within the governmental system were operating within a set of assumptions about modes of government that were directly at odds with vocationalism.

Whyte has termed this 'bureaucratic'. This, however, may not be the most useful term for what appears to be a defence of a wider model of government.[19] This model has been described as an 'early twentieth century Westminster model' of government. From independence on,

> three core conventions of the Westminster model were absorbed into the Irish system: the doctrine of collective responsibility . . . the principle that individual ministers are answerable to parliament for the functioning of their departments, and a commitment to cabinet confidentiality that has built into a formidable tradition of executive secrecy. (Farrell, 1993: 167)

A number of sources make it clear that MacEntee (and his civil servants) resented what was seen as a usurpation of ministerial prerogatives. This can be seen in the letters and drafts of letters to Dignan and to the NHIS, in various public statements, and in the department's assessment of the plan.

There are numerous examples that indicate that the doctrine of ministerial responsibility was strongly adhered to by MacEntee. In his speech to the Fianna Fáil party responding to Dignan's comments, he remarked:

> If I were to admit for one moment that the Chairman of the Committee of Management of the National Health Society was entitled to demand from the Minister who appointed him the reasons for any answer the Minister might give in pursuance of his responsibility to Dáil Éireann then the relationship which exists between the Chairman and the Minister, as laid down in Act of Parliament, would be reversed, and we would have the interesting position that a Minister would be responsible to his appointee for his decisions and policy.[20]

He continued:

Ministerial appointees must be persons who will be meticulous to confine themselves to those functions which the Minister appointed them to discharge and, especially, will not arrogate to themselves functions which attach to the Minister or, if not particularly to him, then to the Government as a whole.

In the *Report of the Inter-Departmental Committee on the Health Services*, it is argued that the plan would, in effect, abolish the system of central health administration, under which a minister or parliamentary secretary responsible to the Oireachtas is charged with the duty of initiating measures for the improvement of public health and the supervision and financing of their execution by local authorities: 'The removal of health administration from out of the political sphere has been advocated by the protagonists of particular schools of social reform in other countries. Our Constitution gives no countenance to such a radical departure from the principles of democratic control.'[21]

The calls for vocationalism in Ireland, then, met with hostility because they were seen as an attack on a firmly held tenet of government. Irish politicians, self-described as 'the most conservative minded revolutionaries in history' had never questioned the *mode* of government in Ireland. Successive Constitutions had enshrined, and indeed, strengthened the Westminster style of government that focused on the power of the executive. In this, Ireland, together with the UK, has been said to diverge from a more 'consensual' decision-making process visible in many European countries (Gallagher, Laver and Mair, 2001). This style of government is not conducive to 'subsidiarity', and made a social insurance system which was administratively centralised under ministerial control an outcome more in tune with the political institutions of the state and the political culture of policy-makers.

The final nail in the coffin: Norton and the NHIS

The increasing unlikelihood of a vocational solution is underlined by a memo on the proposed new Department of Social Welfare in November 1946 that discussed possible future lines of development.[22] An appendix to the memo discusses the question of administration, pointing out the overlapping bodies administering the social-welfare schemes. This points out that no major economy can be made while the different schemes exist in separate compartments – only when all the different schemes lose their identity in a new unified scheme can any considerable saving be expected. This requires identity of scope, the single card and the single stamp.

> Probably the biggest single problem in the question of unified administration is the position of the National Health Insurance Society. As long as Sickness Insurance would require a separate form of administration mainly because of the existence of the Society, no considerable progress can be made. If the full benefit of the establishment of a Ministry of Social Welfare is to be realised there seems no practical alternative to abolishing the Society and transferring all its functions to the Minister.

It was to fall to the inter-party government and the Minister for Social Welfare, William Norton, to take the final steps in relation to the NHIS. The question of administration was addressed early by Norton, even before he finalised the draft 1949 White Paper on social security. On 10 June 1948, a memo on the future of the NHIS was circulated to the government. 'The Minister for Social Welfare has in preparation unified and comprehensive schemes of social insurance and social assistance . . . This examination has disclosed certain problems of administration – of which a major one is the position of the National Health Insurance Society.'[23] The memo stated that the proposals which the minister hoped to bring before the government would include a proposal that the society be abolished and that its functions be transferred to the minister. However, Finance, which had been consulted on this, made a number of objections to the proposal to abolish the society.

Finance disagreed that its abolition would necessarily involve greater economy.[24] Much of Finance's argument drew on the *Commission on Vocational Organisation Report* and the Dignan plan to argue that vocationalism 'has distinct advantages over the alternative method of bureaucratic control'. Had a body similar to the NHIS existed in Britain, it was possible that it might not have been abolished but might have continued in operation as part of the Beveridge plan:

> Considerable public opposition may be expected to the abolition of the National Health Insurance Society as an example of the insatiable appetite of bureaucracy for swallowing up organisations which are perfectly capable of fulfilling their functions.

In fact it might be argued that from the points of view of efficiency and economy some of the Social Services work could profitably be transferred from the Department to the Society and this course was suggested by Dr. Dignan, Bishop of Clonfert and former Chairman of the Society.

Finance appended an extract from the Dignan plan to its submission in support of this point of view. As we will see in Chapter 6, however, the Department of Finance, under its Fine Gael minister, opposed virtually every aspect of the White Paper, and it is questionable whether its approach represented a genuine commitment to Catholic social thought, as opposed to a genuine opposition to the proposed social-welfare scheme.

In the event, Norton succeeded in having his proposal carried by the government, although there are some anomalies in how the decision is recorded.[25] However, the decision allowed the 1949 White Paper to be unambiguous on the question of the NHIS:

> The new scheme will call for a comprehensive review of administrative methods with a view to securing the most efficient and most economical results from the co-ordination of the different services, including the absorption into the Department of Social Welfare of the National Health Insurance Society, the existence of which as a separate organism operating only part of the unified scheme would be quite anomalous. (Department of Social Welfare, 1949: 33)

Putting this into effect was quite torturous, however, and it took two years between the decision made above and the translation of the proposal into law (McCullagh, 1998).

Despite the fact that this decision ran counter to the expressed preferences of the Church, opposition was muted. The 'considerable public opposition' envisioned by Finance does not appear to have materialised. There *was* a response from within Catholicism, as individuals and organisations commented on the developments in social security from the publication of the Dignan plan on. For example, the Rev. Professor Lucey (later Bishop of Cork) remarked on the response to the Dignan plan: 'most people could not but have an uneasy feeling that . . . the Government has little use for schemes for which it cannot take the credit or which propose to curtail rather than extend its own sphere of control.'[26] Likewise, the Catholic Societies Vocational Organisation Conference objected implicitly in its response to the White Paper. The statement it sent to the Taoiseach in February 1950 pointed out that the White Paper envisioned administration of the scheme devolving entirely on the state. It referred to the section of the White Paper (quoted above) that argued that the administrative arrangements on the Continent were not present in Ireland, and that establishing them '*ab initio*' would be difficult. 'Are we then to accept the position that in this matter we have proceeded so far in the direction of Statism that there is no turning back and that the line of least resistance should be followed?'[27]

These, however, were, by and large, isolated examples which merely highlight the absence of a response from the institutional core of the Church. There appears to have been no correspondence between the hierarchy and either the various Ministers for Social Welfare or the Taoiseach on any aspect of the social-security plan. Norton forwarded an advance copy of the White Paper to McQuaid on 25 October 1949, but there is no record of any response.[28] Likewise, Lee (1979) has commented on the surprising lack of reaction to the Vocational Commission's report, even within the Catholic press.

On the surface, then, the central argument of this chapter may appear to be that the institutional legacies of British rule outweighed Catholic Church preferences in this period. This argument would imply, first, that a corporatist-type social insurance scheme would have reflected the policy preferences of the Church for vocational structures and, second, that the absence of these structures consequently indicates the Church's failure to achieve its preferred social policy outcomes. However, this conclusion would almost certainly underestimate the extent of Catholic influence in the period, and would leave many aspects of the controversy surrounding the Mother and Child Scheme unexplained. Rather, the argument is that institutional legacies were central *only* because the Church's adherence to vocationalism was weak. A close examination of the 1952 Act raises questions about the widely held perception that the Church in this period was actively committed to vocationalism, and that this commitment underlay its activism in health. However, other explanations may have to be found for the Church's role in health, since its stance on social welfare indicates what I term 'benign indifference' to state activism in the field of social welfare. It is to this that I now turn.

'Benign indifference': the Catholic Church and social security in Ireland

The processes by which Catholic social teaching might influence social policy are central to understanding why vocationalist ideas had little appeal to the Irish Catholic Church. As outlined in the previous chapter, accounts of the influence of Catholicism on social policy have generally rested on measurements of Catholic power expressed in terms of control of government; that is, on Catholicism as expressed in Christian-democratic parties (Wilensky, 1981; van Kersbergen, 1995; Huber, Ragin and Stephens, 1993; Huber and Stephens, 2001). But there are other ways that religion can influence policy. Castles (1994) points out that these processes are likely to be diverse:

> Religious beliefs may influence policy because individuals with such beliefs behave differently from those without them, because interest groups and parties may be formed to promote such beliefs, because the views of those who are influential in policy making may be shaped by such beliefs, or even, in quasi-corporatist mode, because the state delegates to the Church the public regulation of certain spheres of social relations. (p. 20)

Stressing *how* Catholicism seeks to influence government points to a need to take into account 'the political dimensions of religion, for example, the state–church-cleavage' (Schmid, 1996: p. 104). Schmid draws attention to the importance of this cleavage, which was central to the genesis of the Christian-democratic parties, and points to its role in shaping the nature of social-welfare organisation, especially in religiously mixed societies. In many respects, the explanations for the lack of Christian democracy in Ireland are compatible with explanations for the lack of corporatism in Irish social insurance.

Unlike many other countries, the influence of the Church in Ireland was not expressed through a political party. Although Fine Gael, the second largest party, sits with the Christian Democrats in the European Parliament, its historical origins are quite different from Christian-democratic parties generally (Mair, 1999). Christian democracy largely emerged where Catholicism was challenged by secular political forces. As Mair argues, in Ireland, political Catholicism emerged victorious with its values enshrined in the political system and, hence, 'uniquely among the Catholic countries of western Europe, Christian democracy never emerged as a distinct political movement in Ireland' (p. 130).

Instead, the influence of the Church in Ireland owes more to the strength of its position in Irish society generally and the loyalty accorded to it by politicians of all political hues. Arising out of this, the mode of influence characteristic of the Irish Church has been described as 'the politics of informal consensus', where formal contacts between Church and governments were rare (Keogh, 1996: 103–17). Formal contacts were rare because there was, in general, little discord between Church and state. In his classic study of the Church in Ireland, Whyte concluded that between 1923 and 1979, there were only sixteen pieces of legislation on which one or more bishops were consulted or made representations (Whyte, 1980).[29] The areas in which the Church made such representations varied over time, and the 1940s and 1950s probably mark the peak of its interest in social policy.

One feature of this politics of informal consensus is that it relied, to a large extent, on private consultations between government and the hierarchy. Some of MacEntee's quarrel with Dignan concerned Dignan's decision to make their disagreements public – something he regarded as 'a very grave breach of confidence'.[30] The Mother and Child Scheme referred to above became a major debating point only because of the Minister for Health's decision to publish correspondence between him, other members of the government and the hierarchy. This correspondence was intended to be confidential. The Catholic Church in Ireland, then, did not 'run for office' (as a political party) and influence policy through control of government. Instead, the Church was dependent on the extent to which it could persuade governments that they should, for whatever reasons, acquiesce with the wishes of the Church. It relied, to some extent, on a commonality of interest or, where this did not exist (as perhaps in health), on its ability to use its moral authority to persuade politicians to adopt its policies. The Church was aided in this by the fact that its representations were generally not in the public domain.

Although there was diversity within the Church on this, it is clear that many members of the hierarchy were not automatically hostile to an extension of a state role in the provision of social services. Nor were they necessarily hostile to the extension of social insurance. As we have seen, Dignan was broadly supportive of a state role in providing compulsory social insurance in Ireland.[31] He commented on the White Paper as follows:

> I am all in favour of a scheme: and I want it to be *national* in the
> sense that virtually all our citizens will be included in it. I want
> it to be *comprehensive* in the sense that it will go far in
> providing all the benefits, monetary and otherwise, that are
> implied in the term 'social security'. And I want an *autonomous*
> committee to administer it. (Dignan, 1950: 104)

Dignan's criticisms, then, focused on two aspects: the fact that it was
not a genuinely comprehensive scheme (due to the exclusion of
farmers), and the fact that it was to be administered by the
Department of Social Welfare rather than an independent committee
organised on vocational lines. But this is very far from a hostility to
state welfare and a commitment to deep subsidiarity. Catholic social
teaching, in Ireland and elsewhere, was concerned not *only* with
countering excessive state power but *also* with achieving some sort of
balance between labour and capital: 'in Catholic social doctrine
subsidiarity is intrinsically linked with other fundamental principles,
such as personalism, solidarity, pluralism and distributive justice'
(van Kersbergen and Verbeek, 1994).

Dignan was not only – or perhaps not even primarily – concerned
with countering state power. His plan was also centrally concerned
with removing the taint of 'pauperism, destitution and degradation'.
Hence, his scheme was welcomed by the Labour Party, one influential
trade unionist even going so far as to suggest that it should be published jointly by Dignan and the Labour Party. The *Report of the
Commission on Vocational Organisation*, likewise, was informed not
only by a dislike of state centralisation, but also by a desire to achieve
a more socially just society. It stressed that 'All would agree that
democracies are bound to make the maximum use of their resources
and to plan economic life in accordance with the dictates of social
justice' (cited in Lee, 1979: 335). Few even of the strong vocationalists were as hostile to state welfare schemes as Hegarty (quoted
above).

In providing a solution to 'pauperism, destitution and degradation', the White Paper and the 1952 Act met much of the demands
of Catholic social teaching as it applied to the Irish situation. Social
insurance, *however* organised, was seen to encourage individual and
family responsibility, and to supplement rather than supplant the role
of the father as provider. The White Paper concludes: 'the scheme
goes a long way towards recognising the proper status of the worker
in a society organised on Christian principles' (Department of Social

Welfare, 1949: 44). Catholic social teaching is referred to at many points. For example, the White Paper argues that a variable-rate scheme increases state compulsion by requiring more than compulsory insurance for key risks at a basic level:

> The flat rate system, which is now well established here, can be held to conform with this view, subject, perhaps to an extension of the plan of additions to benefit, based not on salary or wages, but on family needs. This basis is felt to be more in accord with Christian principles, and indeed, may be related to the special recognition given in the Constitution to the family as 'the natural primary and fundamental unit group of society'.

It is in this sense that I have used the term *benign* indifference to describe the response of the Church. The response was largely benign because many aspects of the plan were, in fact, congruent with the preferences of the Church. And it was indifferent to the apparent discrepancy with vocationalist thought because, in reality, the vocationalist perspective put forward in the 1940s was a solution to quite a different set of problems than actually existed in Ireland. Daly accounts for the 'lack of popular support' for corporatism in interwar Ireland by pointing to the very different historical traditions, and in particular, the fact that in Ireland 'the state supported Catholic values' (1992: 117). The Irish Church had no real need for solutions that defended its interests from a secularising state, since there was little real conflict between Church and state. Those who promulgated extreme vocationalism were essentially a minority; the bulk of the hierarchy was opposed to vocationalist ideas which could threaten not merely its relationship with the state, but its own power base in health and education. 'The Catholic church itself had arrived by 1937 at a satisfactory relationship with the state and complimented this by firmly ensuring that internal radicalism – political and economic – did not disrupt the new consensus' (O'Driscoll, 2000: 140) Finally, among those genuinely committed to 'social Catholicism', some of the most influential were not necessarily hostile to an increased state role in the provision of welfare.

Conclusion

In 1992, Korpi asked why there was no corporatism in Irish social insurance, given the strength of the Catholic Church in Ireland. The answer, perhaps, is that the association between corporatism and Catholicism is not automatic, but is specific to the experiences of core European countries in the period surrounding the birth of the welfare state. It is not so much Catholicism *per se*, as the specific context in which Catholicism was located which is central to explaining the association between Catholicism and corporatism. The patterns of industrialisation, class mobilisation and Church–state conflict which gave rise to the doctrines of subsidiarity, corporatism and Christian democracy in Europe generally were absent in Ireland. Thus, the application of 1911 National Insurance Act to Ireland, while shaped by interventions from the Church, did not reflect the doctrine of subsidiarity. By the 1940s, the generally harmonious nature of Church–state relations in independent Ireland meant that vocationalism was not merely unnecessary, but potentially disruptive, while the institutional legacies of British rule made it unlikely. None of this suggests that Catholicism does not make a difference – merely, that we might expect it to make a difference in highly distinctive ways in different places, and at different times. As Daly notes, 'there may be more than one kind of Catholic welfare state' (1999: 128).

A close examination of the policy processes surrounding social security raise a number of questions about the role of the Catholic Church in Ireland. Perhaps the most striking point to emerge is the contrast between the 'benign indifference' in the field of social security, and the activism in health. The difference between the two has been commented on, though not accounted for, by others: hence, Peillon (1996) attributes 'a great deal of autonomy' to the state in relation to social security, but very little in health (p. 12). As in the previous chapter, the doctrine of subsidiarity might, theoretically, have been applied to state activism in both fields; the discussion of social security demonstrates that the reality was that its tenets were applied selectively. Catholic social thought, it seems, provides a poor guide to understanding the actions of the Irish Catholic Church. We might conclude, therefore, that rather than the doctrine of subsidiarity providing the impetus to activism in the field of health, it was state activism in health which provoked recourse to the doctrine of subsidiarity.

A clearer understanding of the Church's role in shaping the Irish welfare state may require a shift in attention from the theological rhetoric of the Church to a closer consideration of the circumstances that evoke this rhetoric. Thus Barrington remarks that 'The Hierarchy's opposition to the health reforms had little to do with Catholic social or moral teaching and is only understandable as a defence of the interests of the powerful Catholic voluntary hospitals, their consultant staff and associated medical schools from further state encroachment' (2003: 159). However, their focus on broadly moral concerns in connection with the plans for the education of women in respect of motherhood in the health reforms do suggest that their opposition might also reflect what Daly terms a 'traditionalist' rather than 'social' Catholicism which 'shuns modern secular institutions like divorce, abortion rights, and secular schooling' (1999: 105).

What is clear, however, is that their response is not easily understood by reference to patterns of Church activism in the conservative corporatist family of nations. While the Church's contribution to the creation of a two-tier system in health may appear superficially compatible with the focus on the status maintenance in corporatist systems, it is very difficult to describe the Irish health system as corporatist (O'Sullivan, 2004). By and large, corporatist health systems are associated with a strong role for *social* insurance in health care systems, whereas it might be said that the contemporary Irish health care system is distinguished by a strong role for *private* health insurance. Patterns of governance too cannot be described as corporatist, since we do not see employers, employees, insurers and providers embedded in the administrative and governance structures as is the case in varying ways in the corporatist world of welfare (Saltman et al., 2004; Daly, 2001). Thus while we might agree that 'Ireland is probably unique in the extent to which the Catholic Church has influenced the development of health policy' (Barrington, 2003: 152) it does not follow that outcomes reflect Catholic corporatist values (Adshead and Millar, 2004). We might conclude then that the example of social security prompts us to reconsider our conceptualisation of health, and that we need to assess the impact of Catholicism in ways which do not rely on the concept of corporatism.

This chapter has focused on the administrative structures of social insurance, arguing that the outcomes we might expect from the theoretical literature are absent in Ireland, because Catholicism in Ireland was shaped by distinctive patterns of industrialisation and state formation. It is true, though, that this may only partially capture the extent to which Catholicism may influence welfare states, as noted above. For example, redistributive issues were not explored here. Yet this is crucial in considering the contrasting effects of social democracy and Christian democracy. Christian democracy, very generally, might be said to 'reproduce rather than overcome class and status differences' (van Kersbergen, 1995: 152). This may be partially related to the way in which class interests are expressed in Christian democratic parties. Huber, Ragin and Stephens (1993) suggest a distinctive 'multi-class' aspect to Christian democracy:

> Christian democratic parties typically have strong bases among farmers, the petite bourgeoisie, professionals, and even sections of the haute bourgeoisie, in addition to wage and salary earners, and they advocate class compromise and class harmony in their internal operation as well as in their approach to governing. (p. 741)

The administrative structures of social insurance, revealing though they may be of the factors shaping social insurance, can only take us so far.

Embedded in the account above is a suggestion that the response of the Catholic Church to social policy needs to be considered in relation to its location in a broadly agricultural country, as indicated by its response to the 1911 National Insurance Act. Much the same can be said for the response of many Catholic thinkers to developments during and after the Second World War. Thus Lucey's response to the Beveridge Plan, while referring briefly to Christian social teaching, mostly stressed that Ireland should not necessarily plan along the same lines as an industrialised country like Great Britain: 'The majority of our people are property-owners, not wage-earners or salaried officials, and they own enough property – land, shops, etc. – to be in a position to provide for themselves and their families by their own efforts' (Lucey, 1943: 43). Indeed, Adshead and Millar's (2004) account, although stressing the impact of conservative Catholic social teaching, present an explanation which in many important respects prioritises the role of conservative *rural* (or property-owning) values as a key explanatory factor.

The Irish social insurance system owes much to the legacies of British rule. Policy choices that reflected British experiences con-strained later policy-makers; hence, the Irish social insurance system has much in common with that of the UK. However, the choices that policy-makers took in the 1940s and 1950s also reflected the nature of Irish society in the period, and the social insurance system was also shaped by indigenous pressures. It is, perhaps, this combination of the shared experiences of core countries (via colonisation), and the divergences from traditional paths to industrialisation and modernisation, which makes Ireland difficult to classify in the worlds of welfare. One of the central factors which lie behind divergences from the Beveridge model in Irish social security is the centrality of agriculture in both economic and political terms, and the following chapter examines the extent to which agrarian influences have structured outcomes in Irish social security.

CHAPTER FOUR

Farmers, Workers and Welfare: The Social Politics of Land in Ireland

Introduction

'on the road of segregating our population into two warring factions of 500,000 working farmers on the one hand, and 700,000 employed persons on the other, nothing but disaster lies ahead'.[1]

In 1944, two deputies from the National Labour Party put forward a motion calling for the unification and coordination of all social services under a Ministry of Social Services, and for all in employment to be brought under the provisions of a comprehensive scheme of social insurance.[2] Seán MacEntee, who, as we have seen, was the politically astute Minister for Local Government and Public Health, requested a full note from his department:

> Inherent in the proposed scheme of social security is the analogy between conditions in this country and those in Great Britain where the vast bulk of the people are homogeneous, industrialised and urbanised. Do the movers of the motion mean to include in 'gainful employment' those working on their own account? Would not the difficulties of including under a 'comprehensive scheme of social insurance' people working on their own account such as farmers and artisans, who represent such a large proportion of our population, be very great?[3]

For the next eight years, and through two changes of government, the problem of reconciling the interests of workers and farmers was a common thread running through the diverse issues surrounding the drafting of the 1952 Social Welfare Act. In the Irish context, however, workers were rural and agricultural as well as urban and industrial.

As the introduction discussed, while the impact of the Beveridge plan is evident in Irish outcomes, a central point of differentiation is the absence of universality. One key reason for this was the centrality of the agricultural sector in Irish political and economic life. The long history of the 'land question' in Ireland, its impact on social structures and its expression in national mythology and in party politics structured debates and outcomes. In fact, agrarianism was so fundamental to the process of state formation, and had an impact on so many diverse aspects of Irish political life, that it is sometimes difficult to separate it from the nature of the state itself. As Bull notes in his study of the land question in Ireland, 'the issue became so important in national life that it shaped the future of Irish nationalism and the shape of the society which emerged out of the nationalist struggle, creating between the issue of land and nationalism a nexus which was so strong that one issue became effectively a metaphor for the other' (1996: 4). As the land question interacted with nationalism in nineteenth-century Ireland, it shaped the emerging party system, was embedded in the developing administrative structures of the state, and contributed to deeply rooted beliefs about the nature of the society itself. Agrarianism in Ireland shaped both the state and the wider society.

As Chapter 1 discussed, debates about the impact of social class on the Irish welfare state have tended to focus on the weakness of the left. There has been, until recently, very little attempt to assess the role of agrarianism in shaping social-policy outcomes (see Fahey, 1998b and 2002, discussed below). In fact, the shape, structure and political organisation of farming interests were crucial in deciding outcomes. Thus the first response of policy-makers to demands for comprehensive social insurance was to assess how this would mesh with a primarily agricultural economy with a high proportion of self-employed or independent workers. But this did not translate into a simple dichotomy between 'agrarian' and 'urban' interests. Rather, it opened a debate in which the competing demands of 'privileged' versus 'unprivileged' groups were addressed through the prism of the Irish party system, where the social bases of party support may be obscure, but nevertheless exist. In their attempts to chart a policy course tackling redistributive issues that encompassed diverse agrarian groups, as well as the interests of 'privileged' urban workers, policy-makers had in mind a particular vision of what was seen as a primarily agrarian society. In some respects, though, this vision was one which only superficially matched the reality of agriculture in post-war Ireland.

All three governments who considered the issue shared, in some important respects, the same institutional framework. Yet there were important differences, too. As we've seen, the period witnesses what has been described as a central 'watershed' in the development of the Irish party system. The emergence of the first coalition government, expressing the underlying logic of proportional representation, marks a departure and points to the dynamism inherent in any political system, but perhaps especially in a state little more than two decades old. As we will see in the following chapters, social policy was a central element in the internal politics which ultimately doomed the first experiment in 'inter-party' government. A close examination of decisions taken on social security opens up the manner in which social-class interests are expressed in the Irish party system, and adds to our understanding of how interests are embedded in institutional settings.

Agrarianism and welfare state theory

Although the land question is acknowledged to be one of the key issues in Irish history, the role of agrarianism in the development of social policy in Ireland has only recently attracted any attention (Cousins, 1997; Fahey, 1998b and 2002; Carey, 2005). In comparative terms, this is perhaps not surprising. Farmers seldom feature in explanations of welfare development; in many respects, this is because key explanations are predicated on the process of industrialisation which rendered agriculture a subsidiary force. For many theorists, as we have seen, welfare states implicitly, if not explicitly, arose as the agricultural sector declined relative to a growing urban-industrial sector. This is not to say that there has been no interest at all – farmers figure largely in Baldwin's (1990) restatement of a social explanation for welfare states, they have been cited as actors in explanations of American exceptionalism (Alston and Ferrie, 1985; Gilbert and Howe, 1991) and Dutton (2000) has argued for their role in shaping the development of the French welfare state. Most recently, Watson (2005) has suggested that agrarian issues played a role in influencing the late-developing Spanish welfare state. But it is fair to say that they have generally been seen as much less significant in shaping welfare outcomes than their working-class sparring partners. To date the various authors cited above have not been considered collectively as constituting an agrarian perspective, largely because agrarianism, while central to these accounts, has not always been the key independent variable.

Those authors who *have* prioritised agrarian issues have generally prefaced their accounts by stressing their neglect in the field generally. Hence Petersen's study of the emergence of welfare in Denmark presents it as 'an important corrective to general theories regarding the emergence of welfare states' (Petersen, 1990: 70). Petersen examines the Danish 1891 old-age pension, a non-contributory, tax-financed scheme, and argues that it was essentially a response to agrarian demand and pressure. 'Conventional thinking maintains that social security systems emerged in response to the social consequences of industrialisation. The timing and nature of Danish social legislation, however, followed from agricultural conditions' (Petersen, 1990: 71). Dutton (2000: 410) critiques an urban bias in his description of the importance of French agriculture, remarking that 'the fair treatment of rural populations is hampered by a silent presumption that only urban workers or their allied political parties could muster the necessary influence to effect reform'. Likewise, Fahey (2002: 62) remarks that 'academic analysis has conventionally defined [agrarian policy] out of the picture as far as welfare state development is concerned.' This general neglect means that the theoretical literature on agrarianism and welfare states is not extensive enough to permit an account of what an 'agrarian' welfare state might look like – as opposed, for example, to the social democratic or Christian democratic regimes discussed in the previous chapters. However, from the disparate existing accounts, it is possible to draw out some tentative suggestions about what one might wish to consider in terms of conceptualising an agrarian impact on social policy.

An obvious starting point is Scandinavia, 'where the introduction of a uniform and egalitarian national system can be traced to a class compromise between the industrial workers and the small farmers' (Flora, 1986: xx). It is perhaps not surprising that agrarianism has long been recognised as a factor influencing welfare state outcomes in Scandinavia since 'political agrarianism' in the shape of agrarian political parties has also been essentially a Scandinavian phenomenon (Gallagher, Laver and Mair, 2001). In his account of the key factors underlying the different welfare regimes, Esping-Andersen (1990) stresses the fundamental role of rural classes in building class coalitions. His analysis is particularly useful, both in stressing that rural classes were central for welfare outcomes, and in pointing to some factors which might explain divergent outcomes. Hence he points to the importance of whether agriculture was labour-intensive or capital-intensive, and to the nature of the political organisation of agricultural interests. He suggests that Scandinavian farmers were 'politically articulate and well-organised', and hence had a greater capacity to negotiate political deals. However, his general comments that 'the rural classes were decisive for the future of socialism' (p. 30) points us to a problem with his and other accounts of developments in Scandinavia. This is that despite the recognition of an agrarian dimension, outcomes in Scandinavia have generally been integrated into an essentially social democratic narrative.

Baldwin's (1990) account is primarily concerned with reconsidering this 'labourist' or social perspective on welfare states, and rests partially on a reconceptualisation of the factors shaping Scandinavian welfare states, since they have been seen as one of the clearest exemplars of the triumph of social democracy. The 'labourist' perspective is one which 'regards the welfare states of certain countries as a victory for the working class and as evidence of the left's ability to implement universalist, egalitarian social policy on behalf of the least advantaged' (p. 55). Baldwin argues that the focus on the industrial working class as the motivating force behind solidaristic welfare outcomes is simplistic. He does not argue that social class is irrelevant but, rather, that the class interests which have shaped policy outcomes have varied. Workers as a class have not always coincided uniformly with categories of high risk; those with most to gain from solidarity have differed over time. Hence Baldwin attempts to shift the focus from one which assumes a straightforward link between a particular class category and risk category, and thus to shift the association between one particular class and solidaristic legislation. Solidaristic measures, he argues, have triumphed when 'otherwise privileged groups realised that they shared a common interest in reallocating risk with the disadvantaged' (p. 292). He returns to the origins of solidaristic welfare in Denmark and Sweden, and suggests that the egalitarian, universalistic outcomes were determined 'at the behest of parties and classes not associated with the left' (p. 63). The traditional picture of the factors shaping Scandinavian welfare states has neglected the fact 'that it was the outcome of battles between a rising agrarian bourgeoisie and entrenched, but declining, bureaucratic and urban elites' (ibid.). For Baldwin, then, agriculture is used to provide support for wider arguments about the social bases of solidaristic welfare states, rather than being an argument about the agrarian roots of welfare states. But, in the process, he provides a useful account of how social policy might be shaped by agrarian social classes.

In Denmark, for example, Baldwin argues that the universalism of the 1891 Act (see above) 'was the result of farmers' hopes to improve labor conditions during the agricultural crisis of the late nineteenth century' (p. 64). A key factor was the structure of the agricultural sector, since the rural workforce included cottagers and smallholders, making it difficult 'to distinguish between the dependently employed and the self-employed' (ibid.). Baldwin locates debates in a broadly political context: farmers felt they were denied the representation to which they were entitled, and social policy became an element in the struggle between this perspective as expressed by liberals, and the conservative representatives of the urban professional and manu-facturing classes, and aristocratic estate owners. The 1891 Act represented a compromise position that met farmers' demands in a number of ways. It eliminated the need for employers' contributions, which was important since farmers were the largest group of employers. It avoided higher wages (which a contributory scheme would have implied), important in the low waged agricultural economy. It prom-ised to benefit the rural world at the expense of the urban world, since the countryside contributed proportionally less to central government's revenues than the cities. And it fulfilled the important condition of making rural life more attractive. 'Because farmers sought to please a labor force that included both wage earners and smallholders, limiting welfare to the dependently employed, not to mention the urban working class, was out of the question' (p. 75).

Petersen (1990) echoes many of these points: in particular, pointing to the double role of smallholders as both independents and as dependently employed, implying that coverage limited to wage-earners would have been problematic. He also locates the emergence of the 1891 Act in the wider political context, arguing that the influence of agriculture on the Danish 1891 Act can be traced to 'agricultural conditions, pressure from farmers, and political circum-stances which empowered farmers to enforce their demands' (p. 70). These two accounts direct our attention to the particular structure of agriculture (in this case both the employing role of farmers, and the double role of small-holders) and the wider political context in which agriculture was located as the context of events in Denmark at the end of the nineteenth century.

Baldwin's (1990) account of the emergence of the 1913 'people's pensions' in Sweden also points to the importance of the agrarian social structure. The long-term solidaristic outcome of universalist, tax-financed policy generally associated with social democracy was, in fact, determined by initial decisions which reflected 'the farmers' narrow, but persistently pressed demands' (p. 93). A central factor was farmers' desire that they should not be excluded from 'new forms of statutory beneficence' (p. 83). His account points to differences between the Swedish and Danish case, in how parties mediated class differences, and in the structure of the agrarian sector. But both cases provide support for a perspective which sees agrarian social classes as important in shaping social-policy outcomes.

These accounts are useful in clarifying the role of agrarian factors in Denmark and Sweden, but a central question is whether agrarianism is essentially a Scandinavian phenomenon only. A number of more recent accounts suggest that it has played an unacknowledged role in other welfare states. Hence Dutton's (2000) call to 'bring the countryside back in' is based on his analysis of developments in France. He argues that attempts from the 1930s on to extend an industrial model of family allowances to agriculture 'triggered a revolt against employer-controlled social welfare that opened the door to large-scale state intervention and, ultimately, to the massive reforms that form the basis of France's current welfare state' (p. 378). Central to his argument is the structure of French agriculture, with farm size being a crucial variable. Larger farms, he argues, most closely resembled factories, while small holding peasants, a particularly important group in France, often relied on family labour, or employed small numbers of employees (sometimes paid in kind). Living standards of employees and employers were frequently similar. The centrality of small and medium-sized agricultural enterprises meant that 'the line between employer and employee upon which employer-based welfare in industry and commerce rested was not so easily determined in agriculture' (p. 387). As a result, the system of family allowances which had been designed by industrialists as part of a wage strategy targeted at well-organised urban workers did not translate to the more diverse smallholder world of French agriculture (p. 392). Hence, there was a need to provide, not just for workers, but also for 'small-holding *chefs de famille*' (p. 392). He traces events in the evolution of family allowances between 1936 and 1945, arguing that the structure of French agriculture led to the reshaping of the system of family allowances, culminating in an extended role for the state. There are parallels with the Scandinavian case, in that the distinction between farmer and worker was less clear cut than in industry, requiring welfare solutions which were not targeted at employees alone. In accounting for the introduction of governmental assumption of fiscal responsibility for family allowances, Dutton also stresses the interaction of two overlapping ideological factors: the importance of 'a rural ideal of a fecund countryside, teeming with family farms' (p. 399) and the interaction of these views with pro-natalist ideas. He concludes his account of the role of French agri-culture in shaping family policy with the hope 'that other national histories might be similarly interrogated' (p. 410) to counter the urban bias and neglect of agrarianism. Watson's (2005) account of more recent events in Spain might be considered in this light.

At the heart of her analysis is the thesis that the creation of unemployment benefit emerged from the need to find a solution to southern Spain's agrarian social question following the transition to democracy in the late twentieth century. Agrarian factors are not the central focus of her concern – instead she is primarily concerned with arguments about the particular role of political parties and the use of social policy as a weapon to undermine political competition, and I do not engage with the details of her argument on this. She locates her account within what she sees as 'the paradigmatic discussion of agriculture's role in shaping welfare state development' (p. 3). Thus, as here, she begins by considering the standard interpretation of the Scandinavian 'red–green' alliance which stresses that agricultural producers, not dependent on the sale of labour power, were not interested in welfare reforms *per se*, but traded social protection for the industrial working class in exchange for price supports. As outlined above, this broadly labourist or social-democratic thesis has been critiqued (Baldwin, 1990; Petersen, 1990). However, Watson's focus is to stress that this account treats the agricultural sector as an undifferentiated mass, and ignores that fact that landless peasants are in fact dependent on the sale of their labour power.

Watson argues that the nature of the unemployment benefit system introduced in Spain in 1983 needs to be understood in terms of the complex relationship between agrarian unions and the strategic needs of their associated political parties.[4] For our purposes, however, what is important is that the conflicts centred on contrasting solutions to rural poverty stemming from excess agrarian labour, in the broader context of long-standing calls for land reform. Solutions needed to encompass a heterogeneous rural structure, including a 'notoriously conservative' smallholding peasantry in northern Spain, and a large landless working population in southern Spain. Given this hetero-geneity, challenging property relations was problematic in electoral terms. The solution – a non-contributory rural unemployment subsidy, public works, and an occupational training program – was aimed at tackling rural employment in the context of de-industrialisation by enabling rural workers to remain in the countryside.[5] Hence, although Watson's account, again, is not primarily intended to promote an agrarian perspective on welfare states, it does suggest that the interests of and structure of the agrarian sector was central to shaping outcomes. That her account is focused on conflicts within and between socialist and communist unions and parties merely under- lines the fact that the agrarian sector needs to be located in wider political and institutional configurations.

Finally, some US researchers have suggested that the organisation of agriculture in the American south was a factor retarding welfare growth, while others suggest that agriculture adds to our under- standing of the state–society interaction (Alston and Ferrie, 1985; Finegold, 1988; Gilbert and Howe, 1991). Alston and Ferrie (1985) put forward an explanation for why US government did not grow faster in the 1930s which prioritises the structure of agriculture in the south. They argue that southern agricultural landlords retarded the growth of old-age insurance because of its perceived effect on labour relations: 'Federal provision of welfare threatened planter pater- nalism and thereby undermined the dependence of agricultural labour on landlords' (p. 96). The New Deal, they argue, would have offered a substitute for paternalistic benefits, decreased the value of planter paternalism, and made it more difficult to obtain cheap and loyal labour (p. 103). The ability of southern agricultural landlords to resist the New Deal can be traced to institutional factors that facilitated their social and political dominance. Rural élites 'were able to control the election of senators, congressmen, and even governors in some cases' (p. 104). Alston and Ferrie's key argument is that their research has important implications for the belief that special-interest groups always force an expansion of the welfare state, but their research also contributes to the thesis that the structure of agricul- tural interests can contribute to shaping social-policy outcomes. Indeed, agricultural factors seem fundamental to understanding the New Deal and its associated welfare outcomes.

Finegold argues that 'to understand the development of many welfare states, and especially to understand public social provision in the United States, we must analyse the role of agriculture as well as that of industry' (1988: 200). He stresses two key legacies which reflect the impact of agriculture: the initial exclusion of farm workers and farm owners from the social-security, old-age insurance

programme, and the emergence of food stamps as a central programme of aid (food stamps, which are administered by the
Department of Agriculture, reflect the politics of agriculture, argues
Finegold). He is concerned with explaining why agriculture in the
USA had these particular outcomes, rather than others, and he argues
that 'arrangements for representation and administration through the
state organisations and party systems of the American national government have determined the extent to which agricultural interests
would influence social provision' (p. 232). He echoes some of Alston
and Ferrie's (1985) comments in stressing how these administrative
and representational arrangements prioritised the perspective of
commercial farmers, especially southern plantation owners. Finegold
is clearly operating from within a statist or institutionalist perspective; hence, he stresses the role of bureaucrats and experts within
the administrative structures which surround the agricultural policies
of the New Deal. This statist perspective on the role of agriculture in
the US has been critiqued as neglectful of the role of class interests
(Gilbert and Howe, 1991).

Gilbert and Howe (1991) examine the social origins of state-
building in the USA as part of their contribution to what they term
the 'state vs. society' debate. As Chapter 1 outlined, one criticism of
institutional, or statist, perspectives is that they take insufficient
account of class structures in the wider society: Gilbert and Howe
(1991) are concerned with exploring how the interrelations between
state and society contribute to shaping policy. As with Baldwin
(1990), then, their perspective is less with arguing for agriculture as a
primary factor shaping welfare states, and more with using New Deal
agriculture policy as a case study to illustrate the centrality of class
relations to the policy process.[6] They take issue with statist perspectives on the New Deal agriculture policy. They examine agricultural
state institutions (such as the US Department of Agriculture and
related organisations), concluding that, as the state's institutional
capacity developed in the agricultural arena, it did so 'in a way that
increased the class capacity of the dominant farm groups, subverted
that of oppositional groups, and structurally privileged the former
within the state' (p. 208). They also examine the structure of farming
classes across three key agricultural regions. One of their central
points is that the class structure of agriculture varied across different
regions, meaning that agricultural policy had to deal with extremely
divergent interests. So, while, as we have seen above, plantation
sharecropping was dominant in the south, capitalist agriculture

dominated in the Pacific West, and family farming in the Midwest, Plains and northeast. Their analysis outlines complex power struggles within diverse state institutional settings, focusing on how the interaction between state structures and class forces influences policy outcomes. The nature of their research means that they do not reach a particular conclusion about the impact of agrarianism on social-policy outcomes. Rather, they suggest that the structure of agriculture is central and, moreover, that its interaction with evolving state structures can privilege certain groups, and not others.

The diverse accounts considered here cannot be thought of as constituting an agrarian school. Rather, this section has abstracted the agrarian content from accounts which in many cases have quite different underlying theses. However, considered collectively, they are supportive of an argument that the agricultural sector has shaped welfare outcomes cross nationally to an extent which may be insufficiently acknowledged. They differ very considerably in their accounts of the role of agrarianism: thus in the USA it needs to be considered in tandem with race and in the context of the particular US party system, in France a central element was widespread views of a rural ideal, in Spain conflicts between socialist and communists were to the fore, and in Scandinavia the electoral representation of farming interests was central. Thus they draw our attention to the importance of recognising diversity: in terms of land ownership, in terms of the role of agricultural labour, and in terms of the relationship between the agricultural sector and the state. In effect, they suggest that we need to bear in mind that the term 'agrarian' can apply to quite diverse types of agricultural settings, that we are concerned not just with farmers, but with agricultural workers also, and that there may be varying outcomes depending on how these diversities interact with state and political structures. Beyond this, it seems likely that more case studies are needed before any generalisation about the impact of agrarianism can be made. What, then, of the Irish case?

Ireland: the social politics of land

Until very recently, agrarianism has featured little in explanations of Irish welfare state development. O'Connell and Rottman (1992), who (as we have seen in Chapter 1) provide one of the few theoretically focused studies of the Irish welfare state, do not mention agrarianism at all. This reflects the focus of their study, which is on evaluating core theoretical perspectives. Since these core perspectives neglect agrarianism, it is perhaps not surprising that agrarianism has been neglected in Ireland. Agriculture has occasionally featured in accounts of Irish welfare state development, but usually as exemplifying the type of society which preceded the flowering of the welfare state from the 1960s. So, Cook (1982) remarks that social-security growth is associated with 'the rapid transformation of Ireland from a rural to an urban society and from an agriculturally based nation to an increasingly industrialised one' (p. 136). He comments on the 'consistent inverse relationship' between the proportion of social-security expenditure as a proportion of GNP and the agricultural labour force as a percentage of the economically active population (p. 137). The growth in manufacturing and service employment leads to income insecurity in urban occupations, where people lack the 'protection and ultimate security of the land'. Similarly, Maguire (1986) remarks that the most active phase of welfare growth coincided with (among other features) significant changes in the structure of production and employment. Growth in wage employment led automatically to an increase in the numbers covered by the social insurance system, and there was pressure to expand the system to cover a wider range of contingencies. In effect, these accounts restate the link between industrialisation and welfare development, and the association with agriculture is essentially negative – that is, the less agricultural employment, the more social spending.

More recently, though, agriculture has begun to take on a more central role. Cousins (1997) includes agriculture as one of the neglected influences on the development of the Irish welfare state. By the nature of his study, however, his reference is brief. He cites work arguing that farmers in the 1970s and 1980s benefited significantly from direct transfers from the state, and refers specifically to farmers' exclusion from the social insurance scheme, which is, of course, a central concern of this book. Finally, Fahey (2002) argues explicitly that agrarian social classes have influenced the formation of the Irish welfare state, and I discuss his work in some detail here.

An important aspect of Fahey's argument is that he links agrarianism with familialism. Hence, he suggests that recent insights into the role of the family in structuring welfare regimes can be brought together with Baldwin's insights into the role of agrarianism. Neither has been taken far enough; 'They can be added to by being brought together and developed into a wider focus on the role of the family economy in the evolution of welfare regimes' (p. 52). The primary argument justifying yoking together what seem to be very

different ideas is that agriculture is an example of family-based production continued into the twentieth century in many modernising
economies. Fahey is concerned with two interrelated questions. The
first is to do with family-based production, which he suggests can be
seen as de-commodifying labour by organising work relations on the
basis of kinship rather than the wage contract. This raises the question
as to whether state support for the family economy can be seen as
support for de-commodified labour relations and, thus, an indirect
means of social protection. The second question he is concerned with
is a development of this, and concerns the focus of much public
policy on support for the small family farm: 'To the extent that we
assess state intervention on behalf of the family economy as a form of
social protection, then its strong agrarian focus adds a new dimension to the question of the agrarian influence on the welfare state'
(p. 53). In effect, then, he argues that in promoting a rural society
based on non-wage labour, agrarian policy 'tended to de-commodify
labour and therefore merits being evaluated as a functional adjunct to
state welfare provisions of the usual kind' (p. 62).

This chapter endorses Fahey's arguments that the Irish case indicates that the agrarian dimension of social policy has 'greater significance in welfare regimes than has yet been adequately recognised'
(p. 51). There are, however, some aspects of the impact of agrarianism not addressed by his analysis. These relate to a common theme:
the question of how agrarian interests are expressed in the Irish
political system. The best illustration of this is to consider his central
claim that 'massive state intervention in social and economic life
designed to promote small-scale family farming was a core element in
"social policy" broadly defined' (p. 51). In the course of his article, he
gives many examples, drawn generally either from the example of
land purchase and redistribution or from his micro-study of housing.
So land-purchase schemes from 1870 to the 1940s are included, as
are a series of housing Acts from the early twentieth century until as
late as the 1970s. These are all examples of 'state intervention' – but
what is not addressed is that the period witnessed a revolution in
terms of state-building. The Irish Free State of the 1930s and 1940s is
fundamentally different from the UK state of the 1870s. Indeed, the
state which emerged at independence was one which was *itself* fundamentally shaped by the agrarian policy of the colonial period. Fahey
does not distinguish between the two states, but it seems likely that the
motivation of Gladstone's Liberals and de Valera's Fianna Fáil had
different roots, even if both were concerned with agrarian issues.

A secondary (but related) concern is that of the structure of agriculture. Fahey has focused on 'the small family farm' in his analysis. He cites the decline of rural wage labour and its replacement by family labour: 'The family economy distributed the fruits of production to workers within household production units according to concepts of need and entitlement that had little to do with the strict calculus of returns to labour which the wage system embodies' (p. 58). Resulting from this, family farming offered a more natural and wholesome form of social protection than state welfare and this, in turn, contributed to shaping a distinctive welfare regime. However, while the 'family farm' is, indeed, a fundamental unit in Irish society, there is more diversity in farm structures than Fahey's account encompasses. Additionally, he does not consider the way in which agrarian interests are structured politically, and the often bitter and divisive battles over land that have contributed to the shaping of the Irish party system.[7] Agrarianism is central to Irish social policy, but its impact encompasses a wider set of actors than 'family farmers'.

The discussion above suggests that, while we might expect agrarianism to have had an impact on Irish social policy, it is difficult to generalise about what exactly its impact might be. This is particularly the case with social security: the outcomes congruent with agrarian interests are highly dependent on the structure of agriculture. Moreover, how those interests are translated into policy outcomes is important. For example, did agrarian interests outweigh those of other actors, such as industrial interests? To understand the impact of agrarianism on Irish social policy, we need to consider the evolution of agrarian politics in Ireland. There are two distinct periods – before independence, when the impact of agrarianism is expressed through legislation emanating from Westminster, and after independence, when agrarianism is expressed through a domestic political and party system. I begin by looking at the legacies of the colonial period, before turning to look at events in independent Ireland.

Legacies from colonialism: cultural and institutional factors

In his study of the Irish land question, Bull remarks: 'It is an issue which to be understood must be firmly set in both an Irish and a British context, for as a problem it is the product of the interaction of two societies and two cultures' (1996: 5). On independence, the Irish state inherited a number of legacies from this complex interaction –

the previous chapter has already touched on the centrality of inherited modes of thought at the heart of government. Agrarian issues usefully highlight the extent to which we need to cast our net quite widely in considering the institutional legacies in which post-war policy-making was located.

Perhaps the most obvious legacy of the colonial period (in terms of agrarian issues) is a particular pattern of landholding that, in turn, became associated with a wider set of values and beliefs (Fahey, 1998b and 2002; Hannan and Commins, 1992). These beliefs have been described as 'rural fundamentalism', and see agriculture as the source of national prosperity and, in Ireland at any rate, see the family farm as the natural and desirable form of agrarian structure. From 1870 on, a series of land Acts transformed patterns of land-holding in Ireland. 'In 1870 only 3 per cent of the occupiers of Irish agricultural holdings were owners of those same holdings; by 1916 this figure had jumped to 64 per cent and was still rising' (Ó Tuathaigh, 1982: 167). The outcome has been said to be the creation of a 'stable, conservative, land-owning peasantry' (Hannan and Breen, 1987: 43). Undoubtedly, then, a key legacy was the creation of a system of peasant proprietorship linked to widely shared beliefs about the centrality of agriculture. This chapter discusses the impact of this legacy on the evolution of social security in more detail below. Yet we need to take conflict as well as consensus into account in considering the cultural legacies of the colonial period.

The agrarian agitations of the nineteenth century may have bridged social and economic divisions in Ireland, but they did not eliminate them. Indeed, these divisions shaped the nature of the demands made in the agrarian campaigns (Bull, 1996). A central division was between 'the prosperous tenant farmers of the eastern side of the country and the impoverished tenants of the poor western side' (p. 139). Agrarian agitation had ultimately to encompass the grievances of both; redis-tribution of land as well as tenure reform became, hence, a key element. But land redistribution 'had potential for social divisiveness, as it contained within it the seeds of distributional conflicts between major agrarian classes' (Fahey, 1998b: 4). From the nineteenth century on, attempts to suppress, minimise or redirect the demands of poorer, landless elements in rural Ireland has been a constant feature of Irish agrarian politics (Bull, 1996). We need, then, to be alert to the lega-cies of a particular type of agrarian policy: one that needed to juggle with internal divisions, even as it pursued apparently consensual aims. 'Agrarian grievances were the fabric out of which skilled political leaders crafted an entity in which diversity of interest was consolidated into strong institutional form' (Bull, 1996: 142). One outcome is a relatively substantial administrative legacy that left agrarian issues located at the heart of the state. A second is the impact on mass-electoral politics from their foundations right through to elections in the post-war period. Finally, we can see the legacies in social-policy outcomes both before and after independence. I consider each of these briefly before moving on to look at independent Ireland.

State activism in relation to land in Ireland has a long history and, consequently, left independent Ireland with a substantial administrative legacy. Bull (1996) suggests that legislation as early as the Encumbered Estates Acts of 1848 and 1849 'marked the beginning of active intervention by parliament in the problems of land tenure and management in Ireland' (p. 2). Initially, intervention was targeted at the role of the landlord, but a shift from around 1870 saw tenant farmers become the focus of parliament's attention, and legislative interventions (ibid.). As we have seen, the outcome was a fundamental and revolutionary change in landholding patterns. But the process of transforming landholding structures left institutional legacies, too. The Act of Union, while ensuring that legislation originated from Westminster, did not lead to uniform legislative and administrative development across the United Kingdom. Various governmental agencies, boards and programmes were introduced in Ireland either earlier than elsewhere in the UK, or solely in Ireland (Daly, 2002). As I suggested above, nineteenth-century agrarian agitation encompassed both land-tenure reform and land redistribution, and dealing with both these aspects left administrative legacies. The creation of *ad hoc* administrative bodies was widespread in the Irish administration; at the end of the century, Ireland was said to have 'as many boards as would make her coffin' (Chubb, 1992: 213). Two key examples are the Land Commission (1881) and the Congested Districts Board (1891). Both were set up towards the end of the century to facilitate in the transformation of landholding patterns. These two bodies brought issues of land redistribution into the heart of government before and after independence. The Land Commission, which had been reconstituted in 1923, published its final report in 1987, and was not finally wound up until 1992 (Jones, 2001; Dooley, 2004b).[8] Agriculture had an additional voice with the foundation of the Department of Agriculture and Technical Instruction (DATI) in 1900. This 'marked a new experiment in Irish administrative and economic history'. Side by side with the DATI was a consultative Council of

Agriculture comprising 102 members, selected essentially by the county councils. The first secretary of the DATI described it as 'one of the governing authorities of the nation, a Department of State, representative of the Crown, of Parliament, and of local authorities of the country, which has been constructed by the will of the Irish people of all parties and [is] the first representative institution of the kind in their possession' (cited in Daly, 2002: 17). Arising from the long history of agrarian agitation, then, and the diverse demands which this encompassed, the concerns of a wide section of Irish agriculture, from landless labourers through to prosperous farmers, had an institutional existence at a time when industrial workers were struggling to achieve the right to organise in trade unions. This pre-dated independence but remained a feature of independent Ireland because of the persistence of administrative structures in Ireland. Daly comments that if any government department epitomises Fanning's (1978) claim that there was considerable continuity before and after independence, it is the Department of Agriculture (2002: 102). As we will see, one outcome was that the agricultural sector had no need to campaign to get its interests considered in the policy-making process.

Equally important is the fact that the evolution of electoral politics in Ireland is inextricably bound up with the land question. Out of the struggle for the 'land of Ireland for the people of Ireland' emerged the first modern Irish political party, making the story of agrarian politics a part of the wider story of mass electoral politics in Ireland (Coakley, 1999). The 1885 election, said to mark the birth of modern Irish party politics, witnessed the emergence of nationalist domination of the south. The Irish Parliamentary (or Irish) Party, whose origins lie partially in the 1879 Land League, 'stood for Home Rule for Ireland, for defence of Catholic rights and for the principle of state intervention to promote the interests of tenant farmers' (p. 11). The party dominated elections in the south for thirty years, until the watershed election of 1918 witnessed its eclipse by Sinn Féin. Hence, fundamental aspects of Irish political culture pre-date independence and the party system born from the civil war. The commitment to British parliamentary practices and procedures, seen as so central in the previous chapter, can be traced to this long participation in the evolving democracy of the UK. Secondly, the centrality of the land question is carried over into the new party system born in the cauldron of the civil war.

Finally, we can see an embryonic impact on social policy. We have already seen this when the previous chapter discussed the 1911

National Insurance Act. As I argued, the Church opposed the Act, not on theological grounds, but on the grounds that it was not appropriate to Irish conditions, which were agricultural rather than industrial. The outcome was a scheme that differed in some fundamental respects from that operated in the wider UK. Not all of this can be attributed to the impact of agriculture, but Barrington's account does imply the centrality of the agricultural structure of Irish society. Perhaps the most interesting point about the outcome, though, is that the exclusion of medical benefit indicates the emergence of a domestic politics capable of influencing policy, and policy outcomes which are the result of interaction between the politics of two societies. This domestic politics was one that, as we have seen, had needed to fashion a consensus about land which skated over divisions. It is possible to argue that social policy was part of the process of maintaining this consensus, and that this would continue to be a feature of social policy in independent Ireland. We can see this if we consider briefly the case of housing policy.

As outlined above, Fahey's argument about the agrarian roots of Irish social policy rests partially on housing, and on initiatives which pre-date independence. His example of housing is notable, not merely because he argues that Irish housing policy has agrarian roots, but because of his suggestion that it indicates a 'trade-off' to tackle these divisions between landed and landless interests. Constitutional nationalism, he suggests, did not accept that land should be shared out between farm labourers as well as tenants and, instead, opted for a 'trade-off between land for farmers and housing for agricultural labourers' (Fahey, 1998b: 8); hence, the 1883 Labourers Act, which began a process of shifting responsibility for housing to Boards of Guardians (Bradley, 1988; Fahey, 1998b). It provided cheap housing for rent to farm labourers, subsidised out of local rates. The 1906 and the 1911 Labourers Acts further facilitated the development of housing, and 42,000 cottages were provided in the twenty-six counties by 1922, while 24,000 more cottages were built between 1945–64 (Bradley, 1988). Fahey (1998b) comments: 'Public housing in Ireland was thus remarkable for the essentially agrarian origins of the campaigns which gave rise to it and the dominance of peasant rather than proletarian concerns in providing the underlying dynamism of those campaigns' (1998b: 9). There are, then, grounds for arguing that from the inception of modern electoral politics in Ireland, politicians sought to sustain an ideology in which land owning was of central ideological importance, while defusing, where possible, the claims of the landless through targeted social and economic policy.

On independence, then, agrarianism had left multiple legacies that both shaped the institutional context of the policy process and structured the manner in which those interests were represented politically. Additionally, it might be suggested that social policy had emerged as a device that could usefully defuse distributional conflicts threatening a nationalist consensus that rested on obscuring economic divisions. What impact would independence have? Perhaps surprisingly, one impact that it would not have would be the emergence of an agrarian party.

Agrarianism and electoral politics in independent Ireland

Although the land question was so central in nineteenth-century Ireland, one of the striking features of Irish political life has been the absence of a strong agrarian party. Despite the size of the rural population in Ireland, and the centrality of the land question, there has never been a successful agrarian party. For Lee (1989), the absence of a strong agrarian party reflects the relative homogeneity of urban and rural society in Ireland, and the existence of an integrated, national polity. It is unclear, though, whether homogeneity can account for the absence of an agrarian party since, as we have seen, the reality of the agrarian sector in Ireland is that there has, in fact, been a diversity of interests in rural Ireland. Even by the 1940s, there was no clear overlap of interests between the still quite considerable class of agricultural labourers, the strong farmers of the east and south of Ireland, or the small subsistence farmers of the west.[9] In grappling with redistributive issues in the post-war period, policy-makers sought to walk a tightrope not only between the competing demands of urban and rural Ireland, but between the conflicting interests of differing agrarian groups. What was especially problematic was that the evolution of electoral politics in Ireland meant that all the political parties represented some aspect of agrarian interests.

Typically, agrarian parties have been said to spring from the urban–rural cleavage identified by Lipset and Rokkan in their influential account of the origins of European party systems (Gallagher, Laver and Mair, 2001; Urwin, 1980). Agrarian political parties mobilised around this cleavage in the late nineteenth and early twentieth centuries, but only Scandinavia experienced enduring and significant agrarian parties well into the twentieth century. In Ireland, agrarian parties have fallen into the category of 'minor' parties, albeit winning around 10 per cent of the vote at certain times (Coakley, 1990).

Coakley (1990) commented that two cleavages have been reflected in the history of Irish agrarian parties. These two cleavages are 'the cleavage between the agricultural population and urban dwellers, and the cleavage *within* the agricultural population between landed and landless groups' (Coakley, 1990: 280–1). To this, we might, perhaps, also add the lesser divisions between large and small farmers. While the distinction between landed and landless is important, and was a major issue for post-war policy-makers, it is not always easy to make. This is because the categories of 'small farmer' and 'labourer' merge into each other. Some who were primarily labourers but had plots of land would return themselves in the census as farmers, while some would describe themselves as labourers. These problems are of long-standing origin. 'In the case of post-Famine Ireland the boundary between agricultural and other occupations is unusually indistinct, since numerous shopkeepers, priests, teachers and artisans occupied farms, while many "agricultural labourers" and farmers augmented their meagre earnings by working in winter and wet seasons as stone-breakers, road-workers or railway navvies' (Fitzpatrick, 1980: 67). Furthermore, amongst farm workers, there were other divisions, too. Bradley (1988) identifies four, and Breen (1983) also remarks on a subdivision within paid labour on Irish farms. There is, for example, a conceptual distinction between 'farm servants' and 'agricultural labourers'. The distinctions between farmer and labourer interact with, and feed into, distinctions between large and small farmers. Most obviously, large farmers were more likely to employ labour (of whatever type) while, as noted above, small farmers sometimes doubled as labourers (Bradley, 1988; Breen, 1983). We are, then, dealing with a heterogeneous agrarian society, but one in which drawing clear boundaries between different groups is extremely difficult, leading to severe problems in identifying the precise nature of agrarian interests. The interests of agricultural labourers might, at times, coincide with those of farmers (in terms of broad economic policy, for example) but might conflict at other times (on issues of rates of pay and working conditions). A continuing issue, though, was the demands of the landless, and we need to consider how these were expressed in the Irish party system.

Some thought that the struggle for independence would provide the opportunity for the grievances of marginal groups to be heard.

The early decades of the twentieth century witnessed widespread unrest among smallholders and landless men (O'Tuathaigh, 1982). Initially, Sinn Féin sought to capitalise on these grievances by developing an agrarian policy with some radical dimensions, and by participating in a variety of rural campaigns centred around the claims of the landless (Rumpf and Hepburn, 1977). This radicalism was short-lived, however, and an order went out to Irish Volunteers not to participate in cattle-driving and ploughing, 'as these operations are neither of a national nor a military character' (p. 21). During 1919–20, agitation over land was heightened. Indeed, this period has been described as 'the zenith of trade unionism on the farm' (Bradley, 1988). The ITGWU was seeking to organise labourers, there were incidents of agrarian violence, and farmers sought to organise into a Farmers' Union to resist calls for wage increases. Land Courts were established by Dáil Éireann, but these aimed more at protecting the rights of property and allowing for the national struggle to take predominance than to pursue any radical aims. A Dáil Éireann decree in 1920 stated: 'That the present time when the Irish people are locked in a life and death struggle with their traditional enemy, is ill chosen for the stirring up of strife amongst our fellow countrymen; and that all our energies must be directed towards the clearing out – not the occupiers of this or that piece of land – but the foreign invader of our country' (quoted in O'Tuathaigh, 1982: 171).

Within the bitter divisions of the civil war, agrarian unrest continued. Although the main issue may have been the Treaty, there were, nevertheless, socio-economic dimensions (Dunphy, 1995). Among these, agrarian divisions played their part. A number of authors have noted a tendency for Cumann na nGaedheal to take support from large farmers, while anti-Treaty forces were frequently supported by small farmers and the landless (Ó Tuathaigh, 1982; Dunphy, 1995). The reasons for this tendency are not difficult to deduce. 'Put very simply, those with least to lose, and everything to gain, tended to oppose the treaty in the hope that an alternative settlement might give them enough land to support their families or some security of livelihood' (Dunphy, 1995: 34). Among the anti-Treaty side were those whose ideology was radical on social issues, as well as those whose radicalism was more tactical. The defeat of the anti-Treaty forces, however, largely spelled the end of this era. 'The hopes and dreams of radical land reformers, the articulate leaders and the desperate landless men of the west and south-west, could not be realised' (Ó Tuathaigh, 1982: 175). By 1923, it seemed that agrarian radicalism had largely ended, trade unionism had been 'defeated', and agricultural interests began to express themselves along the lines of the party system created by divisions over nationalism.

Consequently, Fianna Fáil has frequently been seen as carrying the banner for the hopes of the landless and small farmers. In the same way, though, that Fianna Fáil cannot be said to be a labour party in all but name, neither can it be said to be an agrarian party in disguise. In his inimitable fashion, de Valera captured in the Constitution the complexities surrounding attitudes to the rural social structure. Bunreacht na hÉireann stated that the state shall direct its policy towards securing 'That there may be established on the land in economic security as many families as in the circumstances shall be practicable'.[10] This had the virtue of combining an acknowledgment of the desirability of the land-owning ideal with a recognition of the practical difficulties in implementing it. Moreover, perhaps in an implicit recognition of the scale of the practicalities, the article is one of the non-binding Directive Principles of Social Policy. Early policy had certainly prioritised a land distribution policy which appealed to small farmers and labourers. But this, after an initial burst of activity, was limited by practical issues, and moreover was in itself a divisive policy in some respects both within Fianna Fáil and within the agricultural community (Dooley, 2004a). Moreover, the economic war (and the partial retention of land annuities by the Irish state) hit farmers hard. In addition, Fianna Fáil increasingly sought to appeal to an urban working-class base as it became more of a catch-all party in the period (Dunphy, 1995). Thus early social reforms (discussed in more detail below) sought to retain Fianna Fáil's constituency of small farmers and agricultural labourers as well as that of urban workers, and others. As well as housing, unemployment assistance in 1933 and non-contributory widows' and orphans' pensions (1935) were deliberately targeted at groups failed by insurance – among them being a diverse selection in rural Ireland. Commenting on this, Lee notes; 'It was one of the innumerable ironies implicit in the pursuit of "self-sufficiency" that among de Valera's attractions for the people of the west, not least of the Gaeltacht, was the increase in state handouts from the apostle of rural self-sufficiency' (Lee, 1989: 186).

Despite this, the emerging party system did not always dovetail neatly with the political aims of rural Ireland, and the first thirty years of independence saw recurrent attempts to organise agrarian parties. The earliest attempt to represent agrarian interests was the Farmers' Party (set up as the political wing of the Farmers' Union), which contested every election from 1922–32 (Manning, 1979; Gallagher, 1976). It won seven seats (with thirteen candidates) in 1922, fifteen seats (with sixty-four candidates) in 1923, but declined thereafter to three seats in its final election in 1932 (Coakley, 1990: 281). Gallagher argues that, while its nucleus was 'relatively wealthy farmers', who constituted its TDs, it also probably attracted support from labourers. This is based on the fact that its support was related to the proportion of farm labourers in an area – although Gallagher does note that this may simply reflect the presence of large employing farmers. Certainly, it attempted to appeal to labourers, as one election advertisement indicates. 'If your Employers prosper you prosper. Support the Farmers Party, which has at its heart the welfare of our common Industry' (quoted in Gallagher, 1976: 47). Manning remarks that it was never really a coherent political party and TDs tended to act more as independents than as members of a political party.

> Its policy was vague and generally negative – it opposed and constantly railed against government extravagance and waste; it was suspicious of civil servants, saw no need for a Department of External Affairs or for the ESB. It couldn't make up its mind on whether it was for free trade or protection and even on questions of agriculture had little that was constructive or positive to say. (Manning, 1979: 51)

The entry of Fianna Fáil into the Dáil in 1927 forced the party to align itself along civil-war lines, indicating, again, the extent to which nationalism and the agrarian dimension cross-cut each other. In the 1930s, a series of short-lived organisations culminated in the Centre Party, which won eleven seats in the 1933 election. A key issue was its stance on ending the economic war with Britain. Gallagher's analysis again suggests a support base of farm labourers; Labour (generally supported by labourers) won its lowest-ever share of the vote in this election. In September 1933, the Farmers' Party merged with Cumann na nGaedheal and the National Guard to form Fine Gael. The best known of the farmers' parties is Clann na Talmhan.[11] Formed in 1938, it contested its first election in 1943, and I discuss it in more detail below.

The story of agrarian politics outlined above is generally well known, but the extent to which the politics of agrarianism is embedded in the Irish party system has sometimes been underestimated. While no successful agrarian party has been able to sustain a long-term existence, electoral politics emerged from agrarian struggle, and diverse agrarian interests found an expression in the three main political parties. We need to place post-war policy choices in this context. Policy-makers had to juggle distributive choices with an eye to assuaging a diversity of groups whose interests did not necessarily coincide. Conflicts of interest occurred both within rural Ireland, and between rural and urban Ireland, and policy-makers of all shades were alert to these conflicts as the party system was buffeted by rural dissatisfaction in a period when agricultural issues had taken on a new political salience.

The electoral emergence of Clann na Talmhan in 1943 points us to an awareness of both the continuing existence of rural issues, and to diversities within rural Ireland. Traditionally, it has been seen as 'arguably the last electoral hurrah of Davitt's smallholders of the west and south-west' (Ó Tuathaigh, 1982: 185). Although mostly identi-fied with the west, Varley and Curtin (1999) draw attention to some diversities in its origins which I return to below. Gallagher's analysis suggests that 'Clann na Talmhan's emergence reflected a dissatis-faction in the poorest areas of the country not just with Fianna Fáil but with the whole party system as it then existed' (Gallagher, 1976: 55). It was unlikely that Seán MacEntee, for one, would have missed the message implicit in its success. Indeed, he referred to it and its leader Michael Donnellan with what seems like unnecessary ire in a meeting at Ballinasloe in 1942, where he 'described Clann na Talmhan and the Labour Party as an "unholy alliance". They had "Hitler" Donnellan with his totalitarian party in Galway, and "Stalin" Duffy and Larkin in Dublin as allies' (cited in Duggan, 2004: 103).[12]

The centrality of agriculture was also underlined by the agrarian unrest centred on attempts to unionise agricultural labourers. As Bradley (1988) notes, the perception that agricultural labourers had effectively died out by the beginning of the first World War means that this period is poorly documented; the following, therefore, is drawn almost entirely from his account. Bradley notes that earlier attempts to organise labourers foundered on the problems of rural unemployment, emigration, and a lack of financial and organisational resources. Yet agricultural labourers, while undoubtedly in decline, remained a substantial class in the early 1940s, albeit unevenly distributed geographically (see further discussion in Chapter 5). In 1943, the Workers' Union of Ireland (WUI) began to organise farm workers, resulting in the formation of the Federation of Rural Workers (FRW) in 1946. The main issue was the demand for a weekly half-holiday and a week's annual holiday with pay. An increased demand for agricultural labour coupled with a rising cost of living provided a fertile breeding ground for discontent. Dublin, Meath, Wicklow and particularly Kildare were the main counties initially involved, reflecting the areas where farm workers were concentrated. Strike action at a variety of locations around Kildare prompted the *Standard* to condemn the dispute: 'a war of sabotage has swept over North Kildare . . . where the FRW, a body organised from Dublin, is in conflict with local farmers on issues which seem to us to be more political than social or economic' (cited in Bradley, 1988: 84). The 'national emergency' sparked by bad weather and which led to a call for volunteers to save the harvest led to a temporary truce, and the formation of the Labour Court led to an agreement to refer the dispute to it.

The Kildare strike prompted labourers in Cork to organise. Seán MacEntee was moved to comment that the FRW agitation was political on behalf of Mr Norton's 'International Labour Party' (p. 90). On 10 July 1947, the Labour Court reported; while recognising the right of labourers to free time, it essentially found that the practical problems in applying the principle were too great. The outcome was that, while a settlement was reached with farmers in some areas, in others it was not. Hence, the 1948 election also reflected these issues to some extent, and four FRW representatives were elected. The Agricultural Workers' Holidays Act 1950 was passed in 1949, giving workers a legal right to paid holidays. In addition, the Agricultural Wages Board granted a five shilling increase in all areas, a decision the new Minister for Agriculture, James Dillon, declared was 'most deplorable' (p. 92).

Conclusion: in search of a 'proper solution'

As was the case with the discussion of Catholicism in the previous chapter, debates about reform need to be located in the context of existing provisions. In this case though, the central area of concern is the nature of provision for agriculture. The broad context was one where a patchwork of social provisions existed which had grown on an *ad hoc* basis before and after independence. While there was no consistent pattern whereby social services were seen to be the preserve of urban industrial workers, nevertheless, the two groups were frequently treated differently. Some services were aimed exclusively at industrial workers, while others incorporated agricultural workers as well. Within this overall context, agriculture was also the main recipient of a variety of state initiatives aimed solely at developing agricultural resources. However, the debate about reform reflected the fact that much social legislation had been concerned with low-paid industrial workers, and explicitly excluded the agricultural sector. Both the Conditions of Employment Act 1936 and the Holidays Act 1939 excluded farm employees, so that in 1946, a nine-hour day and six-day week for agricultural workers were still legal, as the dispute outlined above suggested. Likewise, agricultural labourers were specifically exempted from the Industrial Relations Act 1946 (establishing the Labour Court) except for section six, making provision for investigation of disputes in agriculture. They were, however, were included in the 1933 Unemployment Assistance Act, but this allowed for the exclusion of agricultural workers during periods when it was thought that employment would be plentiful. From 1935 to 1947, such an order was made each year for the months of July and August (Bradley, 1988).

Agricultural workers, along with others, were eligible for children's allowances, old-age pensions, blind pensions, non-contributory widows' and orphans' pensions (all subject to a means test), limited unemployment assistance, home assistance, free allotments and (only to constantly employed agricultural employees) national health-insurance benefits. Services available more or less exclusively to the non-rural community were national health and unemployment insurance, workmen's compensation, and contributory widows' and orphans' pensions.[13] In effect, insurance schemes were largely limited to industrial workers – but the rural population had recourse to a range of tax-financed income-maintenance schemes. It might be said that the distinction largely concerned the financing of social services rather than the receipt of social services, and this was to be the key issue in post-war debates.

The debate around the Widows' and Orphans' Pensions Act 1935 usefully highlights some of the reasons why industrial and agricultural workers had been treated differently in social legislation of the period. Calls for a widows' and orphans' pension had been made throughout the late 1920s and early 1930s by the Labour Party, but had been largely ignored by the Cumann na nGaedheal government. Shortly after taking up office, Fianna Fáil set up a committee to examine the issue, leading to the *Report of the Committee of Inquiry into Widows' and Orphans' Pensions*. The committee considered that the major question before it was whether the scheme was to be one of contributory insurance or some other principle. In the process, it considered this issue at some length, and was, the report said, mainly indebted to the ILO's surveys of social insurance. The committee divided in its views on whether a contributory or non-contributory scheme should be adopted, but the overwhelming majority suggested a non-contributory scheme, largely in response to the existence of a large smallholder class.[14] As noted in the introduction, contributory schemes were seen to have various advantages, in that they provide an absolute guarantee of benefit in a way which encourages responsibility and self-respect. The absence of means testing avoids penalising thrift, and moreover, is administratively efficient as well. Yet after much consideration, the committee found it impossible to provide only for a contributory scheme, and thus a non-contributory benefit was also introduced. The key reason for this was the large size of the agricultural sector, as the Minister for Local Government and Public Health, Seán T. O'Kelly remarked:

> It is true to say . . . that out of the whole population of workers in the Saorstát whose means are little more than sufficient to provide the ordinary necessities of life, there is a large number of persons who are not in receipt of cash wages at regular intervals. The principal class of this type is the small working farmer whose level of subsistence is comparable with that of the urban wage-earner, and who requires, to the same extent at least, to be protected against the loss which his premature death might bring to his wife and children. No proper solution of the difficulty of applying a scheme of compulsory contributory insurance to persons of this class has yet become apparent. Their inclusion in the scheme is, however, regarded as imperative and it has been decided to include in the Bill provision for the payment of non-contributory pensions to the existing and future widows and orphans of agricultural 'small-holders', where the valuation of the holding does not exceed £8.[15]

As early as the 1930s, then, problems with applying contributory schemes to farmers were clear to policy-makers. A decade later, however, the context of reform had shifted considerably. As we've seen, policy-makers had recognised that there was 'ever growing public demand for greater measures of social security, supervised and administered by the State'.[16] The international trend seemed to suggest that contributory social insurance was the 'modern' approach, and thus policy-makers struggled to find ways of applying contributory schemes to the Irish situation. As described above, they did so in the midst of widespread dissatisfaction in much of rural Ireland, and in a society with widely shared views about the distinctiveness and value of agrarian society.

A central point which this chapter has sought to make is that the continuing diversity of Irish agriculture in the period is an important background to debates. By the time Irish economic policy shifted on its axis in the late 1950s and early 1960s, much had changed. Mechanisation, depression and emigration meant that the 1950s saw, finally, the death of the agricultural labouring class; from then on, the agricultural sector was undeniably more homogenous.[17] But this lay in the future. In the 1940s, the confusing categories of small farmers and labourers were a sizeable and dissatisfied grouping whose interests' policy-makers struggled to meet. The way these interests were expressed is crucial: the diversity of interests between different types of farmers, and between landed and landless classes, together with the primacy of the national question, meant that rural Ireland had never succeeded in forming a successful political party capable of transcending these divisions. Thus one of the problems Clann na Talmhan faced was the existence of 'tensions and divisions between the interests of big and small farmers, and between those practising different types of farming' (Varley and Curtin, 1999: 68–69). Nor had the agrarian sector yet formed well-organised interest groups to carry their interests into the policy making sphere. Yet, nevertheless, their interests were represented electorally and ideologically at every stage of the policy process.

The importance of agriculture to shaping social policy in Ireland has been generally neglected. To a large extent, this is because there has been a general consensus that 'the land question' had little relevance in independent Ireland. As Dooley (2004b: 175) notes, there has been a 'general assumption among political, social and economic historians that there was no land question after 1922, that the land act of the following year defused all potential for future agrarian unrest by completing the transfer of ownership from landlords to tenants'. However, as both Dooley (2004a, 2004b) and Jones (2001) have demonstrated, the land question remained a live issue until well beyond the post-war period, and remained important both to intra- and inter-party relations at least until EEC membership fundamentally shifted the context within which agrarian policy was shaped. While their work focused on land redistribution, the following chapter illustrates that tensions around varying patterns of land ownership in rural Ireland would also shape the broad context of social policy making in the period. The legacies of choices made in this period mean that agrarianism can be said to be a fundamental factor shaping distributional outcomes in the contemporary Irish welfare state.

CHAPTER FIVE

Two Warring Factions? Social Security and Agriculture in Post-war Ireland

Introduction

In 1922, the Minister for Industry and Commerce answered a Dáil question about extending the 1920 Unemployment Insurance Act to agriculture: 'Farmers would be definitely opposed to it, labourers either hostile or indifferent. The collection of contributions would be difficult, and the prevention of abuse in administration troublesome. So much employment in agriculture is of a temporary or casual nature that the claims to benefit would be high and the expense considerable.'[1] When the question of insuring farmers was considered in greater detail during and after the war these concerns would be repeated, and would give rise to distinctive solutions in the policy sphere of social security. At the heart of the debate was the problem of devising forms of social provision which would be applicable to both urban and rural areas, and to a diverse agrarian economy.

This problem was one which occupied the minds of policy-makers until almost the final hour, indicating the range of issues involved in reconciling the interests of diverse groups. While Fianna Fáil and the inter-party governments faced similar challenges and constraints in attempting to devise solutions to these varying interests, they differed considerably in how these problems were experienced. Their dissimilar experiences reflect the fact that class interests are expressed very differently in single-party governments and coalition governments. As theoretical perspectives on the Irish party system suggest, both governments were essentially cross-class – but class interests were aggregated differentially in the two governments. Thus the two Fianna Fail ministers – James Ryan and Seán MacEntee – faced very different challenges from those faced by Labour's William Norton. Norton's was probably the harder task, as he faced a fairly hostile internal environment in the inter-party government. While he had some support from colleagues on the Left, he faced stiff opposition from Fine Gael ministers and from James Dillon, as well as the Department of Finance. Ultimately, this opposition combined with the collapse of the government doomed his proposals.

A second issue which is illustrated by a close examination of the policy process is that policy-makers were constrained by policy models which were in many ways inappropriate to Irish conditions. However, devising alternative solutions was difficult for a variety of reasons. The most obvious was that existing models of provision were a constraint in terms of both ideas and institutions. The Beveridge model combined with existing social insurance provisions was to some extent a strait-jacket, which militated against the development of a model of social security which more closely reflected indigenous social and economic circumstances. An alternative model, however, would have required a paradigm shift amongst policy-makers, and the ideological or ideational circumstances necessary to underpin this were absent in the period. This would have long-term implications: when paradigmatic change in the social and economic policy process did occur it would be super imposed on the existing social security model. Thus the distributional outcomes which reflected the agrarian structures of the 1940s and 1950s would be carried forward through the processes of state-led industrialisation which lay in the future.

To some extent, policy-makers clearly perceived the nature of problems outlined above. Thus as the previous chapter noted, MacEntee's first response to calls for a coordinated scheme of social security was to consider the problems involved in applying a scheme devised for a 'homogeneous, industrialised and urbanised' society to the very different circumstances of 1940s Ireland. Moreover, a memo on the subject of social insurance of independent workers was prepared by the ILO in November 1944 at his request.[2] However, it would be far from easy to resolve the 'very great' problems involved. As we have noted already, there was, at first, no clear conception of what exactly might be meant by social security, never mind a detailed analysis of the redistributive consequences of risk spreading across diverse urban and rural groups. These concepts emerged piecemeal as concrete issues were tackled by a succession of ministers and their civil servants.

Initial considerations: the problem of subsistence agriculture

MacEntee received a number of notes in response to his call for comments on the difficulties of applying a scheme of comprehensive social security to Ireland. One response, that of Dr James Deeny, chief medical officer of the department, presciently raised a point that would be to the fore in later debates. He remarked: 'in this country owing to the existing organisation it is almost impossible to introduce any kind of social legislation which will not benefit one class more than all other groups and which will not be to the prejudice of one class more than others. A benefit to the unemployed working man in the town inevitably hits a small farmer.'[3] Farmers figured largely in his analysis. The people in this country, he comments, are in a peculiar position, in that they have probably a greater degree of social security than elsewhere. 'For example, the Irish farmer, who constitutes the main economic group in this country is among the very few in Europe to own his own land. Therefore we have in Ireland a great group of people with a wide distribution of a relatively large individual capital who have in this way insurance, an insurance which is enhanced by the small demands of their low standard of living.' He agreed that a measure of social security would be of benefit to the small farmer, but remarked it was difficult to see how such a development could be implemented under existing conditions. Nor, he commented, was there a spontaneous demand from the vocational agricultural organisations for such a benefit.

Initial wide-ranging considerations such as this were, however, relatively quickly superseded by more focused concerns. A memo entitled 'Considerations attending the problem of extending Social Insurance in Ireland with special reference to the Rural Community' clarified some problems, and it is worth examining it in some detail.[4] The memo begins by suggesting that 'The greatest problem of all is how to apply Social Insurance measures to a population half of whom are unoccupied and half of whom are in the rural community.' The rural community is divided between farmers, shopkeepers and small tradesmen, their relatives and children, and agricultural labourers, a high percentage of whom are only casually employed. The memo continues with a brief survey of the situation abroad. Of twenty countries in 1932, not including the USA and UK, only two insured farmers and the self-employed for old age, disability and health services. These were Sweden and Denmark. This, the memo notes, was based on 'a long tradition of mutual insurance by co-operative groups and the State merely enforces compliance with a system already developed extensively by individual initiative.' At a later stage, New Zealand, Belgium and Germany inaugurated schemes for the rural community. 'The deduction to be drawn is that a few countries where agricultural life was becoming highly organised had begun to include agricultural workers and farmers in social insurance schemes.' The memo notes that, while Sweden and Denmark are in the same income group as Ireland, the social and economic conditions were very different. First of all, the high degree of civilisation attained in these countries may be said to be largely due to long, peaceful development. There were other factors, too. In the case of Denmark, land division had been completed before the end of the eighteenth century, while universal education and universal franchise were introduced in the early nineteenth century.

Turning to consider what might be done in Ireland, the memo discusses the necessity of 'completely rehabilitating' the agricultural community – a campaign to increase agricultural productivity is an essential contribution to the development of social insurance. It foresaw problems inherent in any attempt to insure the agricultural community: 'in this country it is commonly thought that great difficulties will be experienced in persuading the agricultural community that they should pay cash contribution towards social insurance. Many farmers live almost on a subsistence basis and many effect their purchases by the medium of exchange, little or no cash passing.' The system of agricultural marketing was 'primitive in the extreme', though collection of contributions might be possible where farmers receive periodic cheques for produce in creamery areas. However, it 'is possible that there is a class of rural dweller who under no circumstances would be capable of paying any contribution which would prove economic having regard to the cost of collection'. Hence, adoption of the English system of collecting standard contributions would be most difficult. The memo presents a view of a primitive subsistence agriculture, where the 'agricultural community' would be unable or unwilling to pay contributions. Initially, then, no real distinction is made between farmers and labourers; all are members of a broadly subsistence agricultural community. How accurate was this picture?

In 1946, just under 50 per cent of farms were under 30 acres, a figure which might be said to be subsistence level (Breen et al., 1990: 191). On these farms, the 'relatives assisting' and those who might be irregularly employed certainly presented problems in an attempt to draw them into a social-insurance scheme. Should farmers have to pay insurance contributions for their sons (or other relatives) engaged in labour on the farm? This was a serious issue, given the large number of 'relatives assisting' in the Irish agricultural system. According to the 1946 census, about 35 per cent of agricultural occupations were relatives assisting.[5] Considering how to treat these in a contributory scheme would certainly be problematic. Moreover, farmers in the subsistence farm category presented in themselves a problem in terms of social provision.

An equally central concern was the question of agricultural employees. Contrary to the perception that agriculture in the period can be characterised unproblematically as 'family farming', there was a relatively sizeable paid workforce in the agricultural sector. The 1946 census records total agricultural occupations as 593,653, a decline from 643,965 in 1936. Of these the bulk were farmers and relatives assisting. However, what were described as 'other agricultural occupations' were just under a quarter of all agricultural occupations at 140,295. The category of other agricultural occupations was relatively diverse, and included farm managers, foremen, gardeners, nurserymen, foresters and woodmen. The majority however were agricultural labourers, numbering 113,812 in total. This figure accords roughly with that given by the inter-party Minister for Agriculture, James Dillon, in the debate on the Agricultural Workers (Holidays) Act 1950. Echoing the discussion in the previous chapter of the problems of arriving at an accurate figure, he pointed to the difficulties of measuring the sector, and said that the 'nearest figure we care to offer as an estimate, and we do it with reserve, is 85,000 permanent and 50,000 to 51,000 casual'.[6] Bearing problems of measurement in mind, then, paid employment in the agricultural sector lay somewhere between 18 per cent and just under 25 per cent of all agricultural occupations, depending on whether we focus narrowly on agricultural labourers, or more broadly on all paid employment in the sector.[7] Agricultural labourers and other agricultural employees were not only a relatively substantial subset of the agricultural population in the period, but were an important section of the paid workforce as a whole. Agricultural labourers comprised around 13 per cent of the total occupied population in 1946 if farmers and relatives assisting are excluded. Thus Labour's Sean Dunne, who was active in organising farm workers in the period, and who introduced a bill in 1950 to give agricultural workers a weekly half-day with pay, claimed that they were 'the largest group of workers following one occupation, and employed for wages'.[8] There were, however, profound regional variations. As Bradley (1988) notes, agricultural labour was particularly important in twelve Leinster and east Munster counties. Thus in Leinster as a whole 'other agricultural' occupations comprised around 40 per cent of the total agricultural workforce, and agricultural labourers specifically comprised just over 30 per cent of the agricultural workforce. The figure of 30 per cent applies generally to those Munster and Leinster counties where agricultural labour was concentrated (Bradley, 1988: 10–13). In Connacht, on the other hand, only 9 per cent of agricultural occupations were made up of 'other agricultural'.

We have, then, a farming sector with some large employing farmers on one end, and very small farmers on the other, who probably slid into the category of agricultural labourer. The National Farm Survey of 1956–57 found that, while 31 per cent of western and north-western farmers were classified as subsistence, fewer than 3 per cent in the south and 9 per cent in the east and midlands could be so classified (Hannan, 1979: 32). 'The western system of production co-existed with a highly developed capitalist farming system which had been characteristic of most of Leinster and Munster since the mid-eighteenth century' (p. 35). The discussion of agricultural unrest outlined above fits in with this picture. Yet it was not the picture we see expressed in policy documents, written initially not by politicians, but by civil servants. Here, the perception of policy-makers seems to be that the agricultural sector as a whole was essentially subsistence, and thus insurance was highly problematic. The diversity of the agrarian sector, outlined above, was at best touched on. It might be argued that one legacy of the agrarian struggle was a picture of rural Ireland which only imperfectly matched the reality, but which was so deeply ingrained that it had become embedded at an institutional level.

Of course, a central issue was that, while insurance presented administrative and other difficulties, it was very clear that those who were at the subsistence end were in as much, if not more, need of assistance as industrial employees. This was clarified as consideration of social-service reform became more focused. This is clear in a memo written in advance of the setting up of a Department of Social Welfare.[9] This acknowledged that social-service reform was also applicable to the agrarian sector: 'The economic condition of many small-holders and self-employed artisans is no better than that of wage-earners, and for them and for their families (as in the case of wage-earners) the occurrence of illness, disability, premature death and old age may have serious consequences. They need protection against these risks just as much as the wage-earner.' However, the memo noted that development of insurance of independent workers has been slow generally, and has usually occurred in association with an intensive development of local friendly societies heavily subsidised by the state. Again, the main difficulty that the memo foresaw was the collection of contributions. This was 'a difficulty which varies inversely with the margin between income and subsistence. In the case of the small-holder producing mainly for his household's consumption, where the cash income is small and precarious, this difficulty is regarded as insuperable.'

Importantly, though, the memo offered four possible lines of development, which implicitly acknowledged variations within the agricultural sector. It is worth looking at the various suggestions put forward. The first possibility was to recognise that social insurance could only be applied to employed persons, but to include agricultural labourers for unemployment benefit. Those outside the scope of the scheme would be provided for by a centrally administered national assistance scheme 'with rates of benefit approximating more closely to those of the insurance schemes but all subject to a means test.' A second possible line of development would be to include old age and workmen's compensation under social insurance, again only for employees. A third route was to include independent workers in social insurance, with certain limits. For example, there would be an income limit of £500, the self-employed would not be insured for unemployment and there would be restrictions on the extent to which they would be covered for sickness. This path presented difficulties, however. One was the 'well recognised difficulty of exacting contributions from small-holders'. Additionally, the 'convenient machinery' of collecting the contribution through employers at time of paying wages was missing. A major problem was the income limit – in effect, this would mean a type of means test would need to exist, thus losing one of the main benefits of social insurance. I return to this point in the next chapter; as we will see, rather ironically, an income limit was included, but it was focused on urban rather than rural workers. The last possible line of development was to adopt the principle of compulsory contributory insurance for all in a unified scheme on the model of the British national insurance scheme.

No decision was recorded before Fianna Fáil left office in 1948, but there is an indication that they had decided that the self-employed would be excluded. This is in the speech made by William

Norton when introducing his bill (outlined below). Norton remarked that, in 1947, a conference took place between representatives of the Department of Social Welfare and representatives of the British Ministry of National Insurance. 'At that conference, the secretary to the Department of Social Welfare was instructed by the then Minister for Social Welfare to inform the British representatives that, in his approach to the problem of social security, that he did not, at that time, intend to cover within the scope of a comprehensive Bill any but the employed classes'.[10] Before moving on to look at events under this government, it is worth reviewing some of the implications of these early considerations of reforming social security. The obvious point is that the issue of the self-employed or independent workers was clearly seen by policy-makers as a key issue to be considered, but the approach to be taken was not resolved quickly. However, a starting point was a perception that it was subsistence farming which formed the barrier to a comprehensive scheme. Although this group was only one section of the farming community, early responses tended to see them as the key group. Even later, the problems of collecting contributions from this group continued to be seen as a major stumbling block. Gradually, we see some recognition that larger farmers existed, in that means testing was suggested as a possibility. But this was seen to present a problem in that it would negate the very thing that made social insurance desirable.

A second and related point was that social insurance was not seen as a stand-alone package. One possible response to the problem of subsistence agriculture was to exclude the self-employed. But if this were done, it would require *enhancing* social assistance for excluded groups. The perception that social assistance could compensate for exclusion from social insurance is crucial. Finally, there was initially little awareness shown that agricultural employees were a distinctive sub-group within the rural economy. Agriculture was not an industry employing close to 140,000 workers in concerns of varying sizes – it was a society composed of subsistence smallholders who either would not, or could not, be made to pay contributions, and for whom alternative routes to social security almost certainly needed to be devised. It was to fall to William Norton to move beyond these general lines of inquiry to arrive at a concrete scheme where abstract issues were expressed in actuarial terms, and where costs and benefits to various groups emerged relatively clearly.

The inter-party government: farmers against labourers?

In this period, Fianna Fáil was still seen as being concerned with representing the interests of small farmers and labourers. What of the inter-party government? Considering how the interests of the agricultural sector were represented in this government is not easy. An obvious starting point is Clann na Talmhan, generally said to be the representatives of smallholders. However, they were perhaps not well served by their member in government; the party leader, Joe Blowick, who became Minister for Lands, is described by McCullagh as 'a somewhat inarticulate man' (1998: 45). He comments that his colleagues had little respect for him, and that a regular attendee at cabinet meetings cannot remember a single contribution from him. He appeared to lack charisma (Lee, 1989). In that he was representative of the disaffection of small farmers and agricultural labourers, his presence alone was perhaps important. A more vocal representative was the Minister for Agriculture, James Dillon. Dillon, having parted company with Fine Gael over the issue of neutrality, was an independent TD at the time (Daly, 2002). He was the son of John Dillon, a founder of the Land League and an Irish Parliamentary Party MP (Manning, 1999; Daly, 2002). His interest in the agricultural sector was profound.

Noel Browne, silent on Blowick, had more to say about Dillon. He was 'a shallow person with an unoriginal and uncreative mind' who 'refashioned other people's ideas for use in support of his consistently mean, conservative, small time prejudices' (Browne, 1986: 205). Certainly he had a strong interest in the agricultural sector. Daly (2002), comments that he saw himself as an heir to Patrick Hogan.[11] He told Dáil Éireann that he had 'sought to crystallise the agricultural policy of this Government in the aphorism: "One more cow, one more sow, one more acre under the plough"' (cited in Daly, 2002: 277). In particular, he was the driving force behind the Land Rehabilitation Project (Lee, 1989). This, Lee comments, had more political than economic merit, being almost certainly an attempt to attract the constituency which Clann na Talmhan had indicated was ripe (p. 303). Dillon himself, as we will see below, rated it above social security in terms of its merits to the agricultural community. In addition, Fine Gael might perhaps be said to represent the interests of some large farmers, and as discussed in more detail below, Labour represented the interests of both agricultural labourers and industrial workers. As a result, the coalition represented the diversity of Irish agrarian life and was perhaps a government divided by its conflicting views of what the interests of the agricultural sector might be. Thus, the inter-party government was certainly cross-class, but as we'll see, this was a source of some conflict throughout the term of government. In particular, the Labour party which held the key social welfare ministry in the period was to face problems in this respect.

The assignment of the social welfare portfolio to Labour leader William Norton, who also held the position of Tánaiste, reflected the importance which the party attributed to social security policy. A number of authors have pointed to the importance of the social welfare bill as the party's 'keynote piece of legislation' (Puirséil, 2002: 55; see also McCullagh, 1998). Before turning to look in detail at Norton's failed attempt to bring this scheme to fruition, it is worth spending some time clarifying the problems Labour encountered in terms of developing policy in the area. One problem, perhaps, was that wider divisions in the labour movement deflected attention from policy formulation. However, both wings of the Labour movement might have been expected to share a broadly similar constituency, and thus were generally representative of urban trade-union interests. There are indications (discussed below) that this constituency had a perception that farmers were paying less than their due and that reform of social security should tackle this. However the Labour movement was also representative of rural labour: Norton's own Kildare constituency contained one of the highest concentrations of agricultural labourers in the country. Bradley notes that Norton had 'championed the farm workers' cause regularly in the past, sponsoring bills for holiday legislation, so that he could be expected to use influence for them now' (Bradley, 1988: 91). In more general terms, the Labour party in the period has been described as 'reformist, timid, non-socialist and anticommunist' (Gallagher, 1982: 6) and its social policy position was framed within this context.

As we have seen, the ten points of policy for government released by the inter-party government included a commitment to the introduction 'of a comprehensive social security plan to provide insurance against old age, illness, blindness, widowhood, unemployment, etc.'. However, it is not clear that the Labour party had a coherent idea of what this might look like in practice, although their views were clearly strongly influenced by the Beveridge proposals. From shortly after its publication, they began to grapple with the question of social service reform. Hence a sub-committee under the chairmanship of Louie Bennett was established in 1943 to examine questions relating to Social Services 'and to make proposals for their reorganisation and improvement so as to prevent overlapping and wasteful expenditure of public money'.[12] Owing to its 'multifarious commitments' work proceeded slowly,[13] but they produced an *Interim Report* on *Social Services* sometime towards the end of 1945.[14] They produced a second document entitled '*The Financing of Health and Social Security Measures*'[15] which seems to have been circulated in September of 1945, but which had not received detailed consideration by the Administrative Council as late as March of 1947.[16] The 1946–47 report also refers to 'a large volume of statistical material which was assembled by Mr. Arnold Marsh' in early 1946.[17] (Arnold Marsh was a member of the social services sub-committee.)

The two papers produced by the sub-committee make it clear that a considerable extension of social security was envisioned. Thus the *Interim Report* recommended the acceptance of the principle of a national unified scheme of social security, in which 'subject to the available resources' all persons would receive benefits, and all in receipt of income would contribute.[18] It recognised that many sections of the population were not provided for, including 'many thousands of agricultural workers and small farmers, as well as teachers and others, who are either not provided for at all, or for whom provisions are grossly inadequate'. It envisioned a wide range of benefits: sickness, disablement, unemployment, children's allowances, school meals, maternity, marriage, widows, orphans, old age and funeral benefits. However, it recognised that there would be financing implications, which were outlined in the *Interim Report* and addressed at more length in the financing document. Both of these recognised problems with a contributory scheme and considered adaptations. Thus the *Interim Report* points to the fact that 'the inclusion of the rural population in the scheme creates a fresh problem – that of arriving at a contribution rate which will come within the means of low-paid agricultural workers and farmers and farmers with incomes little above subsistence level and will, at the same time, go a reasonable distance towards meeting the cost of the scheme.'[19] They suggested that contributions would remain a feature of the scheme, but would be graduated by income. These would stay weekly for wage-earners, but for others, they would be assessed on the basis of income tax 'and would, in fact, be similar to other direct taxation'. This proposal was, it seems, 'a special social security tax' and part of the cost of services would also be met by other means from state funds. A key feature though would be that 'all persons will receive benefits according to their special needs, and all persons in receipt of income will contribute'.

The financing document went somewhat further.[20] It proposed 'that instead of the mixum-gatherum system of collecting workers' contributions, employers' contributions and a state contribution we should instead institute a graduated system of contributions based on personal incomes, which would be paid by people of every class'. This they remarked went a little further than the New Zealand system. The shift, perhaps, was because they envisioned including 'some of those people who have hitherto paid less than their share'. Farmers are not specifically identified here, although in attempting to estimate farmers' incomes the paper remarks that 'at least we know that farmers are undertaxed'. Clearly, one problem was the lack of precise figures on which to base costings. Thus the paper points out that 'the computations have been made hastily and have not been checked. They are based on inadequate data. They should be right to within a million or two, but they cannot be relied on any more than that.'

The Administrative Council decided to prepare a policy statement on social security for the 1947 conference, but found it did not have sufficient information. Consequently, it remarked that the draft report which was to be submitted to the Kilkenny Conference of that year was to be regarded 'as of a tentative nature only'.[21] This report seems likely to be that entitled 'National Scheme of Social Security: A Statement of Labour Policy'.[22] It is different in many respects from the two documents above. Running to 25 pages, the bulk of it is a general discussion of the meaning of social security, the extent and nature of poverty in Ireland, and the preconditions on which any scheme must be based. These preconditions were, in effect, increased productivity and full employment. Increased productivity was necessary because 'Frankly, the present level of production in this country is too low to permit of adequate incomes being provided for all'. It listed a range of contributory and non-contributory benefits, the bulk of which are to be contributory, and included specific contribution and benefit levels. It did not address any of the issues in relation to financing discussed above. Instead it simply pointed out that the 'proposals are based on the assumption that unemployment will be entirely eliminated from our national life'.[23]

However, as noted above, these proposals were tentative, and the election manifesto for the 1948 election simply called for 'a broad scheme of social security on a contributory basis aided by exchequer contributions'.[24] Thus Norton appears to have entered government committed to a comprehensive scheme which would provide a range of new and enhanced benefits, and which would in general be more redistributive, but without having resolved some of the problems which had been tentatively identified by the social services sub-committee some years earlier as springing from the inclusion of rural classes. When he entered government, he inherited a substantial body of work, much of which had focused on the problems which the self-employed sector presented for a contributory social insurance scheme.

Privileged trade unionists: the retreat from universalism

On taking office, Norton was faced with answering the questions which had so far been posed, but not resolved by the previous government. An early memo posed the question of 'whether the immediate scope should be confined to those working for an employer only, leaving the self-employed and others to be absorbed, if feasible, at a later date?'[25] The draft scheme put forward by Norton did not, however, include farmers. A memo on this notes: 'The question of extending the scope of insurance outside the employed classes is found to be, by and large, a question of whether the farming class should be incorporated, and it has been reluctantly decided that, for the time being at least, it is not practicable, all things considered, to take this course.' The draft states that the problem is, however, being kept in view and, if there is a general desire for it, every effort will be made to overcome the administrative and other difficulties involved when the new scheme is underway. Very early on in his term of office, then, Norton took the decision, with apparent reluctance, to limit insurance to the employed class and, at this moment, a 'comprehensive' social insurance scheme no longer existed, with all the implications this involves for risk spreading and distribution.[26]

On one level, his decision is entirely understandable. As we have seen, Labour had failed to clarify or resolve the issues involved, and Norton inherited considerations which stressed the problematic aspects of inclusion. Thus, as we have seen, the ILO and a number of internal memos had indicated 'insuperable' difficulties in collecting contributions from a large subsistence class. Faced with a government representing diverse views and lacking clearly worked out alternatives, a pragmatic individual such as Norton might be expected to cut his losses on this point, at least in the short term, and concentrate on winning what he could for his core constituency of employees.

The decision to exclude farmers did not, in any sense, end the policy debate. Rather, it gave it a new focus. Two issues were responsible for it continuing to be a key issue. The first was that exclusion was read as privileging urban over rural interests. The second was that excluding farmers did not mean excluding all agrarian groups. A key question now concerned where agricultural labourers were to stand in the new scheme. These interrelated issues were to be to the fore of public, if not private, debate.[27]

Norton's submissions to government were keenly alert to the distributive consequences of social insurance along a number of dimensions, and on this, he clearly drew heavily on the advice which he was receiving from civil servants. (The following chapter discusses in more detail the commitment of key officials to a broadly inclusive Beveridgean scheme.) As outlined in the introduction, compulsory risk pooling is one of the key factors which influence the redistributive impact of social insurance. Thus the White Paper defends the decision to exclude the self-employed:

> It may be that, all things considered, the best solution of this problem is not to attempt to include such persons in the compulsory insurance scheme, but to retain for them the assistance schemes relieved, as far as possible, of any objectionable features. If that be so, it should be recognised that all the advantages do not lie with those who are in the insurance scheme. The insured person may, with some justification, feel that a more equitable spreading of risks would be secured if all classes were included and that he is obliged through taxation to contribute on equal terms towards assistance schemes from which he may expect little in return, whereas the non-insured person makes no special sacrifice for the assistance schemes corresponding to the insured persons contributions. (Department of Social Welfare, 1949: 15)

The White Paper's plan balanced an awareness of the way insurance works with an attempt to meet the needs of the agrarian sector. This was in relation to agricultural labourers. As noted above, prior to this, neither agricultural nor private domestic workers were insured for unemployment benefit. As we have seen, Labour was committed to more inclusive social security. Did this mean that agricultural labourers were to count as employees under the terms of the scheme? This presented problems on two fronts. On the one hand, the tripartite nature of financing meant that farmers would be called upon to make contributions. Second, there were concerns that the contributions required from agricultural labourers would have implications for agricultural wages in an era when this was a matter of occasionally violent unrest. As the White Paper noted: 'The rate of wages payable generally in these classes have nearly always been lower than in most other occupations, and it is undeniable that a heavy rate of contribution would represent a real hardship and frequently a real difficulty, as in many cases remuneration take the form largely of board and residence' (Department of Social Welfare, 1949: 17). Norton attempted to retain distributive equity and meet the demands of both labourers and farmers by creating a 'low-wage' group with lower contributions and, crucially, lower benefits. He hoped that having a low-waged group (rather than an agricultural labourers' group) avoided the creation of different classes based on differences in types of employment or, indeed, residence. There was some limited precedent for this. The Widows' and Orphans' Pension Act of 1935 had allowed for lower rates of contribution and benefit for agricultural workers: contributions for this group were half the rate while benefits were four-fifths the normal rate. The scheme was sent to all departments on 8 April 1949 and a range of responses was received. As discussed in more detail in the following chapter, Norton was deluged with memos on the scheme from his governmental colleagues. I focus on those relevant to an agricultural perspective here, and discuss broader issues in the next chapter.

Two main sources took up cudgels on behalf of farmers: the departments of Agriculture and Finance. It is probably most useful to begin with Agriculture, the preserve of James Dillon. The situation, as Agriculture outlined it, was clear.[28] According to the 1936 census, there were 1,300,000 persons 'at work'. Of these, approximately 700,000 were employees – 'largely trade unionists in protected occupations'. Over 500,000 were farmers and members of their families assisting them on the land. The majority of these, claimed Agriculture, were working on small farms of up to 30 or 40 acres and the livelihood of practically all of them depended on selling their produce in a competitive export market:

> The White Paper proposals are, in essence, that about £15 million a year should be paid in various benefits to the 700,000 employees (largely trade unionists) . . . of which sum considerably over one-half would be provided by the 600,000 non trade unionists, who are mostly small farmers and their families, whose average

income per head is less than that of the beneficiaries under the Social Security Scheme and who will themselves receive no benefit.

Agriculture argued that:

> an attempt to put the White Paper proposals into operation would cause a social upheaval. Farmers are slow to take any extreme measures but the manifest injustice of the proposals would give rise to insuperable opposition among the farmers, and it would be expecting too much of human nature to think that they would not attempt to take any retaliatory measures. Farmers also are capable of using the Strike weapon by resort to subsistence farming, as they clearly began to do towards the end of the Economic War.

The proposals, continued the memo, were clearly not worked out in relation to Ireland, but were inspired by what is being done in other countries:

> The Beveridge Plan was framed to suit conditions in a highly industrial community and pronouncements by Lord Beveridge and his associates indicate that they would be the last to describe the Plan as one for export. Indeed if Beveridge were asked to draw up a Social Security Scheme for Ireland, there cannot be the slightest doubt that he would produce something quite different from the White Paper proposals and from what is being attempted in Great Britain.

The minister's criticisms of the draft White Paper did not imply that he was not in favour of social-service reform. It meant that reforms should be strictly related to Irish conditions. An example of 'standing solidly on the economic and social realities of our economy' was given: small farmers should be able to qualify for the old-age pension without having to go through the formality of conveying the farm to the sons 'in pursuit of a family arrangement'. Any valid conveyance should suffice. This, plus a pension at 65, would deal with the problem of farmers who 'hang-on' until extreme old age to the demoralisation of the eldest son who is middle-aged or elderly before he gets the farm and can marry.

The memo also briefly mentioned the question of agricultural labourers: 'Such questions as the effect of large deductions for contribution from the wages of agricultural workers on their ability to meet their day to day needs and the effect of an expensive contributory social insurance scheme on employment in agriculture should also be carefully considered.' The memo concluded by remarking:

> We should not delude ourselves with the idea that social security plans are more than a palliative. In this country the fundamental method of improving the economic condition of all classes is to increase agricultural productivity and to secure remunerative export markets. In a sense the Land Rehabilitation Project is the best social service that has ever been introduced into this country, because it is designed to increase everybody's real income, without attempting to regulate the method or purposes for which the earner shall direct its outlay.[29]

In defence of Agriculture's position, the department's submission looked at the funding of the scheme, arguing essentially that much of the state subvention would, in fact, be collected from the farming community. 'What would the Government say if the Department of Agriculture proposed to relieve agricultural land from the onerous burden of rates by means of a levy on trade unionists without any corresponding benefit to the latter, on the ground that as they have no land to relieve, it is not practicable to bring them within the scope of the proposals?'

Two months later, a second memo was presented.[30] It begins by again drawing attention to the large number of farmers and their families. Looking at the benefits offered by the scheme, it remarks, 'In our special conditions where so large a section of the population are not wage-earning employees, it appears to me that the benefits of Old Age Pensions, Widows Pensions, Orphans Benefit, are excellent and susceptible of material development.' Again, the memo makes the point about qualifying for the old-age pension without an inquisition into the reasons for passing on the land. It also makes an interesting point regarding the extent to which the scheme can be thought of as an insurance scheme: 'The introduction of the insurance element into the whole proposal appears to me to be illusory, because on examination it is really an abuse of the word "insurance" to describe a scheme under which the beneficiary contributes one-fifth of the total cost of the benefits. If it desirable to provide for substantial transfers of income, then I think we should do it, but not on a basis of concealing our true purpose.' The memo concludes that an excellent White Paper can be prepared setting out the ultimate levels at which services will be established, accompanied by an estimate of the period of time over which their realisation will have to be extended. This, it suggests, would provide a framework for successive governments to fill bit by bit.

> On this road, real and valuable progress can be made; on the road of segregating our population into warring factions of 500,000 working farmers on the one hand, and 700,000 employed persons on the other, nothing but disaster lies ahead, and in the recurring conflicts which must eventuate, not only shall we fail to make progress, but the national income out of which all our plans must be financed, will proceed to melt away, as the farmers revert slowly to subsistence farming rather than producing the maximum surplus of which they are capable, because they feel that an undue share of the surplus will be taken from them in the form of imposts designed to provide benefits in which they can never hope to share.

As discussed in more detail in the next chapter, the response of the Department of Finance to the draft White Paper was also over-whelmingly negative. Among a wide range of objections were those that rested on the position of the rural community. Finance argued that the proposed scheme failed to take into account differences between conditions in Britain and Ireland:

> agriculture is relatively ten times as important in the Irish econ-omy as it is in Britain; there, only 5% of the working population is engaged in agriculture as against 50% here and agriculture yields less than 3% on the national income as compared with our figure of over 30%. Our dependence on agricultural exports for the maintenance of our standard of living makes it essential not merely to avoid raising production costs but to secure a lowering of them to the utmost extent.[31]

Particular problems were foreseen with the inclusion of agricul-tural labourers, given the seasonal nature of their employment. Neither farmers nor their workers would appreciate the necessity for paying contributions, which 'would be a serious imposition on the agricultural labourer . . . and would doubtless result in pressure for a further increase in agricultural wages which in turn would bear heavily on the small farmer and tend to upset the rural economy.'

Norton commented on the problems of responding to such a range of objections, but did submit rebuttals of the points in the memo.[32] On agricultural labourers, he commented that:

> This matter has received very careful consideration. The Minister considers that no class will better appreciate the new scheme than agricultural labourers. Insofar as the seasonal feature of their work is a necessity, it is essential to provide unemployment insurance and so help to stem rural depopulation. In the view of the Minister for Social Welfare, agricultural workers ought not to be treated in this matter as inferior to industrial and other workers.

He commented in some detail on Agriculture's memo.[33] He begins by summarising Agriculture's argument that it was inequitable that, as taxpayers, farmers contribute to a scheme from which they themselves would not benefit. Norton replied: 'The Minister for Social Welfare desires to point out that the only way any class can secure the benefits of the scheme is by including it within the scope of the scheme. He gathers from the absence of any comment or suggestion on this point that the Department of Agriculture do not wish to recommend the inclusion of farmers in the compulsory scheme.' Given that farmers are not be included, the key question is, then, to what extent the farmer is to be reasonably treated in regard to what he pays in general taxation and what he receives from the general revenue of the state. On this, Norton argues that he cannot agree with the Department of Agriculture's view that the main burden of the redistribution of national income, which the scheme will involve, will be shouldered by the agricultural community. He makes two further points. The first is that in terms of the burden of contributions, only a small number of farmers are employers and, of these, it must be presumed that they are in a position to pay contributions. Second, it needs to be remembered that, whatever their respective incomes or standards of living may be in normal times, the employee has, in adversity, nothing to correspond with the farmer's land and its potential for providing the means of subsistence. 'It is with conditions of adversity for the employee that the scheme is mainly concerned and not with relative standards of living.'

Despite these and other objections, the bill was given the go-ahead by cabinet in December 1950, subject to two amendments, both of

which related to farmers.[34] Norton had, in fact, introduced a bill in
July, apparently without formal governmental approval (McCullagh,
1998; Cousins, 2003). This was thus withdrawn and amended as
agreed. The first amendment was to allow those who were members
of co-operative societies to insure themselves through their societies.
This allowed for retention of tripartite funding, with co-operatives,
farmers and the state all contributing. Second, another concession
was that a farmer whose rateable valuation was £30 or less could
draw an old-age pension on reaching seventy without deduction if he
transferred his holding to a son or daughter. In 1937, approximately
278,006 holdings, or 73 per cent of the total, were below £30 in
valuation (Central Statistics Office, 1960).

   In this shape, the Social Welfare (Insurance) (No. 2) Bill finally
reached the Dáil, where the exclusion of farmers was central to the
debate. The *Irish Times*, in a largely favourable review of the scheme,
made particular mention of these amendments.[35] The amendments
went some way towards correcting the weakness of the White Paper
in neglecting farmers, but did not go far enough. For one thing, it was
'doubtful whether half the farmers in the country belong to co-
operative societies, and those who do so belong are apt to be the
wealthier of their kind.' The old-age-pension provision was useful in
discouraging the traditional practice of 'hanging on to the holding'.
But it seemed unlikely that the concessions would obviate the
farmers' widespread distrust of social insurance. 'Those of them who
employ farm labourers complain loudly enough – though, seemingly,
with little reason – about the present wage-scales, and do not relish
the thought of an insurance scheme that will take 3s. 6d. *per* week
per man out of their pockets.' The article went on to comment that
poorer farmers may resent exclusion, and farmers' sons in particular
('possibly the second largest group in the country – outside of
housewives – outside its scope') will be even more dissatisfied.

   The *Irish Times* was correct. A large number of co-operative and
other farmers' organisations wrote expressing their opposition. All
were hostile and made similar points: these were that, on the one
hand, farmers would get no benefit from the scheme but, on the
other, would have to contribute both in taxes and in contributions.
This would also have the effect of driving up agricultural wages. For
example, the Knockavardagh Co-operative Creamery Society wrote
that the scheme would lead to malingering by agricultural workers.
In fact, it would make small farmers sell their holdings, become
agricultural labourers and thereby be eligible for benefits under the

scheme.[36] A district conference of farmers from Co. Tipperary in the IAOS (Irish Agricultural Organisation Society) resolved that the scheme would impose grave burdens on employing farmers, but confer no corresponding benefit. Also, it would lead to unwillingness to work at wages which the agricultural industry would bear.[37]

A flavour of the most oppositional responses can be gauged from the criticisms of P.D. Lehane, elected as a Clann na Talmhan representative. Lehane, a representative of the Cork Farmers' Association, cited Dignan's argument that the proposals violated distributive justice in imposing burdensome taxation on the whole community to pay benefits to a new, privileged class of wage earners.[38] He was critical of the perspective that the bill staved off communism.

> I believe the way to counter communism is to give property to as many people as possible. Anyone who has something to own will not be so keen on dividing it with someone else. This Bill unfortunately, puts the person who owns anything in a worse position than the person working for someone else. At the same time, it puts an imposition on the self-employer and gives him absolutely no benefit. Take, for instance, the lads round the street selling papers, the unfortunate woman in Moore Street or the Coal Quay in Cork selling her fish, the shopkeeper in a village, the rural blacksmith, the man with the small plot of land. All these people are self-employed and are completely excluded from benefit but they will be called upon to pay considerable sums in general taxation for benefits to bank managers, directors of the Electricity Supply Board and so on, who will be included for benefit under the Bill.

He reiterated the standard argument that 'the only wealth we have must come from the soil'. In response, a Cork Labour deputy remarked that 'Deputy Lehane is a member of an association which is more or less confined to the superior type of farmer in Cork – they call them, I think, "gentlemen farmers".'[39]

In the Dáil debate, Norton defended the scheme on many grounds. Among them was the key point that the small farmer was still eligible for benefit under the old-age-pensions legislation. 'When it is realised that 75% of the £7,000,000 paid each year in old age pensions is drawn in rural areas it will be seen that the old age pensions are of more value to the agricultural community than to townspeople.'[40]

Outside the Dáil, he continued to defend the exclusion of the self-employed, as reported in the *Irish Independent*:

> People who complain . . . that farmers are not included in the scheme say the whole scheme is bad and yet they want the farmers included in that bad scheme. What is the position with respect to the farmer? So far as the farmer is concerned he has got an agricultural factory in his farm. He owns the land and he can never be idle once he attends to that land because there is always work to be done on the land. Unemployment is not a problem with him. If he has not got sufficient land to keep him fully occupied and he works on another job then he is covered for the purpose of this Bill, but so long as he is a farmer with an agricultural factory at his disposal he can never be unemployed. If he happens to be sick he is not obliged to suffer loss of wages like the factory or road or shop worker, because, unlike them, he is not expected to give personal attention to his farm and that can be done in a variety of ways.[41]

Norton also pointed to some wider financial implications. He pointed to the Land Rehabilitation Scheme as a 'free grant' to the farming community, and to the relief of rates on agricultural dwellings. As Cousins notes, this was not an argument well designed to appeal to the large self-employed class (2003: 170). The stress on the benefits to rural Ireland of assistance schemes and other forms of tax-financed expenditure may, however, have been a useful approach if Norton had been seeking to make common cause with a small farm and agricultural labourer sector in defence of a tax-financed system of social welfare. But this would have had to be predicated on a very different model of solidarity, one based on a design of social security which reflected indigenous realities more clearly, and which was, perhaps, explicitly directed at cementing a red–green alliance. As the previous chapter discussed, for a variety of reasons, tax-financing proved attractive to agrarian groups in other countries, for precisely the reasons which made contributory schemes problematic in Ireland. However, the lure of Beveridge, and the weakness of the left's policy formulation process ensured that this did not occur. As it happens, it was a Fianna Fáil minister who – briefly – explored alternatives which sought to bridge the urban/rural divide.

Fianna Fáil: from subsistence agriculture to subsidising agriculture

On attaining office, Fianna Fáil was in the situation of having to live up to comments which it had made in the debate on Norton's bill. It had certainly opposed Norton's bill, but was careful, in doing so, to avoid any indications that it was thereby opposed to improved social security. Lemass, in particular, was clear about this. Clarifying that Fianna Fáil was in agreement that a comprehensive scheme was needed, he remarked that 'This Bill has created a problem for us.'[42] The dilemma was whether Fianna Fáil should accept what was good in it, or reject it and leave the way clear for a better scheme. 'On the whole, it seems to us that the defective character of this Bill justifies the Dáil in rejecting it, but on the understanding that its rejection would be accepted by the government as an indication that a better Bill was desired and desired promptly.'[43] However, he went on to comment: 'As one of those who had, perhaps, more individual responsibility than any other for pushing ahead various schemes of this kind, and had always looked forward to the day on which we could claim to have here as satisfactory a system of social security as any other country enjoyed, I am anxious that we should do nothing to arouse public hostility to the idea.'[44] His wider public attempts to balance opposition to the scheme with promises of better Fianna Fáil schemes attracted acerbic comment from the *Irish Times* columnist, Aknefton, in his comments on a speech made by Lemass at the Synge Street Past Pupils' forum. Lemass was 'the man who would allow nobody to be more revolutionary than himself' and made proposals which were 'far and away beyond what the most left of the leftists would have dared to suggest as practicable'.[45] Somewhat tongue in cheek, the columnist remarked that he must be prepared to answer some pertinent questions:

> Statistical evidence proves beyond doubt that the degree of direct taxation contributed by the farming community is relatively negligible. Presumably, Mr. Lemass, in accordance with the tenets of strict social justice, has some plan whereby the farming community will contribute to his plan in exact proportion to the benefits it hopes to receive. It would be interesting to learn the details of Mr Lemass's proposals in this respect. Is he thinking, for instance, of a capital levy on the farming community?

Fianna Fáil's main opposition spokesman on social welfare, Jim Ryan, was more specific about what could be expected from Fianna Fáil. Ryan had been Minister for Agriculture between 1937 and 1947, and briefly became Minister for Social Welfare in 1947, when the new department was created.[46] He did not argue the point about the exclusion of the self-employed to any great degree. He agreed that the ILO's position – that a scheme should cover all employed persons including the self-employed – 'cannot be done in this country anyway and I suppose it would apply to any other country too.'[47] He continued:

> The self-employed small farmer was mentioned by the Minister. He may enjoy a fair standard of living. Many deputies who know conditions in rural areas know that if you happen to enter a small farmer's house when he is having a meal that it is a good meal, just as good probably as the meal of what he would consider a highly-paid artisan in the City of Dublin. He is reasonably well dressed and pays his way so his standard of living is not so bad. But one of the great difficulties the small farmer has is the want of ready cash.[48]

Although shopkeepers might be a bit easier, there were still problems with collections. 'Every Party then is agreed I think that we shall not look for contributions from the self-employed.'[49] But he did have some alternative suggestions. These were that 'wherever a scheme is applicable to practically the whole population, the only fair way to finance it is through taxation and that, wherever it is applicable to a certain class, we should try to get that scheme financed through a particular scheme applicable only to that class.'[50] He went on to say that old-age pensions and widows' and orphans' pensions were needed by all classes, except, of course, the very wealthy.

Consequently, on becoming the new Minister for Social Welfare in 1951, Ryan attempted to use this as the basis for a new approach to social security. In doing so, Ryan felt he had signalled these changes in his response to Norton. A memo on 28 December outlined the new scheme.[51] As outlined above, the debate surrounding inclusion or exclusion had centred on the ability to pay or collect contributions, reflecting policy-makers' perceptions that self-employed groups were problematic in both of these respects. Ryan proposed something very different: differing *needs* for a service would be the basis of whether a scheme should be contributory or non-contributory. Hence, social-welfare schemes should continue to be of two classes – contributory and non-contributory. However, in the development of social-welfare schemes:

> the principle should be followed that where a service (such as unemployment or disability benefit) is mainly needed by employed persons it should continue to be on a contributory basis, but that there should be no extension of the contributory scheme outside that class and that, in fact, where a service (such as widows' and orphans' pensions or old age pensions) is needed equally badly by employed persons, self-employed persons and others it should be on a non-contributory basis financed entirely by taxation . . .

The memo envisioned substituting a means-tested, non-contributory widows'- and-orphans' pension for the contributory pension, which would be abolished. However, two groups would be exempt from means testing – persons insured under the proposed contributory insurance scheme and persons with agricultural holdings of valuations not exceeding £25. Second, there would be an old-age pension from age 70 for men, and 65 for insured women, as part of the new, non-contributory scheme, with the same means-test arrangements. Insured workers, though, would receive higher pensions on the grounds that they tended to be more dependent on cash income than non-insured workers, and over half lived in urban areas. There would, hence, be no contributory old-age pension, as Norton had envisioned, but the requirements for receiving unemployment benefit would be relaxed from age 65 for men and age 60 for women. Finally, there would be an income limit of £600 for compulsory insurance. The proposals, therefore, moved radically away from the concept of risk-pooling in social insurance and envisioned joining the employed, self-employed and others in a national, tax-financed scheme for several key risks.

It is clear, that the main advantage of these proposed changes was that they seemed to offer the prospect of solving the conundrum of providing enhanced social security for workers, without being seen to do so by excluding farmers. Workers could pay contributions for schemes they alone needed, farmers could be covered by non-contributory tax-financed schemes. However, it would still not solve the problem of agricultural labourers. Ryan agreed that agricultural and domestic workers would be included, and insured for unemployment benefit for the first time. However, he addressed the problem of lower wage rates in the agricultural sector with elegant simplicity. He drops Norton's 'low-waged' groups. Instead, he proposed that agricultural and domestic employees would pay lower contributions, but he did not suggest that they therefore receive lower benefits.

In this memo, Ryan noted that 'the full implications of these non-contributory proposals have not yet been worked out' and proposed introducing the contributory sections first. The 'working out' of the proposals was to be much more difficult than he had envisioned. In particular, the proposal to abolish contributory widows' and orphans' pensions proved problematic. A key question was what would be done with civil servants, and those employed by local and other public authorities, who were insured for these pensions only: this is discussed in more detail in the next chapter, which focuses on debates about this particular group of workers. However, there were also objections to the proposals in relation to agricultural and domestic workers. One problem was these proposals involved a subsidisation of agriculture. Ryan himself had been clear about this in his memo:

> The justification for this distinction, involving a larger State subsidy for the special classes, rests on two arguments: first, that these classes are not at present insurable for unemployment benefit and it would involve too great an increase to raise their contributions to the general level, and, secondly, that the employers in those classes are not in the advantageous position of ordinary or commercial employers for profit who can – even by way of individual action – normally pass on additional charges of this sort to the consumer in the price of goods sold or services rendered.

Departmental officials had already signalled some problems with these proposals: 'With regard to the proposal that farmers should be relieved of all or some of their liability to pay contributions, I do not think the farmers are quite so bad as they are made out to be, and that they would meet their obligations like the rest of the community if so much attention were not paid to their needs and necessities.'[52] This comment previews a shift in the response of other departments. Under Norton, most of the criticism focused on the way in which the scheme omitted farmers. Now, it is the subsidisation of farming which is the problem, and a range of responses argue that farmers can, in fact, well afford to pay insurance contributions.

Finance (now under Seán MacEntee) was not impressed. The general principle about the distinction between contributory and non-contributory schemes was invalid. 'This novel principle appears to be based on the assumptions that all the classes concerned pay appropriate amounts in taxes and that general taxation is a proper and fairer method of finance than special contributions. These assumptions are, however, invalid.'[53] One reason was that foodstuffs were not taxed but were heavily subsidised, and indirect taxes could often be avoided and were often arbitrary and uneven; 'if, therefore, the widespread benefits envisaged by the Minister for Social Welfare are to be provided out of taxation, it would be necessary to cut the subsidies on, say, tea and sugar, reduce the agricultural grant, and perhaps even impose a tax on the ownership and occupation of land or property.'

The proposed treatment of agricultural labourers and domestic servants by Social Welfare met with equal criticism. The suggestion that lower contributions should earn equal benefits was 'entirely objectionable'. Finance pointed to the inequity involved. The best course might be continued exclusion. Failing that, they should either pay lower contributions and get lower benefits, or pay the same rates of contribution for the same benefits. 'There is no justification for asking taxpayers in general to shoulder extra and unwarranted burdens for the benefit of agricultural and domestic workers and their employers.' Farmers were reasonably prosperous, and those who employ agricultural labourers should be able to pay the contributions payable by ordinary employers. Moreover, farmers were virtually free from income tax and enjoyed substantial remissions of rates. Finance also commented on the old-age-pension proposals. On this, there were a number of objections: £25 was too high a limit, Poor Law valuation was faulty and, in many cases, those on a farm of £25 valuation had other means. Finance contrasted the position with that in the 1951 Social Welfare Act, where farmers had to divest themselves of their property (in favour of sons) in order to qualify for the old age pension, while Ryan's proposals allowed them to retain ownership of the farm and still qualify.

MacEntee's comments present farmers in an entirely new light – no longer the subsistence farmers excluded from benefits but forced to pay destructive contributions that would weigh heavily on the rural economy. Rather, they are suddenly a prosperous group who are already favoured by public policy generally, and who should receive no further subsidisation. This shift, however, probably merely indicates that the department was adept at finding grounds to criticise any proposals for spending public funds, particularly given the growing realisation of the harsh economic realities that the country faced (Cousins, 2003). More particularly, MacEntee is noted in this government for his deflationary stewardship of the economy, and the harshness of his 1952 budget (Bew and Patterson, 1982; Lee, 1989). His assignment to the Finance portfolio has been interpreted as a (temporary) victory over the very differing approach which Sean Lemass was attempting to win the party over to in the period (Murphy, 2003). Thus the bulk of Finance's memo was devoted to outlining the economic problems facing the country. This focused on inflationary pressures, a hugely unfavourable trade balance and a large budget deficit: 'No responsible Minister for Finance could in existing circumstances be expected to take on the Exchequer additional burdens of the magnitude contemplated by the Minister for Social Welfare.' The essence of Finance's argument was that the cost of improvements in social welfare, if introduced, should be met by 'raising the contributions payable by the persons who will be eligible to benefit from the scheme'. Thus, perhaps rather surprisingly, the memo approvingly quotes the ILO on the superiority of insurance schemes as a means of improving social welfare. Insurance-based schemes safeguard the respect of the beneficiary and have advantages over assistance schemes that are financed out of general taxation and so depend 'entirely on possibly uncertain budgetary provisions'.

Industry and Commerce, too, took a sanguine view of farmers' finances, arguing that the arguments in favour of lower contributions for agricultural and domestic workers were unconvincing: 'In present circumstances it could be argued that both farmers and agricultural labourers can afford to pay full contributions'.[54] It was also doubtful whether farms having a valuation under £25 were uneconomic and 'accordingly there is no clear case for exempting the owners of such farms from the Means test'. As an aside, the memo was also critical of the proposals to give unemployment benefit to domestic servants. 'If such a scheme is in operation it is going to be even more difficult for anyone to get domestic help.'[55] Finance, it might be noted, had been critical of this too: 'No case founded on social justice can be made for subsidising the cost of domestic service for the better-off classes at the expense of those who cannot afford servants at all.'[56] A second problem was the possibility of abuse. 'The relation between employer and employee in this class is peculiarly personal and employment often terminates for very slight causes including personal idiosyncrasies of both employer and employee. The existence of unemployment benefit might tempt workers to leave their present employment when they might otherwise continue to work.' Hence, either exclusion or lower benefits was the desirable outcome.

Under the weight of the combined objections from his own officials (discussed in the following chapter) and fellow government ministers, Ryan caved in on some key points, notably the idea that tax-financed schemes for common risks should be the way ahead.[57] This is not surprising, for a number of reasons. For one thing, the increased expenditure involved was problematic in a context where extremely negative financial realities were becoming clear (Cousins, 2003). Moreover, they involved a radical shift, and one which it seems had the support only of Ryan himself. It is clear that a fundamental shift would require some degree of critical mass behind it in the government, and in the absence of this, the importance of policy legacies in shaping both ideas and outcomes in the period was crucial.

The outcome was that the new bill was along familiar lines (see Appendix 1). But among a number of significant differences between his and Norton's bill was the retention of the suggestion that (male) employees in agriculture would pay lower contributions while receiving the same benefit as other groups. Ryan defended this proposal in the Dáil. He was clear about the level of state subsidy involved. It would mean the state contributing four-fifths as against the farmer's one-sixth and the male agricultural worker's one-sixth. 'This course, I admit, gives a marked bias in favour of agriculture, but the Party on these benches will face the criticism on that issue. Agricultural workers, and farmers, are less well organised than their industrial and urban counterparts, and they cannot so readily shed increased charges or win compensation in the way of higher wages.'[58]

The 1952 Act thus had a number of features which sprang from the agrarian nature of the economy. First, of course, was the exclusion of the self-employed, predominantly farmers. Smaller farmers would of course continue to be eligible for tax-funded assistance, and as Norton had pointed out, rural Ireland benefited disproportionately from the old age pension in particular – side by side with the 1952 Act went 'higher non-contributory old age pensions at age 70, subject to a very liberal means test'.[59] The proposal in the Norton bill, that a farmer whose poor law valuation did not exceed £30 could transfer his holding to a son or daughter, no matter for what reason, and thus qualify for the old age pension, had been previously enacted by Ryan in the 1951 Social Welfare Act.[60] Moreover, (male) agricultural employees and their employers would receive a state subsidy, described as we've seen as indicating a 'marked bias' in favour of agriculture. This bias becomes clearer when we move on to look at the debate about higher-paid workers in the next chapter.

Conclusion

With a few exceptions welfare state theorists – even those stressing politics – have focused on the impact of industrialisation and the concomitant creation of an urban, industrial class as the key to understanding the emergence and development of welfare states. The extent to which this class is organised into or out of power is said to be the crucial factor shaping different welfare regimes. The Irish case, however, suggests that differing patterns of industrialisation and state formation may mean that agrarian social classes can also be crucial in shaping welfare outcomes. What exactly those outcomes are, however, depends on both the structure of the agricultural sector, and on how its (diverse) interests are represented politically.

In understanding the way agrarian interests were expressed in Ireland, the nature of the Irish party system means that we cannot clearly contrast parties that were 'for' agriculture with those that were 'for' industrial workers, though we can point to some differences of emphasis. How, then, did agrarian interests translate into policy outcomes? To understand this, we need to consider 'the relationship among social classes, state structures, and public policies' (Gilbert and Howe, 1991: 204). One key point is that institution-building and state-formation in Ireland meant that, in some important respects, policy-making took place in an agrarian para-digm – farmers' interests did not have to be 'brought' centre-stage, but appeared there as of right in long-established administrative venues. The centrality of 'policy paradigms' has been pointed to by Hall (1993) and this case-study points to the crucial importance of shared sets of beliefs – not always firmly grounded empirically – about the character of rural Ireland which underpinned policy designs in the period. Thus the absence of overarching agricultural interest federations or large agrarian parties in the period did not mean that their interests were ignored, even at times where civil servants rather than politicians were more active in policy design.

This, to some extent, is an institutional explanation for outcomes which stresses long-term patterns of state-formation.

Yet we can overstate institutionalist perspectives and underestimate the impact of the manner in which class conflicts were expressed politically in Ireland. Policy outcomes in social security also represent the attempts of politicians to devise solutions to distributive conflicts in a way that maximised electoral outcomes for them, or met the needs of their respective constituents. Hence, both Fianna Fáil and the inter-party government represented 'cross-class' agrarian constituencies, and sought 'cross-class' outcomes. Both Norton and Ryan's plans tried to placate employing farmers, small farmers and agricultural labourers. They were not identical in the way they mediated social-class interests, but they did share an emphasis on compromise rather than solidarity, although these emphases emerged via different processes. Moreover, they looked for solutions which were capable of responding to both urban and rural interests.

The agrarian slant of policy in income maintenance has sometimes been recognised: thus as we've seen, the 1933 Unemployment Assistance Act has been described by a number of authors in terms of its deliberate appeal to the small farm sector. The agrarian impact on post-war developments however, has rarely been stressed, or indeed recognised. Partially, this is because agrarianism did not shape outcomes in their entirety. Policy-makers were constrained by the logic imposed by earlier policy choices, and by the lure of policy designs from elsewhere. It might be argued that these militated against solutions which may, perhaps, have better suited Irish conditions. The 'striking' failure of Norton to make any sort of alliance with Clann na Talmhan and their small farm base (Cousins, 2003: 170fn) can be partially explained by the fact that, straitjacketed by inappropriate models, Norton seems to have never considered doing anything other than attempt to draw as many groups into a contributory social insurance scheme as political realities allowed, and this may point to failures in Labour's policy formulation abilities in the period. Entering government already broadly committed to a social insurance-oriented scheme, Norton continued along the path of contributory social insurance which the department had already been developing, and which appeared to offer solidaristic solutions attractive to the left. Fianna Fáil's Jim Ryan, perhaps, came closest to devising a scheme which might have more closely mapped onto Irish circumstances. Thus Cousins notes that Ryan's short-lived alternative would, if implemented, have 'brought a more agrarian dimension to the welfare state' (2003: 93). As we have seen, however, this attempt was short-lived, and thus the outcomes we witness in Irish social security in the period reflect the way in which agrarianism was refracted through the lens of the Beverdigean model and inherited colonial legacies.

Chapter 3 drew heavily on institutional perspectives in accounting for the absence of corporatism in Irish social insurance. Among other factors, it pointed to distinctive patterns of industrialisation and state formation, which implied that the doctrine of subsidiarity was less relevant in Ireland than in other European states. This and the previous chapter have examined some of those distinctive patterns in more detail by focusing specifically on agrarianism. The legacies of the interlinked struggles for land and independence in Ireland were embedded in the social and economic structure, and in the party system. Commenting on the long-term effects of this on the wider social structure, Hannan and Commins remark: 'State policy "favouritism" towards the small-farm sector derives from the institutional and cultural context of Irish politics, and from the small-farm and generally petty bourgeois base, of the dominant political party' (1992: 100). The persistence of this class, they argue, constitutes a crucial respect in which the Irish case deviates from the pattern of social development that would be envisioned under the liberal model of industrialisation (p. 104). The centrality of agrarianism in a modern political context demonstrates the distinction which needs to be made between modernisation and industrialisation, touched on in Chapter 1 (Goldthorpe, 1992).

Thus agrarianism is a central part of any explanation for the hybridity of Irish post-war social security outcomes, which as we've seen, is one of the puzzling aspects of the Irish welfare state. The outcomes discussed here represent complex interactions between institutional legacies and class compromises, or between state and society. The next chapter examines these interactions in more detail by focusing on the debates centred on different categories of employees, and points us even more strongly to the importance of the interaction between politics and institutions as the background to understanding distributive and re-distributive policies in the period.

CHAPTER SIX

Institutions and the Politics of Redistribution: Solidarity or Discriminatory Taxation?

Introduction

'the case for general compulsory insurance rests largely on the idea that the more fortunate members of the employed class should stand in with the less fortunate in a common scheme.'[1]

The decision to limit social insurance to the employed class had important distributive consequences, but while these were implicit in discussions of how best to deal with the agrarian sector, they only occasionally featured explicitly. As we have seen, administrative concerns, the financial impact for employing farmers and the diversity of the agrarian sector were the key issues which ran through the discussion. However, when we turn our attention to examine debates which focused on precisely *which* workers should be included in the new social insurance scheme, distributive issues become increasingly visible and thus more fundamental. The central line of division was between those who argued for a scheme which pooled risks between the more and less fortunate, and those who argued that compulsory inclusion of the more fortunate was essentially discriminatory taxation. The outcome was that key groups of workers were excluded from social insurance coverage on the grounds that there was no 'justice or necessity for the inclusion of classes that can never benefit'[2] (Cousins, 1995: 20). Partisan differences are central to explaining these outcomes, and these were particularly visible in the bitter battles within the inter-party government. However, the institutional structures that mediated and structured these differences are also fundamental. In particular, the interaction of the political 'rules of the game' with the cleavage structure of Irish politics created a pattern of party competition with a distinctive attitude to distributional issues: one which combined a non-programmatic approach to social and economic issues with a necessarily cross-class appeal. Cousin's suggestion that the social-welfare system 'would seem to support a class-coalition approach' (1995: 40) points us to look at the way in which class interests were represented electorally. One of the most useful ways of examining the institutional and political context which shaped outcomes is to look at the debates around the position of civil servants and other public sector workers. The question of whether or not civil servants should be included in the scheme is revealing, because it was clear that as a group, they had little if any risk of experiencing unemployment, one of the key risks with which the scheme was concerned. Moreover, they were also well provided for in sickness and old age. The question of whether they should be included thus raised very visible issues around the theme of redistribution.

As the introduction discussed in some detail, a central concept in grasping the solidaristic and redistributive implications of debates about social insurance is the concept of risk (Baldwin, 1990). As noted there, social insurance involves a *compulsory pooling of risk* in a given society, with benefits payable as of right. The redistributive impact of social insurance is predicated to an important extent on the nature of the risk pool. If, for example, only insecure low-paid workers are included, redistribution is reduced, as it essentially involves redistributing amongst these workers themselves. If, however, the risk pool includes more secure workers, then redistribution from the more secure (and generally better paid) to the less secure takes place. Thus a review of the contemporary social insurance system in Ireland described a fundamental principle underpinning the system as the 'Solidarity Principle whereby contributions paid by insured persons are not actuarially linked to benefits at the individual level but can be redistributed to other contributors. It is therefore an expression of solidarity between different earning groups and different generations' (Department of Social and Family Affairs, 2005: 2). Moreover, it is extremely clear that the degree of risk-pooling profoundly affects the extent to which social-insurance schemes are solidaristic.

> The principle of solidarity means in effect that there is not a proportional link between contributions paid by individual insured persons to finance Social Insurance and the vulnerability of the persons covered related to knowledge of differences

> among them in the likely incidence of unemployment, sickness, occupational accidents and diseases, permanent incapacity for work and longevity. (Department of Social Welfare, 1996: 22)

While these issues appear abstruse, they were in fact clear and visible to policy-makers in the period. For one thing, as should now be clear, debates occurred in the context of an inherited approach to insurance-based income-maintenance schemes which had already inaugurated risk-pooling schemes. In 1949, the *White Paper on Social Security* looked back at the 1911 National Insurance Act as follows: 'This introduced the principle of spreading risks over large classes of the population and of financing the costs of benefits by contributions from general taxation and from the prospective beneficiaries and their employers' (Department of Social Welfare, 1949: 1). In the debate on the extension and development of social insurance in Ireland, 'knowledge of differences' in the likely incidences or, in other words, risks between different groups provided for one of the bitterest lines of division among the inter-party government. Although the debates about inclusion and exclusion focused on a range of workers, this chapter focuses in particular at the decisions taken in relation to civil servants and other public-sector workers. The decision to only partially include these workers had long-term effects: until 1995, civil servants and certain other public-sector workers, such as the gardaí, army officers, etc., were the major group of employees who were not covered for full benefits under the social-insurance system. This group, amounting to about 160,800 employees in 1994–95, paid reduced contributions and qualified for a reduced set of benefits (Department of Social Welfare, 1996).

This chapter looks in detail at the policy conflicts that surrounded the decision not to fully adhere to the Beveridgean model in Ireland. Focused debates about particular categories of workers only began with the inter-party government and this chapter begins here. As we will see, a key point is that clear and strong preferences for an explicitly solidaristic social-insurance scheme were put forward by William Norton, while equally clear preferences for excluding 'the more fortunate' were put forward by Fine Gael ministers in particular. The outcome of these long-running negotiations were that this government laid down a formula, carried over into later legislation, which allowed for modifications to be made in relation to certain groups. In tandem with the earlier choices discussed in previous chapters, and with choices across a range of other issues by the Fianna Fáil government which followed, it can be argued that many of the 'hybrid' aspects of Irish social insurance were shaped by the distinctive nature of the Irish party system. To an extent, the (partial) exclusion of civil servants reflects the way in which class interests are expressed and this, in turn, reflects the emergence of particular patterns of party competition over time. I begin by looking at the institutional context within which Irish civil servants were located.

A conservative revolution: old institutions in a new state

The Anglo-Irish Treaty of 1921 provided for the transfer to the new state of the civil servants who had been responsible for the Irish administration. The existence of an Irish administration reflects the crucial fact that the 'union of legislatures was not mirrored by a union of executives' (Fanning, 1978: 1). On independence, the state inherited some 21,000 UK civil servants, out of a total of around 28,000 (Ó Cearbhaill, 1983). The oft-cited Brennan Commission, set up in 1932 to examine the civil service, remarked that:

> The passing of the State services into the control of a native government, however revolutionary it may have been as a step in the political development of the nation, entailed, broadly speaking, no immediate disturbance of any fundamental kind in the daily work of the average Civil Servant. Under changed masters the same main tasks of administration continued to be performed by the same staffs on the same general lines of organisation and procedure . . . The control previously exercised by the Treasury was maintained with unbroken continuity by the Minister for Finance. (cited in Stapleton, 1991: 306–7)

There was some reform on independence: as previously noted, the Irish administration consisted of 'branches of UK departments, specifically Irish departments, and a multiplicity of quasi-autonomous boards, offices and commissions' (Stapleton, 1991: 306). The core legislation governing Irish public administration is the Ministers and Secretaries Act 1924. As Chubb comments, this Act did two main things: first of all, 'it provided the legal basis for the structure and organization of the central administration by designating the extent of ministerial authority in respect of the performance of public functions' (1992: 227). This established the minister as a 'corporation sole', responsible for everything done by the department. Chapter 3 argued in some detail that the mode of government laid down by this Act was an important part of the explanation for the lack of corporatism in Irish social insurance. The second outcome of the 1924 Act was the establishment of departments of state and the allocation of public business between them. It responded to the multiplicity of bodies outlined above by centralising the work of government under eleven ministerial departments and a limited number of independent boards or commissions (O'Halpin, 1991; Stapleton, 1991).

In trying to understand the nature of the key institutions of state, it is possible to identify elements of both continuity and change. It is probably true to say that, until relatively recently, most commentators have tended to stress continuity. Farrell points to the remarkable conservatism of Irish Constitution-makers. 'When it came to the issue of framing institutional arrangements for government and providing safeguards for citizens, the rhetoric of political platforms and ritual denunciation of centuries of British persecution was quickly dropped' (1988: 20). As he points out, Constitution-makers were not adventurous in setting up new structures, and adopted the model they knew best, which was, in most essentials, a replica of the British parliamentary-based cabinet system of government. This model had repercussions for the type of civil service adapted by the new state.

As with other institutional features, there is cross-national variation in the structure, culture and organisation of national civil services. Hence, Gallagher, Laver and Mair (2001) suggest two broad types of European bureaucracies: on the one hand, the 'generalist' UK model inherited by Ireland and, on the other, the more 'technocratic' model of France and Germany. As well as inheriting a generalist model, Ireland has been said to have inherited an 'official civil service culture which is strenuously nonpartisan' (Gallagher, Laver and Mair, 2001: 140). Hence, Chubb remarks that the British inheritance means that 'it was only natural that the Civil Service should remain an incorruptible, non-partisan, and usually anonymous corps whose members, secure in their employment, considered themselves the servants of the legitimate government, whoever they might be. It was also natural that they should tend to conservative austerity with regard to the functions of the state and to their role in public business' (1992: 236).

However, O'Halpin has noted 'a rather more complex process of transition than has generally been recognised' (1991: 293). In particular, he contrasts the apolitical ethos of the independent administration with the 'politics-ridden central bureaucracy of pre-independent Ireland' where the development of the bureaucracy had been influenced by the political and religious circumstances of the country (p. 299). He remarks that post-independence Ireland saw less a continuance than an introduction of apolitical values. A central element of the reforms initiated by the new state was the creation of the Civil Service Commission in 1923, to ensure meritocratic recruitment, as contrasted with what was seen as the 'personal and political patronage' that was a frequent feature of the old regime. Other authors, while noting the centrality of a model that was broadly based on UK lines, have also stressed the modification of the model to reflect the different Irish social structure and experiences.

So, for example, one difference that has been noted was in the background of civil servants. While university education was the norm in the UK, the higher civil service in Ireland was dominated by those who had entered with secondary-level education (Chubb, 1992: 237). A survey in 1956 found that 75 per cent of personnel in the departments surveyed had received their education from the Christian Brothers (O Mathúna, 1956). As Chubb notes, the late introduction of free secondary education implies that 'the children of the poorest, especially the poorest country people, tended to have a Civil Service career barred to them' (Chubb, 1992: 237). On the other hand, the policy of recruiting from secondary schools rather than universities meant that Ireland did not share the 'distinctively upper-class tradition' exhibited by the higher ranks of the British civil service (p. 236). This had obvious implications for the culture and ethos of the civil service. Chubb argues that it shared the 'bourgeois and republican' ethos of the newly independent community (1992: 237). Breen et al. note that, by the 1950s, the Irish civil service had developed its own ethos which was 'meritocratic in recruitment but strongly nationalist in cultural affinities' (1990: 37). They point to parallels between the civil service and Fianna Fáil, arguing that, by the 1950s, they shared a 'basic contradiction' between traditional nationalism and modernisation. Finally, they claim that, by the end of the 1950s, through a redefinition of Irish nationalism begun in the 1940s, a modernising élite within this civil service 'provided the real momentum' for the processes of economic modernisation. One interesting question, then, is whether, in this earlier period, there is any evidence of an embryonic 'modernising mission' among civil servants. As we will see, this is a much easier question to ask than to answer.

Before moving on to consider this question, it is useful to conclude by looking briefly at the specific issue of the place of civil servants in the social-insurance scheme. As with so many aspects of the Irish social-security system, the origins of the debate over the inclusion of civil servants lie partially with the policy legacies inherited by the Irish state on independence, as Hughes (1988) outlines. When the state inherited a central administration under the terms of the Anglo-Irish Treaty, it also inherited pension law and regulations. One of the impacts of the transfer was a reduction in the salary grades of general service and departmental grades because of the different economic conditions in the new state, but the pension law and regulations governing the UK civil service continued to be applied to the Irish civil service. Commenting on the superannuation scheme in the Irish civil service, Hughes remarks: 'The system of occupational pension provision which we now have dates from a number of different arrangements in the 18th century for providing for the needs of British civil servants in their old age' (Hughes, 1988: 104). These obligations were accepted by the government of the Irish Free State, and article 73 of the Irish Free State Constitution formally recognised the legal status of the superannuation Acts passed by the British government since 1810. Broadly, these provided for a pension in return for implicit contributions – that is, pay scales were theoretically below the level they would be at if the scheme did not exist (Chapter 1).

In addition to the pension rights inherited from the British administration, permanent and pensionable employees of the government and local authorities also had relatively generous sick-leave privileges (Farley, 1964). The nature of their employment meant that they were not subject to the risk of unemployment on the same level as other employees, and unemployment benefit was not a central issue. As the Brennan Commission noted, 'it is well understood that the civil service makes its appeal to the well-educated youth of the country by holding out prospects of a safe career with considerable opportunity for advancement, reasonable emoluments according to standards immune from the extreme fluctuations, whether favourable or unfavourable, of the commercial world and ultimate pension' (cited in Hughes, 1988: 115). Consequently, civil servants were not included in the 1911 National Insurance Act. However, there was no provision for widows' pensions. When a contributory widows' and orphans' pension was introduced in 1935 for employees who were insured under the National Health Insurance Acts, civil servants were included for this scheme only.

Among other provisions, the Beveridge Report envisioned abolishing exceptions in social insurance, including those in particular occupations such as 'the civil service, local government service, police, nursing, railways and other pensionable employments' (Beveridge, 1942: 63). Perhaps the first explicit mention of civil-service inclusion in the Irish social-insurance scheme came with the Dignan Report. Discussing the membership of the NHIS as it then stood, Dignan commented that only about 20 per cent of the total population were members, while his scheme envisioned an extended membership that 'constitutes a truly national scheme as 90 per cent (approx.) of the whole population would benefit by it' (1945: 27). In the new society, all employees are included. 'No class will be excluded: Civil Servants, Teachers, etc., all will become members' (p. 27). In the event, the position of civil servants in the social-insurance scheme became one of the most divisive issues for the inter-party government, and I turn to consider the policy debate in some detail now.

A government divided: the inter-party government and the question of scope

The inter-party government which took office in 1948 was, as we have noted, an experiment in Irish political history. A key element of the Westminster model is a stress on majoritarian government. However, this was not always easy to achieve under a PR electoral system; so, for example, Fianna Fáil's first exercise in government in 1932 was a minority one which depended on the support of the Labour Party. Nevertheless, this was the first time a clear division of executive power was attempted. In a number of ways, it put strain on a system which, until now, had been accustomed to single-party government. 'There were significant tensions in the Cabinet, with ideological dividing lines being drawn between parties (or more particularly, between Fine Gael and the rest)' (McCullagh, 1998: 430). Some of the tensions were simply 'ideological'. As McCullagh notes, standard coalition theory tends to stress that coalition parties should be adjacent on a policy scale; this was clearly not the case with the inter-party government. Some tensions, though, were undoubtedly due to the unfamiliarity of coalition government to the participants, as well as to the wider political system. In terms of institutional perspectives, we might say that the 'rules of the game' were unclear.

One indication of the unfamiliarity and suspicion of the incoming government was in its approach to the civil service. As we have noted, the theory of Irish government owed much to the British model, which assumed 'a tradition of political impartiality' (Murray, 1990). Civil servants are expected to be politically neutral and to serve incoming governments impartially – most observers point to the transition in 1932 as a defining moment. However, the incoming government in 1948 was suspicious of a civil service that had served Fianna Fáil for sixteen years and, infamously, opted to exclude the secretary of the Department of the Taoiseach from cabinet meetings. A second, related issue, was the problems in observing the doctrine of 'collective responsibility'. McCullagh (1998) notes multiple examples where this was breached. This indicates that, while all the parties agreed to form a coalition government, the extent to which they all recognised the necessity for compromise inherent in this is debatable. As we have seen, the government began life accepting the need for a 'comprehensive' social-security scheme, but it took virtually the whole life of the government to arrive at a working definition of what that would mean in practice. The key issue concerned scope. It was not until the drafting of the 1949 White Paper was under way that the question of which workers should be included began to be addressed in detail. As the previous chapters discussed, at this point the question of scope had come to refer to the employed class only – that is, were all employees to be included or should social insurance be limited to certain types of employees only?

This general principle that a 'comprehensive' scheme would be introduced, agreed in the ten-point programme for government, was reluctantly accepted by even the most trenchant critic of the scheme, Fine Gael's Minister for Finance, Patrick McGilligan.[3] What would prove to be the ground on which points of principle were fought out was the question of what exactly constituted a *comprehensive* scheme. The exclusion of the self-employed had removed any claims to the universalism of the Beveridge scheme, and consequently, questions as to who then would be included came to the fore. Department of Social Welfare notes on the scope of a bill based on the White Paper makes this clear. It comments: 'by limiting the scheme to the employed class the question of justifying the inclusion of sub-classes like the Guards and the Civil Service is made more difficult: contributions in these cases are to a great extent a tax on particular sections of the community; a tax it is true that is intended for the benefit of their less fortunate brothers but still not a general tax.'[4] The question of the inclusion of civil servants was not a technical question, but one that raised some central points of principle.

The extended battle over the inclusion of civil servants was, to use Baldwin's words, a battle between a vision which attempted to embrace the solidaristic potential of social insurance, and one which attempted to excuse the wealthy and the fortunate from sharing burdens with the harder pressed (1994: 44). As a closer examination of the debate reveals, this battle was not merely implicit, but was addressed explicitly and clearly at multiple points between early 1949 and the final collapse of the inter-party government. Because the battle over the degree of inclusiveness of the social-insurance scheme continued for so long, it is useful to subdivide consideration into two main periods: first the drafting of the White Paper, and then the attempt to translate this into legislative outcomes. Norton fought battles at both points and, indeed, was still responding to objections when the inter-party government collapsed.

In his detailed account, McCullagh (1998) notes that the scheme generally was to be one of the clearest lines of division within the coalition government. In attempting to implement the agreed commitment to a comprehensive scheme, Norton was to encounter an enormous range of objections from his cabinet colleagues:

> I noticed a number of queries, counterqueries, objections, tendering of memoranda on ideological grounds, which accumulated around Norton's proposals with each successive cabinet meeting. One of the last memories of cabinet meetings which I have is of seeing the quarter-inch thick brief with which Norton had earlier introduced his proposals become inches thicker until the final brief was nearly nine inches high . . . This is one of the not-so subtle ways in which the conservative majority party in a coalition can 'legitimately' frustrate radical proposals submitted by the 'minority' parties. One wonders to what extent Norton had collaborated in the delay. (Browne, 1986: 191)

This delay meant that, by the time the inter-party government collapsed, the bill had only reached its second reading and, consequently, its proposals collapsed with the government. McCullagh

(1998) argues that this indicates the 'limits to what could be achieved when in power with a conservative partner' and that left-wing critics of Labour's participation in coalition would argue that this first experience set the pattern for the rest (p. 197). Puirséil (2002) suggests that this perspective was shared by many Labour members, and was a contributory factor to the antipathy to both Fine Gael and coalition which would become evident in the later 1950s. What is particularly interesting about the debate over the social-welfare bill is the clarity with which party-based differences over issues of solidarity and redistributive issues were enunciated. Equally interesting, as I discuss below, is that these issues appear in quite a different guise in the scheme that actually emerges under Fianna Fáil in 1952. The way in which class interests are expressed in the Irish party system have found their expression in policy outcomes, although these may initially be obscure. Nor are they accidental outcomes that were not clear to policy-makers at the time. What can appear minor and technical matters – small variations between groups in contributions and benefits – were, in fact, the standard-bearers for very wide divergences over the aims of welfare, and the question of the place of civil servants in Irish social insurance illustrates this general point well.

The 1949 White Paper

Norton's first sortie into the field was his argument for the inclusion of all employees in the draft White Paper circulated to all departments on 8 April 1949. Paragraph 57 of the draft scheme recognised that, historically, exceptions and exemptions had been recognised for certain groups on a variety of grounds, but argued that these exceptions ought not to continue in the new scheme.

> In a compulsory scheme, it is felt that such privileged exceptions should no longer be retained, and that all members of a particular class – such as all those who derive their living from service to an employer – should stand together and together bear the burden of risks which can be regarded as common to the class as a whole. It is, therefore, proposed to form a single class for employees (i.e. persons working under a contract of service or apprenticeship) to be insured for all benefits, irrespective of the historical privileges of particular sections. This will, for instance, involve the complete abolition of the

wage ceiling as well as the inclusion for the first time of agricultural labourers and domestic servants for unemployment benefit,
and certain civil servants and employees of local authorities and
statutory companies for unemployment and sickness benefits.[5]

As noted above, the circulation of the draft sparked off the
exchange of an extensive range of memos between Social Welfare and
other departments. As might have been expected, Finance (under the
Fine Gael minister, Patrick McGilligan) objected to virtually every
aspect of the scheme – the cost, the growing bureaucracy, the impact
on agriculture, the effect on individual initiative, the marriage grant,
the death benefit, the old-age proposals, and so on. The range of
objections is impressive in its scope.[6] In any event, in forwarding the
comments of Finance on the draft White Paper to the government,
Norton comments 'in view of the general tenor of the enclosed
minute, he feels it would be quite wasteful of time for his Department
to endeavour to reach agreement with the Department beforehand'.[7]

Finance's specific objections to the inclusion of all employees usefully summarises what were to be the key issues in the long-running
debate that followed. Perhaps the central point of Social Welfare's
appeal for comprehensiveness was that employees should stand together
'to bear the burden of risk which can be regarded as common to the
class as a whole'. As Finance points out, however, this ignored the fact
that risks were not common. Three main reasons were given to argue
that these risks were not common: workers already had benefits that
protected them from these risks, the risk (of unemployment, for
example) was essentially not present, and workers had adequate income
to provide against the risks themselves. Hence, insuring those who
fell into any of these three categories was a form of 'discriminatory
taxation' since others would benefit more than they. A range of
problems arose from the three core points above. For example, those
who (like civil servants and certain groups of private employees)
already had benefits corresponding to or surpassing those in the
White Paper would, in effect, receive 'double benefit' arising out of
inclusion. And the taxpayer would, correspondingly, be paying on the
double for some groups. Dealing with this raised several difficulties.
In regard to civil servants in particular, adjustments to encompass this
might be seen as effectively worsening pay and conditions, and raise
claims difficult to resist before the Arbitration Board.

Other departments raised similar points, although they tended to
do so by pointing to particular groups in their domain who fell into

the above categories, rather than by drawing out the general point with Finance's clarity and insight. For example, the Department of Justice urged that the Garda Síochána be completely excluded. Education raised objections in relation to teachers, lay and religious. Defence was concerned about the implications for the defence forces, Posts and Telegraphs referred explicitly to civil servants, and there were also a variety of references to particular groups of employees, such as Guinness workers, whose employees had well-developed occupational schemes, and employees of Coras Iompair Éireann (CIE) and the Electricity Supply Board (ESB) also.[8] 'Messrs Guinness' was regularly referred to in order to highlight the implications for well-developed occupational pension schemes – the questionable implication is that Guinness was merely an example of a wide variety of similar schemes. The Department of Industry and Commerce stressed that in fact state encouragement of private insurance schemes might be the route to take, and suggested that American rather than English lines of development might be followed. Ultimately, the debate was to be narrowed – in what might be seen as a limited success for Norton – to the question of civil servants and certain other public employees. Initially, however, a range of groups who fell into the categories outlined above was used to attack the principle of comprehensiveness.

Objections to comprehensiveness then, either explicitly or implicitly, rested on the key point that risks were not, in fact, common to employees as a whole and, consequently, not all employees ought to be asked to contribute to a general scheme that insured all workers against these risks. The defence of a comprehensive scheme, there-fore, had to rest on grounds which defended inclusion even for those who, for varied reasons, were either not at risk or were protected against risk, and it is, I think, a fair summary to argue that broadly solidaristic arguments were tendered in defence. This is made clear by an examination of an extended defence of the issue of compre-hensiveness by the Department of Social Welfare. On 8 October, Social Welfare forwarded a note prepared in the department to the secretary of the Department of Finance, McElligott, 'on the possibility of excepting Civil Servants, Army, Teachers, Guards, firms like Messrs Guinness etc from the social insurance schemes'.[9] The note argues strongly for an all-inclusive scheme: '*It is therefore, essential to say in the White Paper that all will be brought in*, even though some partial exemptions or modifications are permitted' (emphasis in original).

A range of arguments is put forward to defend this view. All employees should stand together and together bear the burden of their common risk – the risks are common though the provision to meet them may vary. The exception to this may be civil servants, but 'the very existence of this virtual immunity imposes a moral obligation on those privileged to stand in with their less fortunate colleagues'. It goes on to say:

> Exception is regarded as a privilege inasmuch as the element of taxation (by contribution) is thereby escaped by employers and employed. What is often overlooked, however, is that the benefits of the State scheme are subsidised and the excepted person loses the advantage of securing these subsidised benefits. The established Civil Servant and some others may claim that they may expect to derive virtually no benefit from their contributions to Unemployment Insurance, but in reply to this it must be pointed out that they are well compensated for this in the other benefits and that they do not in any case pay for more than they receive (actuarially).

The paper discusses exemption under three grounds:

1. *The absence or smallness of the risk to be covered* The central response to this is outlined above, but the note makes the further point that this principle 'would involve the segregation of classes according to the severity of risks'. This feature had applied in the original national health scheme, allowing some to take advantage of their relative freedom from illness to secure valuable additional benefit, but this privilege was later withdrawn on the grounds that the scheme should be 'national'.

2. *The existence of alternative provision* Here, the central argument is the issue of administrative complexity, given that different groups receive different kinds of provision, e.g. Messrs Guinness and the Munster and Leinster Bank give different benefits and on different grounds. 'This opens an appalling prospect for administration of different rates of contributions, a multiplicity of stamps and a complexity almost beyond imagining.'

3. *The adequacy of income so that those who enjoyed it were regarded as being in a position to look after themselves* The note

argues that, broadly, this attitude could be criticised on the grounds that the better off are not playing their part.

The memo concluded that all the arguments emphasised the wisdom of an all-embracing scheme. It did, however, concede that there may be some justification in the argument that the exchequer would contribute on the double in some cases and 'an intimation might be given in the White Paper that the scheme may be modified in application to certain classes such as these'.

Another indication that the central argument concerned 'the better off playing their part', as well as an indication of Norton's personal commitment, comes from an exchange of letters between Norton and James Everett, the National Labour leader and Minister for Posts and Telegraphs. On 30 May (that is, following the circulation of the draft White Paper), the Department of Posts and Telegraphs wrote to Social Welfare on the question of whether civil servants should get the full benefit of the provisions in the draft scheme. 'If they are not permitted to do so it would seem inequitable to exact full contributions from them; while on the other hand if they are to receive Disability Benefit in addition to full pay when ill, the temptation to malingering would be serious.'[10] Norton writes to Everett:

> If you have not already seen the enclosed letter I should be glad if you would kindly read it and see whether it represents your views on the subject of social security as applied to Civil Servants. I should like to mention that Civil Servants in Great Britain and in the Six Counties are included in the social security schemes there, and I know of no reason why Civil Servants should be regarded as a class apart from the community which they serve and whose employees they are. I do not mind non-Labour people not holding these views, but I thought our own view was that Civil Servants should be included in the scheme, not merely because of its advantages to them but because they should not be exempt from national legislation which affects all other employed sections of the community.

Everett replies that he is in favour and will vote accordingly – 'I feel that the strong should help the weak.'[11] Equally, a Social Welfare memo summarising the response of various departments to the draft White Paper, and referring particularly to arguments that private occupational schemes ought to be encouraged, comments: 'The

Minister is averse to the continuation of any privileges or to the creation of new ones . . . The existence of specially-favoured groups among employees is not conducive to healthy social relations and any special provisions – the implications of which could be very far reaching – would tend to weaken the moral force of a compulsory scheme and unnecessarily complicate administration.'[12]

These arguments for solidarity did not convince other departments. Finance replied in some detail to Social Welfare's memo defending inclusiveness, and the central conclusion is directly opposed to the claims for comprehensiveness. 'The Department of Finance agree that the scheme should be confined to the employee class, but consider that non-manual workers earning more than £500 a year should be excluded, and that the scheme, in its several parts, should, both in equity and on financial grounds, be limited in application to those at risk, as is the practice under the existing scheme.'[13] First, Finance disagreed that the risks enumerated in the White Paper were common to all employees. The 'private collective endeavour' of some means that they can no longer be regarded as at risk and, accordingly, the extent to which the scheme is to apply to a particular employment should be conditioned by the terms of that employment. Furthermore, 'the suggestion that workers are morally obliged to contribute because they are not exposed to risk is fantastic and at complete variance with the principles of insurance.' Broadly, Finance pointed to the duplication of benefit for some, the problem of double payments by the exchequer and the overall cost of the scheme. It argued that those with an adequate income should provide for themselves and disagreed that the administrative problems in determining the range of exemptions were insuperable. In fact, the examination of private schemes to decide exemptions should prove of advantage to the community 'since, in general, every exemption would mean a corresponding saving to the Exchequer'. Furthermore, 'a point which should not be overlooked if exemption is granted is that excepted classes should be treated as if they were in receipt of contributory benefits under the scheme so that they would not be entitled, for instance, to draw non-contributory Old Age Pensions'.

McCullagh (1998) has described in some detail the torturous route of the government consideration of the White Paper, which was beset with continuing delays. A cabinet sub-committee was set up to examine it in July 1949, but its meetings were continually delayed and it failed to resolve key areas of disagreement. On 11 October, general agreement was given to the publication of the White Paper, but the final text was to be considered by a cabinet committee comprising Norton and the Taoiseach, a well as the Ministers for Finance and Defence. Although there is no explicit statement of what the key issue before this committee was, the discussion above and a comparison of the draft and final White Paper make it clear that it was the question of comprehensiveness that was the sticking point.

It is worth considering the personnel of the committee in some detail. In terms of the inter-party government in general, there was widespread opposition to the draft White Paper – probably only the Labour deputies, and perhaps Browne, might have been said to be supportive. McBride (External Affairs) submitted a memo, clearly not the work of his civil servants, which was poorly related to the issues under discussion. This was broadly supportive of enhanced social security, but suggested a combination of policies for full employment with a general tax-financed scheme. His ideas were far outside the terms of reference of the debate and do not seem to have been considered by any of the other ministers involved (though it is worth noting some parallels with Fianna Fáil suggestions, discussed below). However, the opposition from Agriculture (Dillon) and Industry and Commerce (Morrissey) was more considered. Their opposition, however, was generally to much broader aspects of the plan than are being considered here, though Industry and Commerce did have specific concerns about CIE and ESB workers. Given that the ten-point programme for government had, in effect, accepted that a comprehensive social-insurance scheme would be drafted, it may not be surprising that their general opposition did not carry the day – as noted above, the draft White Paper was accepted in principle with the exception of the question of civil servants and other groups.

The two ministers whose opposition to a comprehensive scheme was clearest (as I discuss in more detail below) were McGilligan (Finance) and O'Higgins (Defence) – that is, the two who were, thus, on the cabinet committee to resolve the issue. Both were Fine Gael ministers. The content of the committee discussions is unavailable, but the resultant amendment of the draft White Paper indicates that the outcome can best be described as a stalemate. The issue would continue to be examined. The White Paper stated that:

> In a compulsory scheme, it is felt that all those who derive their living from service to an employer should stand together and together bear the burden of risks which can be regarded as common to the class as a whole . . . The position of Civil

Servants, Teachers, Gardai, members of the Defence Forces and perhaps certain employees of local authorities is receiving further consideration. The problem is being examined to see whether, having regard to the existing schemes of welfare which apply to these classes, they should be included in the scheme or whether it might be advisable to exclude them. (Department of Social Welfare, 1949)

This ends what, in effect, was round one of the battle. Following the publication of the White Paper, the second round commenced with the drafting of a bill based on this. At this point, Norton returns to the issue and a detailed debate between a variety of departments ensues.

Implementing the White Paper: the conflict continues

Following the publication of the White Paper, preparations began in the Department of Social Welfare for the drafting of a bill to implement its proposals. One of the first issues to be considered was that which had been left undecided in the White Paper; that is, the question of modification of the scheme. Information on this was requested from the British Ministry of National Insurance on 19 November:

in our recent White Paper we have had to announce that the question of including Civil Servants, members of the Defence Forces, Civic Guards, teachers and certain employees of local authorities had not yet been settled. My Minister is now anxious to obtain, at first hand, information as to how you have dealt with the problem of including classes (not private groups) which had already adequate welfare schemes for at least some of the benefits.[14]

The ministry's reply was clear. It acknowledged that in the past, some (such as civil servants, police and some local-government and railway employees) had been exempted because the conditions of their service meant they were adequately protected against sickness and old age, and they were substantially free of the risk of unemployment. 'But it is an essential part of the principle of universality . . . that notwithstanding their privileged position in these respects they shall pay the same contributions as other employed persons.' Consequently, the National Insurance Act adhered to the principle of universality and made no provision for the special classes to be excluded wholly or in part from participation in the scheme on the same basis as other employed persons.[15] Perhaps the only (partial) exception was 'members of His Majesty's Forces'. They *were* included as employees, but the Act allowed for 'wide powers of modification' in a range of areas. Civil servants, on the other hand, paid full contributions and were entitled to the full range of benefits. The modifications that were made were essentially to the conditions of service, which avoided 'double benefit' in a variety of ways, and a number of examples in relation to sickness and retirement were given. It seems clear that the technical and administrative barriers to inclusion in the Irish case were not insurmountable, since the situation of Irish civil servants broadly mirrored the situation in Britain. An important point, then, is that the issue of civil servants was quite different from the other key issue of scope – that of farmers – since the arguments based on radically different Irish conditions did not, in this case, apply.

On 12 May 1950, the general scheme of a bill based on the White Paper was circulated to all departments, and Norton returned forcefully to the question of comprehensiveness:

> The Minister has now re-examined this question and wishes to reaffirm his conviction that there should be no departure from the principle of comprehensiveness in relation to the employee class. He is satisfied that the uniform application of the scheme to this whole class is the most desirable course, and he is sustained in this view not alone by considerations of social equity but also by the need to conform to the limits of administrative practicality.[16]

A range of arguments is put forward to support this conclusion. For one thing, none of the classes for which modification is being considered are covered by a scheme that is equal to the proposed scheme as regards both comprehensiveness and benefit level. Excluding these groups would be a retrograde step, ignoring forty years of insurance experience; when sickness and insurance schemes were first adopted, they provided for a range of modifications but later widows' and orphans' pension schemes included many people previously excepted. If civil servants and others were excluded, it would be impossible to resist pressure from others for a similar exclusion, a process which would rob the scheme of all claims to comprehensiveness. It was, therefore, worth restating the general case against exclusion:

> The case for general compulsory insurance rests largely on the idea that the more fortunate members of the employed class should stand in with the less fortunate in a common scheme. Unless this idea is accepted, the scheme should logically involve contributions varying for each individual with the type and degree of risk covered. This completely alien feature, so far as our insurances are concerned, is not in the scheme and it is not proposed to include it.[17]

A variety of departments responded, and Norton submitted a memo to government on 27 June summarising these and outlining the response of the Department of Social Welfare.[18] Generally, as with the responses to the White Paper, the responses concerned the groups that each department felt required either modification of the scheme or exclusion. Hence, for example, the Department of Education expressed some concerns about teachers, especially in relation to disability benefit, since teachers normally received full pay during illness. The Department of Justice expressed concerns about the Garda Síochána. This group already enjoyed substantial benefits, there would be no advantage to them to be included, and they should therefore be excluded. In defence of Social Welfare's case for comprehensiveness, Norton submitted the arguments above (which had been circulated with the general scheme of the bill on 12 May) as an appendix to the memo responding to these points. Generally speaking, the central argument was that, while some modifications might be made in relation to the defence forces, for example, consultations on this should not occur *before* the general principle of comprehensiveness had been accepted by the government. The key issue, then, was the general principle – modifications would be considered only once this had been decided.

The objections put forward by the Departments of Finance and Defence were especially trenchant. Both submitted separate memos to the government two days later, but seem to have discussed their responses beforehand.[19] Defence argued that its separate submission was necessary on the grounds that there was inadequate consultation with it, and because Social Welfare's summary of the minister's views was inadequate. Thus it included extracts from a minute previously sent to the Department of Social Welfare summarising its objections.[20]

In general terms, the memo argued that the majority of arguments advanced in favour of comprehensiveness 'have weight only if it is accepted, as a principle, that there should not be exception or modification for any class'. Familiar arguments concerning the absence of risk or existing coverage were repeated. Referring to Norton's arguments defending comprehensiveness on the grounds of social equity and administrative practicality, the memo notes:

> It is not in accordance with [the Minister's] concept of equity that an officer of the Forces holding a permanent commission, for instance, should be compelled to participate in an insurance scheme from the main risks covered by which he is already safeguarded, or that a soldier who, during his service, will have no need to avail of Unemployment or Disability benefit, should, if insured, be compelled to pay the full contribution. Neither is the Minister convinced that a scheme cannot be devised which would be practicable of administration and, at the same time, have regard to the realities of the situation.[21]

In its submission, Finance comments that the Department of Social Welfare 'press very strongly for a comprehensive scheme and have steadily resisted the exclusion of any groups from the scheme. If this principle is accepted by the Government it will, so far as Established Civil Servants are concerned, give rise to a number of difficulties.'[22] Again, arguments regarding 'double benefit', lack of risk and so on are rallied, leading Finance to conclude that there should be total exemption for established civil servants earning over £500 per annum. Other groups Finance suggested might be exempt included permanent commissioned officers in the army, whole-time army chaplains, judges and district judges, ministers and parliamentary secretaries, National teachers and secondary teachers. Should the decision be taken to approve of a comprehensive scheme, then, a range of modifications was suggested, such as insuring only for widows' and orphans' pensions. Finance also suggested that consultation with staff associations would be necessary.

At this point, it is worth noting that the issue had become one that a variety of civil-service bodies had begun to consider. One reason for noting this is that other concerned groups (such as trade unions generally, or farmers' associations) did not have similar access to the policy process. As a result, it is relatively easy to comment on the perspective of civil servants, whose structural location in the state provided them with the institutional position to clarify their views. In July, the staff side of the conciliation and arbitration machinery for civil servants indicated that they had set up a sub-committee examining the question of participation in the scheme.[23] Between September and November, three bodies who, 'between them speak for the entire Civil Service', made their views known to the Department of Finance.[24] As noted above, Finance was the central department concerned with the staffing and regulation of the civil service, a role inherited from the treasury. Finance comments that there was considerable divergence of opinion between the different bodies. While, in one sense, this is true, in another, a common thread runs through the civil-service position. This was a recognition of the arguments about risk, drawn out above – where the groups differed was on their assessment of the optimum response to this.

The most detailed consideration came from the general council staff panel. In September, it wrote to Finance stating that its view was that civil servants should be included in the proposed scheme on the same basis as other classes – that is, they should receive full benefits in return for full contributions. Should they be included without eligibility for all benefits, then they should correspondingly pay reduced contributions.[25] In November, a more detailed memo was submitted to broadly the same effect, adding that, rather than paying reduced contributions if they were ineligible for some benefits, they would consider full contributions with enhanced benefits in certain areas, e.g. widows' and orphans' pensions. The remainder of the memo concerns the position of unestablished and female civil servants.

The Institute of Professional Civil Servants also wrote to the Department of Finance in October. This organisation represented officers engaged in professional, scientific and technical work who did not come within the scope of the conciliation and arbitration scheme. The letter stated that its members were not disposed to recommend they be brought within the scope of the scheme until the question of establishment for temporary and unestablished offices was decided, and until the reckonability of pensions for these groups was likewise decided. In November, it wrote again to say that it was not seeking the application of the scheme to members above the remuneration ceiling for the Conciliation and Arbitration Board. It remarked: 'this Institute is not opposed to the application of the proposed Social Security scheme to Civil Servants. It does not however, wish to be taken as seeking application of the Scheme to any of its members'. [26]

Finally, the Association of Higher Civil Servants wrote in November.[27] This group did not seek exclusion, arguing that, for reasons of administrative convenience, it may well be decided that exclusion was impracticable. However, since they would have no occasion to claim certain benefits, the state would, consequently, make a substantial saving. The association suggest a variety of approaches to take this into account. One would be a special civil-service widows'-and-orphans' scheme. Otherwise, civil servants should be able to claim all of the benefits or pay lower contributions. It was assumed, the letter notes, that retired civil servants would be eligible for the pension provided under the scheme in addition to the Civil Service pension.

An article in the *Civil Service Review*, summarising the content of a deputation to the Taoiseach from the Conference of Professional and Service Associations, echoes broadly the same points. This conference included representatives of INTO, the Assurance Representatives' Organisation, the Civil Service Alliance, the Irish Bank Officials' Association and the Railway Clerks' Association. Among the comments made was that by the conference spokesman who remarked: 'It was unjust to request people to ensure against a risk which was extremely remote and on that basis exception was taken by the Conference to being included in a scheme where they would be compelled to ensure against unemployment which was for them a very remote risk.'[28] A speaker on behalf of the Civil Service Alliance said that his organisation was 'perturbed lest regulations which had been applied in Great Britain in consequence of the introduction of the National Health Scheme would be applied to civil servants in this country.'

In summary, then, two broadly opposed arguments were clearly drawn out. On the one hand, Norton's arguments for a compre-hensive insurance scheme, where the more fortunate stand in with the less fortunate; opposed to this, on the other hand, stood Fine Gael-led departments and civil-servant associations arguing broadly that the criteria for inclusion should essentially be based on an assessment of risk. The latter argument, in effect, called for a scheme that continued the 'privileged exemptions' of the 1911 and subsequent Acts, and explicitly rejected the (limited) redistribution involved in risk-spreading. These points were not 'technical' aspects, but ones in which the financial implications were clear to all concerned and, hence, the decisions taken reflected clearly opposing perspectives on issues of solidarity and redistribution.

However, in terms of describing the debate in party-political terms, an argument could be made that resistance emanating from the Department of Finance reflected traditional Finance opposition to the spending of public money, and that the key figure here was not McGilligan but the secretary of the department, J.J. McElligott. Equally, Norton clearly drew many of his arguments from his officials, and there is considerable evidence of a personal commitment by key officers to the case he presented. This is particularly visible in a fairly long letter written by W.A. Honohon, an actuary who had been transferred to the Department on its establishment in 1947, and was actively involved in the drafting process (Cousins, 2003: 151). He wrote to the assistant secretary P.J. Keady in June of 1950, as the debates about scope were at their peak.[29] Written on notepaper from the Grand Hotel in Greystones, the letter conveys a strong sense that both he and Keady supported the principal of full inclusion. Thus, Honohan remarks, 'I am very strongly of the view that no exceptions or modifications be made for any classes who are in a privileged position to advance their case.' He describes the approach of the Departments of Justice and Defence as 'narrow and selfish', and suggests (as he does elsewhere) some tactical steps they could take to achieve their aim. His annotations on Finance memos also underscore this strongly. At a number of points it is clear that Norton's case was one which was supported by his officials, and that they shaped the nature of the arguments he presented. It is worth remembering here that while there were solidaristic aspects of social insurance, there were also 'moral' and administrative benefits too, and on many points, arguments about the administrative complexity which exclusions would involve are to the fore.

Nevertheless, this needs to be balanced by the fact that there is also evidence of personal commitments to the positions put forward by key ministers. Thus, in a speech in March 1949, McGilligan spoke openly of the dangers implicit in social security, which could contribute to people losing their sense of independence, and other examples of his generalised resistance have been cited elsewhere (McCullagh, 1998). His 'dislike' of social security was noted on a number of occasions in the *Irish Times*. For example, in late 1950 Aknefton notes: 'Critics of Mr Norton cite his silence in the face of the McGilligan onslaught: admirers point to the fact that, in spite of the open displeasure of the Minister for Finance, the Social Security Bill forges ahead.'[30] There are strong grounds for arguing that McGilligan was personally hostile to an extended social-security scheme. Norton's personal commitment has already been touched on, and he played a personal role in the process at many points. Thus for example, in July 1950, during debates discussed at more detail below, a departmental note points out that Norton had informed his officials that discussion was to be at ministerial level, and that Norton had indicated that his 'intended course was to stand fast on total inclusion'.[31] It can be argued that, during the lifetime of the inter-party government, there was a happy overlap of interests between Finance's minister and its secretary, and between Norton and his civil servants. Perhaps the strongest argument supporting a political dimension will be seen when we consider outcomes under the next Minister for Social Welfare, Jim Ryan. As we'll see, Ryan, unlike Norton, quite clearly did not have a commitment to a comprehensive scheme, and his preferences would ultimately shape several aspects of the 1952 Act.

Certainly, contemporaries interpreted events in the light of partisan differences of opinion. The extent of the objections that hindered Norton had obviously begun to leak into the public domain. On 11 November, Aknefton commented on the possibility of internal governmental opposition, remarking that it was possible that some might decide to vote against the bill or might refrain from voting. Some days later, Cosgrave, in a speech at a Young Fine Gael rally, declared his desire to 'categorically deny' rumours that Fine Gael was opposed to the principle of social security. 'Some form of social security was essential, and he looked on it as a bulwark against the rising tide of Communism, which depended to a large extent on its appeal to those who were in want and distress.'[32] The government had a comprehensive social-security scheme under consideration, he remarked, but it took time to plan a scheme of that magnitude. In fact, as we have seen, much of the delay was due to the range and number of memos that Fine Gael ministers in particular had submitted objecting to diverse aspects of the bill.

Continuing debates about the inclusion of certain groups of workers continued, despite Norton having prematurely introduced a Bill in July (see Chapter 5). One interesting aspect of the erroneous decision to introduce the bill is that Norton received support from Costello for this action, indicating more general support from this quarter, due perhaps to Norton's 'very central role throughout the life of the government' (McCullagh, 1998: 256).[33] In fact, McCullagh utilises the social welfare plan as an example to illustrate a central problem with Costello's style as Taoiseach which was predicated on him acting as mediator, and suggests that the 'endless discussion' in search of compromise often 'resulted in victory for the more conservative elements in Fine Gael' (Ibid). It is worth noting that intra-party ideological differences can occur too, as we will see when we turn to consider Fianna Fáil again below. As an example of the endless quest for compromise, another committee was established (as had occurred with the drafting of the White Paper) to hammer out compromise on the continuing points of disagreement.[34] Finally, in October Norton conceded the point and agreed that the bill would be amended to include the power to exclude some groups, or apply the scheme with modifications.[35] The Bill introduced in July was withdrawn, amended and re-introduced in December as the Social Welfare (Insurance) (no. 2) Bill.[36]

What these modifications may have been in practice is, unfortunately, not known, since the government collapsed in May before the bill had progressed further. During the debate on the second stage, Norton had denied that he had taken a decision to exclude those groups. 'The position is that the Bill includes everybody but there is provision by which the position of certain people may be reviewed and, if the Government thinks fit, they may be exempted, either in whole or in part. But no decisions on that matter have been taken.'[37] However, a later memo in the Department of Social Welfare remarks: 'Mr Norton's intentions with regard to modifying the provision of the Bill under Section 14 . . . had not been finally declared when the last government went out of office. The Minister had, however, tentatively expressed the opinion with regard to Civil Servants that they should be either excluded completely or insured for Widows' and Orphans' Pensions only.'[38] A key question concerns the extent to which this outcome amounted to a defeat for Norton. McCullagh argues that the failure to implement the bill, which in effect arose from the duration of the debate, did amount to a defeat, and that this episode can consequently be read as an account of the limits to this Labour Party – and labour parties in general – in coalition governments in Ireland. It is undeniable that this account points to the implications of the weakness of the Irish left. Resistance from Fine Gael and Dillon both delayed the bill (and, hence, doomed it) and forced Norton to concede key points of principle – though the extent of this concession can only be deduced (that is – what 'modifications' the bill would have allowed for is unknown).

However, it is worth noting that Norton did not concede a salary limit, did not exclude groups with well-developed occupational pension schemes, limited modifications to what was a relatively small group numerically and, it might be argued, was still on his feet and fighting when the final bell went. On one level, the attempt to bring in a comprehensive insurance scheme can be read as a manifesto for what a stronger left might have achieved. As this chapter has made clear, the 'universalism' of the Beveridge plan did appear to promise a solidarity of the more fortunate with the less fortunate, and Norton clearly took this view. However, this interpretation needs to be read in tandem with the arguments in the previous chapter, which suggested that this model of solidarity might not have been appropriate to Irish conditions, and militated against any sort of 'red–green' alliance on redistributive issues.

Norton's credentials as a 'champion of the left' have been questioned, probably most famously and scathingly by Noel Browne. 'Norton was a man of many talents, all dedicated exclusively to his own betterment in society. He was persuasively articulate, and could simulate sincerity and pretended concern with impressive and misleading conviction. He could feel deeply only about his own special needs' (Browne, 1986: 189). Browne also argued that Norton had 'willingly allowed himself to be used by the conservative Fine Gael cabinet, while neglecting the welfare or best interest of the working people' (p. 189). His pragmatism within the inter-party government was noted by contemporary observers and, placed in a wider context, his defence of comprehensiveness was far from radical. He conceded, apparently immediately, any claims to universalism by excluding farmers, despite trade-union interest in including farmers in issues of redistribution. Having said this, it can be argued that Norton accepted (as Browne, perhaps, did not) the 'political realities' which the socio-economic structure and electoral context dictated, and once committed to a contributory scheme, fought his battles accordingly. His commitment can, perhaps, best be observed by contrasting his bill with the quite different outcomes under the next government.

Social Welfare (Insurance) Act 1952

The 1952 Social Welfare Act brought in by the Fianna Fáil government included provisions for the partial exclusion of civil servants and other groups, and included a salary limit of £600. Together with the absence of a contributory old-age pension and the narrowing of the terms for the inclusion of female domestic and agricultural workers, one conclusion might be that the defence of the privileged exhibited by Fine Gael was, hence, displayed by Fianna Fáil. However, what seems more likely to be the case was that the issues of principle represented by the battle over civil servants were not the issues of central concern to Fianna Fáil. Instead, the tight relationship between contributions and benefits, and the associated redistributive logic of social insurance, shackled attempts to express a *different* model of solidarity from that envisioned by Norton. Fianna Fáil's response was conditioned partially by the logic of party competition and partially by the logic of the institutional legacies that faced them. The broader economic context and the ascendancy of MacEntee to Finance were contributory factors also.

The previous chapter has already implicitly suggested some of this when it remarked that the incoming government were tied to promises they had given in the debate on Norton's bill. As we have seen, opposition to the bill was spearheaded in the Dáil by Lemass, who criticised its lack of comprehensiveness (in excluding farmers), the low level of benefits and (importantly) the tripartite financing of the scheme. As the last chapter noted, Aknefton in the *Irish Times* had commented wryly on Lemass' criticisms and expressed some cynicism about how his proposals might be financed. Among other jibes, he remarked that it put Norton in the position of defending 'Inter-party policy as against Labour policy enunciated by Lemass.'[39] This is reminiscent of the general argument that the weakness of the left in Ireland can be accounted for by Fianna Fáil filling the 'traditional' position of the left (for a review, see Mair, 1992 and 1999; Sinnott, 1995, *inter alia*). However, it is far from clear that Fianna Fáil's attitude to social security was 'leftist': certainly, not if we accept the Scandinavian model as an exemplar of a solidaristic approach characteristic of social democracy. However, its approach certainly differed from the generalised hostility clear in Fine Gael, and Fianna Fáil was at pains to indicate this, as Aknefton's comments indicate. Fianna Fáil's response then would need to differentiate it both from Labour and from Fine Gael, and would need to help it regain some of the ground lost to Clann na Talmhan and Clann na Poblachta.

Thus, as we've seen, Jim Ryan's initial approach moved far outside the terms of the debate that had divided the inter-party government and, indeed, away from the Beveridgean model which policy-makers so far had clearly operated within. As noted in some detail in chapter five, Ryan's proposals had moved away from the concept of risk-pooling in social insurance and envisioned joining the employed, self-employed and others in a national, tax-financed scheme for several key risks. Although the concept of risk would still be employed to draw lines between and among groups in this case, what would be attempted was to identify risks that were common across the whole population and to attempt to cover these risks by non-contributory schemes. This was a clear attempt to tackle the thorny problems of a diverse agrarian sector while meeting the demands of the industrial working class, which Fianna Fáil also aspired to represent (Mair, 1992; Dunphy, 1995; Allen, 1997). It is worth noting that the land distribution policies which Fianna Fáil had articulated in the early 1930s were by now deeply problematic (Dooley, 2004a), giving social policy more resonance as a means of retaining support in rural Ireland. But Ryan's proposals to abolish the contributory widows' and orphans' pension were short-lived. They were put forward on 28 December 1951 and were conceded by 17 January 1952, in the face of opposition from Finance and a recognition of administrative complications, some of which involved the position of civil servants. Thus when introducing the 1952 Act, which had abandoned the plans he had outlined in the Dáil debate on the Norton bill, Ryan remarked:

> Some Deputies will remember that on the Second Reading debate on Mr Norton's Bill, I advocated that Widows' Pensions should be financed entirely by the exchequer and not by contributions. I stated my reasons, which for the moment are immaterial, but I also mentioned that no Minister for Finance will readily agree to impose taxation in lieu of an existing source of revenue, even in deference to a colleague's wishes. The present income from contribution for Widows' and Orphans' Pensions is about £1,000,000. I was right. The Minister for Finance did object, and I must add that my own officials were very relieved when I capitulated to that Minister, because they were at their wits end to deal with the position that would arise for those who had contributed for some time towards a Widows' Pension.

Ryan had been aware of some of the potential pitfalls of his plan. Thus in putting his proposals forward in December he reviewed the origins and development of the contributory scheme for widows' and orphans' pensions and remarked: 'It could be argued that there is no need to upset an arrangement which the ordinary person has grown accustomed to and has come to take for granted.'[40] He recognised the financial implications of the loss of contributions, and also recognised that those insured (some 700,000) had acquired rights, and 'means must be found for preserving them'. Ryan also referred specifically to 'the excepted classes', which included over 30,000 persons, 'who were not covered for health insurance or unemployment insurance, but who were brought into compulsory insurance for widows' and orphans' pensions.' Ryan suggested that those 'so circumstanced' would continue, as at present, but those who entered those classes in future would not be compulsorily insured and would be entitled to the widows' and orphans' pension only subject to the means test.

An internal social welfare memo noted some of these problems, which would have them 'at their wits end' in detail. 'Difficulties would . . . be created by the Minister's proposals in the case of persons excepted under the National Health Insurance Acts who are insured for Widows' and Orphans' Pensions only.'[41] This category amounted to about 17,500 men and 12,500 women, essentially those employed in the civil service, by local and other public authorities, and by statutory companies. The memo first pointed out that, as noted above, Norton had 'tentatively' expressed the opinion that civil servants should be excluded completely or insured for widows' and orphans' pensions only. It also made another point. It began by quoting the White Paper's justification that all those who earned a living from an employer should stand together and bear the burden of common risks. 'Whatever reasons, academic or otherwise, there were for the complete inclusion of Civil Servants in the old scheme, those reasons no longer hold.'

A central problem was the old-age-pension provisions, which as we've seen would have given insured workers a pension with no means-test. 'It would be unthinkable to give without a means test an old age pension to a former established Civil Servant on the mere strength of an insurance qualification which is not related by con-tributions to the pension, particularly as such a person would be already drawing a Service pension.' Ryan's scheme, then, had implications which had probably not been foreseen: it is one thing to include civil servants in a contributory scheme, quite another to include them in a tax-financed scheme with a non-means-tested pension. The memo argued that there was 'a great deal to be said' in favour of continuing to offer limited widows' and orphans' pensions in the new proposals to those who were in that category at present.

'If it were considered necessary to grant the privilege in 1935, the like provision is still necessary.'

The memo points out the implications of this for Ryan's plans. 'Logically this would mean a change in the Minister's proposals, but there does not seem to be any more reason for the general discontinuance of insurance for contributory Widows' and Orphans' Pensions than there would be for the discontinuance of National Health or Unemployment Insurance; it does not seem possible to have a contributory Widows' and Orphans' Pension on a limited scale.' Thus the proposals Ryan had envisioned in opposition had underestimated that policy legacies both gave people 'acquired' rights which would be difficult to do away with, and, moreover, failed to encompass the differences within the proposed insured class.

Even after Ryan dropped his proposals, however, there remained some issues to be resolved. This was that of the position of workers in the ESB and CIE. As I mentioned above, even while Norton's scheme was going through the second stage in the Dáil, Industry and Commerce was continuing to press for exclusion. In May, as Ryan's scheme was coming to fruition, a memo from the Department of Industry and Commerce (once again under Lemass) was sent to the government.[42] In an interesting reference to policy continuity across governments, the memo begins: 'The Department of Industry and Commerce has had correspondence extending over some years with the Department of Social Welfare concerning the various proposals for social welfare legislation.' The memo returned to earlier arguments – essentially that the salaried and supervisory grades of CIE and all of the ESB employees should be excluded from the scope of the Social Welfare Bill. Initially, Social Welfare was unenthusiastic. Following a government meeting on 27 May, however, the two departments met on 30 May and hammered out a compromise. With regard to the ESB, permanent and pensionable employees were insured only for widows' and orphans' pensions. This required no amendment because the bill had already allowed for modification under employment by a public authority, building on provisions first introduced by Norton. With regard to CIE, salaried and supervisory staff were dealt with as above; this required a minor amendment allowing for modification for persons employed under 'any statutory transport undertaking'.

Ryan finally introduced his bill to the Dáil on 12 December 1951, and it passed all stages and was signed into law in June 1952: 'After a long gestation period, the social welfare system had finally been born' (Cousins, 2003: 166).

Conclusion

The differences between the proposals in the 1949 White Paper, and the social security system which took its final shape in the 1952 Act are revealing of the long-drawn out policy process and shifts in government in the years between the two. (A description of the final shape of the 1952 Social Welfare Act and a summary of the key differences between it and the 1949 White Paper can be found in Appendix 2.) Perhaps the most salient thing to note is that while there are important differences between the two, nevertheless they are both underpinned by a recognisably similar template. Both proposals were clearly Beverdigean, and both had modified this by effectively excluding the self-employed. Importantly, however, the Norton Bill had included all employees, although as described here, it may ultimately have only been fully applied to private sector workers. It is true that it had also distinguished between low-paid and high-paid workers –but all were included and eligible for benefit, albeit payable at different rates. Moreover all the standard risks – old-age (at 65 and 60), unemployment, disability, and maternity – were covered. There was in addition provision for a death grant. Comparing it to proposals in the UK, there is some justice to Ryan's comment that Norton had done little more than put in the Beveridge scheme and 'take off 2/- all round'.[43]

There were both *quantitative* and *qualitative* differences between the Norton scheme and the 1952 Act. The 1952 scheme was in some fundamental respects 'less' than Norton's plan – but it was different, too, in both its distributive implications, and in how it dealt with different groups. For one thing, in addition to the modification in relation to the public sector which it shared with the Norton plan, employees earning more than £600 were excluded. This limit was amended by regulation six months later to apply to non-manual employees only. As we've seen, only male agricultural workers were included, but this group effectively received a state subsidy to keep their contributions low while maintaining their benefit levels. A very important omission was that old age was not included. This exclusion however was balanced by a 'higher non-contributory old age pension at 70, subject to a very liberal means test'.[44] In addition, the qualification conditions for unemployment benefit were relaxed for those over 65. Any normally insured worker who had reached 65, and who was available for and genuinely looking for work, could draw unemployment benefit continuously. At 70, he would be eligible for the means tested OAP. As the Minister for Finance had remarked during the drafting process, this was 'a substitute form of retirement pension'.[45] As the last chapter discusses, these latter provisions would be play a central role in shaping the development of the Irish pensions system. Thus an important result of the lack of universality would be that those not insured – farmers and others – would receive enhanced assistance provision. There was a maternity grant, in a reduced form, but no death grant. Finally, rates of both contributions and benefits were lower.

What best explains these similarities and differences? Bearing in mind the policy progression across governments and across multiple 'decision points' in terms of scope, it seems clear that outcomes reflect the way in which political processes are embedded in very specific institutional contexts. It is useful to begin by stressing what the two schemes had in common. One of the insights which emerge strongly from a detailed examination of the policy process is just how influential the Beveridge model was. There is general agreement among scholars that the Irish social security scheme which emerged in 1952 was a form of modified Beveridge, and that this also applied to the 1949 White Paper and its associated legislation (Daly and Yeates, 2003; Cousins, 2003; McCashin 2004, *inter alia*). But it is clear that the route to outcomes in the two cases was very different.

Norton fought tenaciously for a Beveridge type scheme, seduced by the solidaristic vision it seemed to promise. Electoral realities, however, meant that the Irish left was a small minority, embedded in an ideologically diverse coalition. The truncated nature of the 1949 White Paper and the associated legislation in 1950 was a compromise forced on him by the realities of the Irish socio-economic structures, and by his more conservative cabinet colleagues. There is some justice in Noel Browne's suggestion, cited earlier, that the failure of the scheme illustrates how 'the conservative majority party in a coalition can "legitimately" frustrate radical proposals submitted by the "minority" parties' (Browne, 1986: 191). But this perspective neglects that fact that Norton's problems were due, not merely to Fine Gael intransigence, but also to problems which were inherent in any attempt to apply the Beveridge model to the very different Irish circumstances. The universalism of the Beveridge scheme – everybody would contribute, everybody would benefit, and all key risks would be provided for – was not just a technical matter, but was in fact fundamental to the nature of the scheme. Excluding as large and ideologically important a group as the self-employed had the effect of pulling a thread which unravelled the entire scheme. Once the philosophical concept of universalism was ceded, there was no longer any logical reason why any particular group should be included, and the question of scope was consequently open to debate. In a government where there was no shared commitment to solidarity, this was a disaster which ultimately doomed the scheme. This was particularly so because of the newness of coalition government in Ireland, which in this period, was an untried experiment where the accepted rules of collective responsibility were stretched close to breaking point (McCullagh, 1998).

In considering how politics influenced outcomes, it is worth noting that this perspective is institutionalist as well as political, since it focuses on the impact of an emerging party system. Thelen and Steinmo, for example, regard party systems as 'intermediate level institutions' (1992: 11) as do other authors (Rothstein, 1996; Mair, 1999). Party systems help to shape outcomes by laying down a patterned set of interactions' which shape the actions of political actors (Mair, 1999: 145). The pattern of coalition government set in train in the period clearly shaped distributional outcomes, particularly since decisions made during the inter-party government were carried over into the 1952 Act.

Considered in this light, perhaps the really interesting question is whether the Irish left might have achieved more had they managed to design a social security scheme which was more appropriate to Irish conditions. One of the best-known analyses of Labour's general political choices in the period is that of Mair, who argues that in 1948 (and again in 1973) 'Labour entered government as part of a wide-ranging inter-party coalition which, given its overall breadth of representation and given its combined social basis, effectively mirrored the inter-party coalition of Fianna Fáil, and as such, while providing an alternative government, proved wholly unable to persuade an alternative politics' (1992: 408). Part of the explanation for the weakness of the left was because it did not seek to mobilise or sustain 'an effective alternative politics' which could have acted as a class-persuader, mobilising a genuinely alternative politics (p. 409). It is clear that, in the 1940s and 1950s, this model of alternative politics could not have succeeded had it been aimed solely at the industrial working class. It necessarily needed to encompass elements of the agrarian sector too – as indeed social democratic parties in other countries did too (Esping-Andersen, 1990). This case-study, I hope, makes it clear that Labour choices in social security militated against their ability to make common cause with small farmers, because the models of solidarity on which the White Paper were based were profoundly unattractive in the Irish context. Yet – as Fianna Fáil seem to have always known – the small-farm sector was not in any way averse to state support, and tax-financed social security may have had some appeal at a time when there was clear rural dissatisfaction with Fianna Fáil, and with electoral politics generally.

Turning to consider the role of Fianna Fáil, however, it is clear that they did not share Norton's commitment to Beveridgeism or to the type of solidarity it embodied. Indeed, it seems clear that they were instinctively sceptical of its ability to appeal to their heterogeneous support base. In their case, the modified Beveridgeism of the 1952 Act reflected a different kind of compromise: one based on the interaction between institutional inertia and the increasingly harsh economic realities of the early 1950s, and the electoral challenges which the party system posed in the period.

Fianna Fáil ministers, acutely aware of the needs of their diverse support base, recognised the inherent problems with the Beveridge scheme: thus MacEntee's virtually instant realisation that it would mesh very poorly with the agrarian structures of the Irish economy, and Ryan's brief attempts to move towards more tax-financed solutions. However, harsh economic realities made such a radical shift impossible to carry. A central point to note is that it was a fundamental ideational and institutional change and would have needed much more momentum to carry it through. Existing modes of provision triumphed, albeit partially because of the wider economic context. Thus the discussion in this chapter illustrates how the position of civil servants and others, both in terms of social welfare and in the wider political system, reflects previous political choices, whether these were made in 1933, with the widows' and orphans' pension, or in 1924, in outlining a particular model of the civil service. Clearly, 'policies, once enacted, restructure subsequent political processes' (Skocpol, 1992: 58).

Thus, instead of attempting to find indigenous solutions, the 1952 Act modified the structures of Beveridge, but did so without concern for a specific model of solidarity. The outcome offered something to all key electoral groups: industrial and agricultural workers got improved insurance protection for some key risks, with the state subsidising agricultural workers and their employers via general taxation. Small farmers made no contribution – but benefited from improved assistance schemes of various kinds. Better off workers were excused from contributing, and public sector workers were cushioned by their superior superannuation schemes (Cousins, 1995). It was thus largely favourable to the proprietal and middle classes, but it is unlikely that this was visible to most workers of the period. The complexity, and the categorical approach it took, obscured the distributional implications of the scheme. Debates about risk-pooling and its distributional implications were clear to policy-makers, but almost certainly obscure to the electorate as a whole. As chapter seven discusses in more detail, it is perhaps this latter feature – the categorical approach taken in the Act – more than any other which would be carried through future welfare state developments.

Ó Cinneide's comments on the 1949 White Paper are also broadly applicable to the 1952 Act. Thus both might be said to have 'represented a compromise between, first, the commitment of a minister with a personal and party agenda; second the professional judgement and preferences of the experts, the civil servants in the Department of Social Welfare; and third, a host of other interests, some selfish and some unselfish, and all of them mediated through the other departments and ministers represented in the Government' (1999: 26). His comments lead us to consider the role of civil servants.

Establishing the precise degree of civil service influence is difficult although Heclo's comment on the way in which 'the bureaucracies of Britain and Sweden loom predominant in the policies studied' (1974: 301) is relevant also to Ireland. Indeed, as Cousins (2003) remarks, only civil servants and ministers were involved: there was no consultation with key interests, and the policy process was effectively closed and secretive. Perhaps the central influence of civil servants lies in the 'incremental, continuous nature of policy-making' (Connolly and O'Halpin, 1999: 263). The 'persistence of influence' of the central administration (as illustrated by Industry and Commerce's persistence on the issue of CIE and ESB workers) inherently suggests a central role for civil servants (Heclo, 1974: 301). Hall (1993) has suggested that this influence is strongest where 'policy paradigms are likely to become intertwined with firmly established operating procedures and departmental routines' (1993: 291). He cites the British civil service as the 'acme' of such settings – it is clear that broadly similar points can be made about the Irish civil service. As we'll see; the same civil servants were active, not just through the events described here, but on through the expansionary period. As we have noted, key civil servants 'tended heavily towards a social insurance approach' (Cousins, 2003: 169). This seems clear in the preliminary notes on the White Paper, which was insurance oriented at a very early stage, despite MacEntee's fulminations against Beveridgeism in the period (Feeney, 2001). Senior officials seem to have been generally thinking along Beveridgean lines, and thus the White Paper was clearly representative of the thinking of the Department of Social Welfare in the period. The later response to Ryan's scheme underlines this further: the opposition of officials to his proposals to depart from the contributory route is clear, and along with the other factors outlined above was important in dooming his scheme

However, there are some important qualifications to be made around the issue of the role of bureaucrats. One interpretation of the centrality of bureaucrats in the policy-making process is that it suggests the autonomy of the state. 'In democratic and capitalist societies, states can be considered autonomous when they create strategies of action independently of capitalists and organised business groups, political parties, interest groups, movement organi-sations, and public opinion' (Amenta et al., 2001: 220). Hall argues that this perspective, which he terms 'state-centric', differs from what he calls a 'state-structural' perspective, which gives 'interest groups, political parties and other actors outside the state an important role in the policy process' (1993: 276). The events described in this and in previous chapters point to an important role for party politicians, albeit one mediated by institutional structures and policy legacies.

At various times, all the key politicians were extremely activist in pursuing particular policy agendas. MacEntee's personal role in events, described in some detail in chapters two and three, needs no further stressing. Ryan too was clearly political in key respects. Thus, for example, in October of 1947 Ryan, 'anticipating discussion in the Dáil' requested his civil servants to include in the White Paper a criticism of both the Dignan Plan and of the Vocational Commission Report. Moreover, he specifically requested that Labour proposals 'are to be criticised but not aggressively'.[46] With regard to Norton, the remarkably long-drawn nature of the policy process bears witness to his reluctance to compromise on key points, even at the final moments. Although in 1952 Ryan failed to fully carry his original proposals, the important differences between his scheme and the Norton scheme can *only* be attributable to political perspectives, since as noted here, they ran directly counter to the preferences of civil servants. Outcomes in social security point us to the complexities of the interaction between politicians and bureaucrats which are not amenable to easy analysis. Thus while the institutional context within which the policy process is located is crucial, so too are political actors speaking to their constituencies. Neither a logic of politics nor a logic of institutions can successfully explain outcomes alone. The case study of social security demonstrates that politics and institutions *require* to be thought of in tandem.

In Search of an Insurance Covenant? Social Security in a Wider World, 1961 to 1979

Introduction

The 1952 Social Welfare Act, together with the 1953 Health Act, brought an end to the post-war period of welfare state development in Ireland. As we've seen, the period was one of both legislative activism and of increasing social expenditure. 'Between 1947 and 1951, public social expenditure doubled from £31.8 million to £62.5 million and increased its share of GNP from 9.6 per cent to 14.9 per cent'[1] (Kennedy, 1975: 11). However, the bulk of commentators have focused on the limitations of reforms, stressing in particular the absence of universalism in both health and income maintenance (Breen et al. 1990; O'Connell and Rottman, 1992; Cousins, 1995, *inter alia*). Thus, by and large, the period is viewed as the key moment at which the Irish welfare state 'lagged behind' developments elsewhere in Europe (Ó Riain and O'Connell, 2000: 310). Chapter 1 suggested that one problem with theoretical accounts of the Irish welfare state is that despite the centrality of the immediate post-war period most accounts begin with the delayed expansion from the 1960s on. It is useful therefore to conclude this book by briefly considering this expansionary phase, and drawing out some continuities and discontinuities across the two periods.

Although there is general agreement that this expansionary phase began in the 1960s, there is rather less consensus on when precisely the period draws to a close. For some, EEC membership in 1973 marks a natural end point – thus authors who lay stress on welfare state development as a concomitant of the internationalisation of the economy see the years 1960–73 as the key expansionary period (Ó Riain and O'Connell, 2000: 335, table 16.2). If we view events through the narrower focus of phases of expenditure, however, it is clear that the while social expenditures began to grow in the early

1960s, they did not peak in 1973. In fact, 'expenditure rose particularly rapidly between 1973 and 1975' (Maguire, 1986: 252). If, instead, we consider policy epochs, then perhaps the publication of the *Report on the Commission on Social Welfare* in 1986 marks an important qualitative transition. But then, so too does the election of the 1987 Fianna Fáil government, which began the process of tackling the severe economic problems of the period, and initiated the contemporary social partnership process. While all of these dates have something to recommend them, none of them work particularly well for the narrow policy sphere of social security, and for considering the themes of this book.

This is because, as Chapter 1 discussed, particular policy areas have very distinctive policy trajectories which do not always map neatly onto macro-level models of welfare state development (O'Sullivan, 2004). As this epilogue argues, there are good grounds for considering 1961 to 1979 as a self-contained period marking both qualitative and quantitative shifts in social security policy. The introduction of a contributory old-age pension in 1961, discussed in some detail in this chapter, not only reflects the impact of a transformed policy process, but marks the beginning of a shift towards the *explicit* adoption of social insurance as the preferred mode of provision in income maintenance. Throughout the two decades which followed, social insurance coverage was not only considerably expanded, but underwent important shifts in how it was conceptualised. These culminated in the decision in 1979 to introduce the PRSI system, a decision which appeared to formalise what we might call the 'Europeanisation' of the social security system. This epilogue therefore briefly traces events between these two dates. It concludes, however, by pointing to an intriguing paradox: despite what seems to be the thrust of policy in this crucial period, Irish social security would subsequently develop in quite a different manner. I begin this account by considering in some detail the introduction of the old-age contributory pension (OACP) in 1961, which marks very clearly both the end of the period with which this book has been concerned, and the emergence of a very different world of welfare.

Sean Lemass and Irish pensions policy: a matter of extreme urgency

On 23 June 1959, Seán Lemass was elected Taoiseach, formalising a paradigmatic shift in Irish social and economic policy making which had been underway for some time. He had been in office for less than a week when, on 29 June, he wrote a short note to his Minister for Social Welfare, Seán MacEntee, stressing his interest in getting started on an examination of the practicability of a contributory retirement pension scheme for insured workers, and including an extract from a speech he intended to make the following weekend:

> I think that we should have a contributory retirement pension scheme for insured workers as they have in many other countries. Many Irish workers have, of course, pension prospects arising out of their existing employments, some based on contractual rights and some voluntary, but there are very many – indeed the great majority – who have not and who, apart from what they can save, have nothing to look forward to in old age except the general old age pension. The working-out of the details of a contributory insurance scheme so as to interfere as little as possible with existing pension schemes, and so as to relate pension rights to the contributions which most workers could afford to pay, is a matter for experts in the first instance and for consultation with workers and employers representatives subsequently.[2]

The situation which Lemass drew attention to was one which sprang directly from the truncated nature of the 1952 Social Welfare Act. The 1949 White Paper had referred to contributory retirement pensions as 'the most important change to be effected under the new social insurance scheme' (Department of Social Welfare, 1949: 24). Despite this though, old age was excluded from the 1952 Act, as we have seen, and this was a source of major concern to workers. As Lemass remarked, it meant that workers had nothing in old age but the means tested coverage of the 1908 pension. The omission was very visible, because at age 70, insured workers and their dependents would often move directly from higher contributory benefits to the lower means tested old age pension.

This situation was in fact one which Sean MacEntee had been considering, focusing in particular upon the situation of widows of insured workers who suffered a sudden drop in income when they reached 70.[3] His preferred solution was to continue the payment of the widows' pension (and disability benefit) after the age of 70, but his officials suggested to him that 'the problem of a drop in income at age 70 would be best met by a scheme of contributory old age pensions.'[4] Earlier suggestions by the Secretary, P.J. Keady, that the key area of reform should be in the area of old age pensions had not seemed to enthuse MacEntee, who commented that the cost of increasing the means tested pension made this an impracticable solution, while a contributory scheme of retirement 'was open to administrative and financial objections.'[5] Despite this, he seems to have mentioned a contributory pension to Lemass – at any rate, Lemass' letter came within a week of the suggestion (above) that a contributory pension would solve some problems in the area.[6] As a result, MacEntee wrote to the Parliamentary Secretary forwarding the Taoiseach's letter, asking for his views 'as a matter of extreme urgency.'[7] With an apparent lack of enthusiasm, he added that 'in considering the matter, you may take it that we will have to accept in principle the eventual introduction of such a scheme.'[8]

Lemass kept an extremely close eye on the subsequent policy process, keeping MacEntee 'under continuous pressure'[9], advising his other ministers that they should deal with the matter 'as one of urgency'[10], and expediting its early introduction into the Dáil. It is clear that, as MacEntee stated: 'The proposed scheme . . . is regarded as having first priority in the Government's programme.'[11] It is worth pausing and considering why the OACP was so urgent that its introduction was one of Lemass' first priorities as Taoiseach. The answer, perhaps, is that the OACP fitted precisely into Lemass' wider concerns at that particular moment and marks the beginnings of social policy as *instrumental* to wider social and economic policy.

As Murphy (2003) has argued, although the publication of *Economic Development* and the *First Programme for Economic Expansion* in 1958 is often taken as the starting point for economic and social change, the roots of this shift lie a decade earlier. Thus while the Department of Finance was tabling its many objections to the 1949 White Paper in the inter-party government, it was simultaneously beginning the twin processes of engagement with a wider Europe and experimentation with new economic models which would accelerate from the end of the 1950s on. Although not a signatory to the Treaty of Rome, Ireland was a founder member of the Council of Europe in 1949, and of the 1948 OEEC, established to distribute Marshall Aid. Murphy has described how the 'initial tentative steps towards engagement with Europe' (Murphy, 2003: 1) involved co-opting economic interest groups into a tri-partite approach to economic management. This was of course particularly the case for Lemass, who 'instinctively knew that the development of the country in economic terms revolved around a corporatist-style arrangement' (Murphy, 1999: 91). Lemass had a history of courting the labour movement in pursuit of Fianna Fáil's electoral interest going back some years, and his broadly urban, trade-union-oriented approach to policy has been noted by a number of authors (Allen, 1997; Bew and Patterson, 1982).

Moreover, Lemass also had a history in the field of social policy. He was well informed and broadly positive – in private at any rate – about the Beveridge proposals, as came across in his comments on Norton's bill, cited in Chapter 5 (Bew and Patterson, 1982; Cousins, 2003). He had been a key instigator of the 1944 Children's Allowance, and had in fact suggested a contributory retirement pension in that same year (Cousins, 2003). Given his strong links with the trade union movement, he had no need to wait till the newly reunited trade union movement called for the introduction of a contributory pension at their very first conference in September 1959 to recognise that this was a core demand of the labour movement generally.[12] Although Lemass left no record of his motivations, it seems unproblematic to assert that he recognised that an OACP would help in the process of co-opting the trade union movement into the emerging internationalised economy. His suggestion that its design should involve 'consultation with workers and employers representatives' underscores these general points. As an aside, these consultations did not take place. As the Secretary of the Department of Social Welfare remarked: 'the officers of the Department could be regarded as sufficiently expert to produce a scheme which would be the best in all the circumstances.'[13] The Secretary was backed on this point by MacEntee, who refers to earlier unsuccessful negotiations, implying that the subject of a retirement pension had been approached under a previous minister, although I have not been able to find any record of this.[14] In the event, it appears that this section of the proposed speech was omitted.[15]

Murphy has suggested that in general terms Lemass set out in this period to establish a 'broadly European style proto-corporatist social democracy' (1999: 99) This may well be the case in relation to wider aspects of his social and economic policy, but the specific design of the OACP does not seem particularly social democratic in ethos. The reasons for this are signalled with some clarity in his proposed speech. Thus Lemass suggested that the 'working-out of the details' of the contributory scheme will be such as 'to interfere as little as possible with existing pension schemes.' In saying this, Lemass drew on awareness from his period as Minister for Industry and Commerce in the 1951–54 government that this was an extremely tricky aspect of designing an old age pension scheme. As the last chapter discussed, William Norton, and to a lesser extent Jim Ryan, had encountered the problem of dealing with workers who had either well-developed occupational pension schemes or private pension schemes. In some cases – that of civil servants, or some ESB and CIE workers, for example – adding a contributory pension might mean that they could receive double subvention from state funds. The omission of old age in the 1952 Act made this irrelevant, but once the decision to introduce a contributory pension was taken, the issue was picked up at precisely the point at which it had been dropped in 1952, and the outcomes in the 1961 OACP drew on earlier debates and decisions. These outcomes are fundamental to the emergence of the 'three-tiered' welfare state which is particularly visible in Irish pension policy, and are worth considering briefly.

The question of how the OACP would interact with the 1908 pension was decided fairly swiftly: receipt of the contributory pension would be a disqualification for the means tested pension – even though, in certain circumstance, some couples would have qualified for a partial pension on means grounds. The interaction of the OACP with private or occupational pensions was decided quite differently. The decision was that there would be provision for existing schemes to alter their terms should they so choose – this had been the solution of Norton's 1950 bill. This was intended to tackle the problem of double benefit, and it allowed occupational schemes leeway to adjust their pensions in the light of the state scheme. However, quite crucially, receipt of a private or occupational pension would not disqualify someone for receipt of a contributory pension. Thus the OACP could be combined with income from all sources *other than* the non-contributory means-tested old-age pension. This decision, in tandem with decisions in the sphere of taxation, would have major implications for the long-term development of the pension system.

Prior to 1961, it was not possible to integrate occupational pension schemes with the state pension, since membership of any occupational pension scheme awarding pensions in excess of 20/- per week meant that members lost their entitlement to either the whole or part of their old age pension (Kaim-Caudle and Byrne, 1971: 4). From 1961, though, those who wished could 'top up' their contributory pensions via occupational pension schemes. Hence Kaim-Caudle and Byrne (1971) in their study of occupational pension schemes remarked that the 1961 Act 'led to a substantial increase in the number of pension schemes for employees covered by social insurance' (1971: 5). Moreover, in tandem with earlier decisions in 1952, it facilitated earlier retirement for some. Although the OACP was not payable before the age of 70, the 1952 Act had introduced quite tolerant conditions for the receipt of unemployment benefit after 65, as we have seen. Thus, following the 1961 OACP, those with occupational pensions could retire at 65, and avail themselves of easy entitlement to unemployment benefit until the OACP took effect at 70 (Kaim-Caudle and Byrne, 1971: 5).

The relevance of decisions taken in these years is indicated by a study of private-sector occupational pensions in Ireland which found that in 1985 there were 2,457 private-sector occupational pension schemes in existence (OECD, 1994). Only 6 per cent of these had been set up before 1960, while 42 per cent had been established between 1961 and 1975 (OECD, 1994: 9). It is important to stress that in understanding the long-term implications of the OACP, decisions in taxation which gradually created large tax expenditures in the pension sphere are fundamental. It is worth noting then that the 1958 Finance Act had already 'created a favourable tax environment for the development of pension schemes as it granted assurance companies exemption from income tax on income arising from pension fund investments' (OECD, 1994: 10). The question of the tax implications of the decisions taken in 1960 seem not to have been discussed, but they were certainly clear to W.A. Honohan, now Assistant Secretary, as a contemporaneous article by him on private pension provision makes clear. Discussing the role of tax concessions in relation to private pensions he remarks that 'a real contribution is made by the taxpayers, in particular the present generation' (Honohan, 1959–60).

I return to some of these points in the conclusion, but the central point to note here is that the 1961 OACP completed the range of risks standard in the period, and thus draws a close to the policy process examined in this book. However, it also points us forward, since it initiates a policy period which appeared to have resolved the debates about the merits of insurance versus assistance in favour of social insurance.

A pressing need for harmonisation: extending social insurance

Given the restricted scope of the OACP (which applied only to the same limited groups as the 1952 Act) MacEntee's ringing declaration that it was 'intended to be the foundation of a new social code based, not upon public charity, but upon a covenant of insurance between the worker and the community of which he is a part and through which he lives and in which he serves' seems somewhat of an overstatement.[16] This is particularly the case because on the surface the 1960s was not an activist period in social security. *Economic Development* had envisioned 'deferring further improvements in the social services until a steady growth in real national income is well established' (1958: 24). It was thus not until the *Third Programme* in 1969 that social policy was explicitly targeted, and this might be thought to explain why it is the 1970s which is the key decade for social security development. However, although it was the 1970s which saw the bulk of legislative activity in the social security field, it is clear that the 1960s laid the preconditions for this in many important respects, even before the publication of the *Third Programme*. There are a number of indications that social insurance was increasingly viewed as the most appropriate mode of provision for most contingencies, and that it was being considered broadly across the full range of social service provisions, although this discussion focuses only on income maintenance.[17] The first indication of a growing insurance paradigm in social security was an occupational injuries scheme introduced in 1967.

In 1955, the second inter-party government had established a committee to examine the occupational injuries system, which was essentially one of employer's liability dating from the late nineteenth century. The committee produced both a majority and a minority report (McCashin, 2004). The majority report recommended retaining and improving the existing system, while the minority recommended that the existing system be abolished and replaced by a social insurance based scheme. Interestingly, this had been recommended to them by the ICTU.[18] Despite the majority opinion of the committee, the government opted to go with the minority ICTU nominated approach, and introduced a contributory scheme. Unfortunately, large gaps in the social welfare files in the National Archives from the early 1960s on mean that the evidence for this period is very fragmentary, and the conclusions here are consequently tentative. However, the evidence that exists points to the emergence of a growing 'insurance mindedness' amongst key policy-makers which helps to explain this decision.

In September of 1967, and again in February the following year, Joseph Brennan, the then Minister for Social Welfare, wrote to the

Taoiseach outlining at some length the course he intended to take in the development of Social Welfare services.[19] These quite detailed outlines were followed in March 1968 by a memo to government summarising some proposed improvements.[20] Brennan suggested, in general terms, that:'As far as possible services will be financed by methods of insurance so that benefits may be granted without test of needs or means.'[21] He pointed to 'necessary and fundamental changes required in our social welfare schemes.'[22] Amongst a range of reasons is cited 'the pressing need to harmonise our social insurance schemes with those of the European Economic Community within the next few years.'[23] Indeed, the requirements of the forthcoming member-ship are cited at a number of points, in particular in relation to the pension age of 70, and the lack of pay-related social insurance. There are other reasons – as he tells the Minister for Finance, Charles Haughey: 'The general public have come to expect some serious development of the social welfare system.'[24]

Thus by March of 1968 Brennan was seeking approval for a number of proposals in the broad areas of social welfare. On the insurance front, these were the introduction of pay-related disability and unemployment benefit, a limited scheme of retirement pensions at age 65, an invalidity pension scheme and a scheme of death grants. Moreover, he sought to extend the scope of compulsory social insur-ance, further develop voluntary insurance, and extend the scope of the occupational injuries scheme. The *Third Programme* in 1969 was therefore able to be specific about the shape of future developments, since it clearly drew on these proposals. It repeated verbatim and thus formalised Brennan's assertion that: 'As far as possible services will be financed by methods of insurance so that benefits may be granted without test of need or means' (Government of Ireland, 1969: 207–8).

The *Third Programme* clarified both that there had already been a trend away from assistance payments, and that the intention was that this would continue. It pointed out that at constant 1958 prices, the cost of insurance payments had increased by 167 per cent since 1958/59, while assistance payments increased by only 15 per cent (Government of Ireland, 1969: 206–7). The aim in general would be to continue to devote an increasing proportion of growing national resources to the extension and improvement of services. A range of named proposals had been approved, and further proposals were being considered. These were those referred to above.

These reforms were introduced piecemeal over the next few years, first under the Fianna Fáil government, and then the succeeding Fine

Gael/Labour coalition from 1973–77. The process began with a retirement pension, invalidity pension and death grant in 1970. In 1974, the income limits for non-manual workers which had been established by the 1952 Act were abolished. As the minister at the time remarked, the 'distinction between manual workers and non-manual workers is a survival from the days when the levels of pay and working conditions of "white collar" workers were greatly superior to those of manual workers. These differences have now largely been eroded and, indeed, the borderline between what constitutes manual work and non-manual work is now very blurred in many areas because of technological advances and developments in skills, as for example, in the field of electronics and computers.' The abolition of income limits meant that the social insurance system expanded to include the bulk of employees: the number of insured people increased immediately by 19 per cent (Kennedy, 1997) and coverage increased from just over half the labour force in 1953 to nearly two-thirds in 1981 (Ó Riain and O'Connell, 2000: 328). For O'Connell and Rottman (1992) the abolition of income limits was crucial, and is one of their illustrative examples of the logic of state action. Together with the extension of social insurance to the self-employed in 1988, they argue that it 'promoted the social solidarity needed to accomplish the extension of social citizenship, and helped to legitimate the extraction of taxes to finance the welfare state' (1992: 235).

The year 1974 was a particularly important one from the perspective of social security, since in addition to the abolition of income limits, income-related benefits for unemployment, maternity and disability were introduced. 'In 1975 the total net estimate of the Department of Social Welfare was nearly double that of 1974' (Kennedy, 1997: 138). Nor, at this point, did there seem to be an end in sight. In setting out the case for pay-related benefits, Brennan had commented that these would be confined 'in the first instance' to short-term benefits, but attention subsequently turned to the issues of pensions, and a Green Paper, *A National Income Related Pension Scheme*, was published in 1976. McCashin (2004) has reviewed the policy debates around the issue of income replacement, particularly in relation to pensions. The Green Paper 'firmly argued a role for an income related pension' but although a White Paper was subsequently drafted, it was never published (McCashin, 2004: 267). McCashin notes that 'governments during this period articulated no consistent policy argument' on the general question of income related social insurance. (2004: 42). In the event, an income related pension was not introduced, and moreover, pay-related benefits were abolished in 1994. The rolling back of the moves towards an income related system means that Ireland is 'one of the few European countries without a mandatory earnings-related pension' (Cousins, 2005: 229).

Finally, the thorny question of the self-employed was examined in some detail in the 1978 Green Paper on *Social Insurance for the Self-Employed*. This clarified that the numbers involved had declined as a proportion of the workforce from around 36 per cent in 1961, to 28 per cent in 1976. Some 65 per cent of the sector, however, was still being drawn from agriculture. In addition, the self-employed remained relatively more important in Ireland than in the EEC generally, with only Italy having a higher proportion (Department of Social Welfare, 1978: 6–7). Notably, 'relatives assisting' had almost halved between 1961 and 1976, and the self-employed were 'an ageing population with a far greater proportion of persons in the older age groups than is the case with the employee population.' The paper pointed out that 'insured persons and their employers finance through taxation a substantial proportion of the cost of social assistance for the self-employed while the latter make only an insignificant contribution through that part of the Exchequer cost of social insurance which can be attributed to general taxation' (DSW, 1978: 28–9). One outcome which the Paper pointed to was that since social assistance was almost entirely financed by the Exchequer, 'the overall proportion of social security expenditure borne by the State is considerably higher in this country than in most member States of the EEC' (DSW, 1978: 27). It concluded that extension of social insurance to the self-employed 'would make for a more equitable distribution of the cost of income maintenance.' It would however, be a further decade before the self-employed were included in 1988, and by this time the economic context had shifted very considerably.

The final legislative initiative of the period was the introduction of a pay-related contribution system (PRSI) in 1979, which abolished the stamped insurance card system and integrated the collection of contributions with the PAYE system. In introducing the scheme, the Minister for Social Welfare, Charles Haughey, remarked that it would 'eliminate the regressive aspects of the present flat-rate contribution system which bears heavily on the lower paid worker.'[25] Moreover, higher paid workers would also benefit since the proposals also envisioned raising the ceiling applying to pay-related benefit.[26] When the reforms and policy proposals outlined here are considered together, it seems clear that as McCashin has suggested, the period was one where 'the framework of policy development remained firmly and unquestioningly within social insurance' (2004: 42). I consider some of the motivation for this in more detail below, but before doing so, it is necessary to point out that simultaneously with this drive towards what might be considered a more European system there were cross-cutting initiatives in the shape of assistance based developments. Over the long haul, these would be equally important.

'Specific categories of the community': filling in the gaps

Although it seems clear that policy-makers of the period felt that ongoing transformation of the economy had ended the long-running debate about insurance versus assistance, the reality was that this was an illusion. In the 1940s and 1950s, policy-makers had struggled with the particular Irish manifestation of a more general problem inherent to the nature of social insurance: that its mode of provision 'as of right' is predicated entirely upon labour market participation. The problems for a society with a large 'self-employed' sector who did not participate in the labour market were obvious. But as these numbers declined, and seemed set to decline further, it appeared that 'a covenant of insurance' was achievable in the new, European and industrialised Ireland.

Irish policy-makers in the 1960s and 1970s were thus subject to precisely the same misconceptions as Beveridge had been in the 1940s. As Glennerster and Evans point out, 'Beveridge's notion that insurance by itself would be sufficient to eliminate want, except for quite exceptional cases, was only tenable if the insured categories were indeed universal' (1994: 66). The flaws in this 'assumptive world' are by now very well known: first, labour market participation is highly gendered, and second, employment generally is not always permanent, full-time, continuous, or accessible to all. Provision for these groups, whose size and relationship to the labour market fluctuates depending on a range of discrete factors, can be very problematic in a social insurance based system.

The various memoranda on social welfare reform in 1967 and 1968 (referred to above) were dominated by the consideration of issues in relation to insurance. But each document contained a short section – somewhere around 10 per cent of the content on average – pointing to some necessary reforms of the assistance side of provision. Brennan suggested that what was required was 'an entirely new approach' to ensure both that public monies were spent effectively and economically, and 'so as to ensure that all citizens of the State who are in need or want, and are ineligible for social insurance benefits, may find it forthcoming not only promptly but adequately.'[27] By early 1968, he had clarified the broad nature of what was required: 'reorganisation of the home assistance scheme with a view to its unification, rationalisation, and its extension to specific categories of the community who are now outside the social insurance and assistance schemes, e.g. deserted wives, persons obliged to attend to old and infirm relatives.'[28]

The Supplementary Welfare Allowance introduced in 1975 famously abolished the last vestiges of the 'odious, degrading and foreign' Poor Law system, conferred a legal right to a (means-tested) minimum payment, and continued the long drawn out process of centralisation of the social welfare system. One its most interesting features, however, is that it did not *actually* rationalise or unify the assistance system in any meaningful way. Thus, for example, it did not create a single common means tested benefit, as, for example, exists in the UK. Instead, it might be seen merely as one of a large number of categorical schemes introduced on an ad hoc basis over many decades. Over the course of the period under discussion, governments almost absentmindedly plugged each gap that appeared in the social insurance system with its own small scheme. Most – although not all – of these gaps concerned women, and thus reflects some of the problems with social insurance referred to above.

The first steps towards developing particularistic schemes for specific categories occurred in 1968, with the emergence of what would later be termed the Prescribed Relatives Allowance. This allowed for an increase in old age or widows' pensions to 'recipients who were incapacitated and were receiving full time care from a "prescribed" female relative' (Commission on Social Welfare, 1986: 41). In 1972, the definition of a 'prescribed' relative was expanded to cover male relatives also. In 1970, a similar scheme covered those whose means were too high to receive a social welfare pension, yet were in need of full-time care and attention. The Old Age (Care) Allowance made a payment to a prescribed female relative caring for an incapacitated person over 70. In the same year, a Deserted Wife's allowance was introduced, followed by a contributory Deserted Wife's Benefit and means tested Unmarried Mothers Allowance in 1973. It is worth noting too the Smallholders' Unemployment Assistance – Notional Assessment (1965) which adopted a more flexible method of assessing the means of smallholders, and which sprang from concerns about the problems of 'small western farms' in the period (Commission on Social Welfare, 1986: 39). Broadly it meant that farmers could increase their income without a decrease in assistance, and led to an increase in the numbers in receipt of the payment to over 30,000 by 1976 (Cousins, 1995: 22–3).

The proliferation of very small scale schemes targeted at very particular groups – occasionally with a matching contributory scheme – seems out of line with the general trend of developments in the period. Although as noted above the evidence for this period is scanty, it seems clear that the various schemes outlined here were intended to be an adjunct to a predominantly social insurance-based system. But retrospectively it can be seen that the categorical and highly particularistic approach taken in the assistance field in this period is emblematic of the contemporary Irish system, and a feature which has been said to distinguish it in particular from the otherwise closely related UK system (Daly and Yeates, 2003). Thus in this period we see the emergence of 'a complex system of categorical schemes directed towards very particular, and often very small, segments of the population' (p. 89).

Perhaps the paradigmatic example of this approach might be the Single Woman's Allowance introduced in 1974, and aimed at elderly single women between 58 and 68 years old. Some 2, 230 women qualified for this in the first six months.[29] The target was elderly women who qualified neither for social insurance (having remained at home, generally caring for ageing parents) nor for social assistance (being unavailable for work). It had broadly similar means test and benefit levels as unemployment assistance (Report of the Commission on Social Welfare, 1986). This particularistic approach is perfectly in tune with the broadly clientalistic nature of Irish political culture, as Daly and Yeates have noted (2003: 91). However, the *possibility* of taking this route was decided to a large extent by the decision in 1952 that social welfare would not be universal: that it would explicitly involve juggling assistance for some and insurance for others, and that even social insurance would distinguish, for varying reasons, between different groups of workers: urban or rural, public or private, highly paid or low paid. The heavily categorical nature of the 1952 Act meant that the general approach of 'tacking on' new schemes directed at particular categories was entirely in keeping with the structure of Irish social security.

The outcome is a complex social security system with approximately 30 different types of cash benefit (Daly and Yeates, 2003: 90) Hence, for example, the Department of Social and Family Affairs list the current social assistance schemes: Old Age Non Contributory Pension, Widow's/Widower's Non-Contributory Pension, Orphan's Non-Contributory Pension, Deserted Wife's Allowance, Prisoner's Wife's Allowance, Lone Parent's Allowance, Unemployment Assistance, Pre-Retirement Allowance, Supplementary Welfare Allowance, Family Income Supplement, Carer's Allowance and Rent Allowance. On the social insurance side, there are currently eleven rates of PRSI, with up to 37 subclasses, and particular provisions relating to special, voluntary and optional contributors (Department of Social and Family Affairs, 2005: 39). The general approach of identifying specific, small scale and restricted needs and applying one of a kind targeted solutions might also help explain what has been described as 'a very unusual aspect of the Irish system' (McCashin, 2004: 63). This is the use of non-cash benefits (free travel, fuel allowances, free television licences, etc.) to supplement cash payments, expenditure on which comprised €296 million in 2002 (Ibid).

Had the policy impetus of the 1970s been sustained, and had social insurance become the dominant plank of the income maintenance system, then these outcomes would be less visible and less important. But although subsequently there has been a very considerable extension of social insurance, economic and demographic shifts though the following decades meant that social assistance has remained fundamental to the Irish system. Discussing both services and cash transfers, NESC remarked that: 'By the 1990s 'the proportion of social spending . . . in Ireland that was means-tested was three times the average for the EU–15' (NESC, 2005: 151). Moreover, the abandonment of income related social insurance and the retention of a flat-rate of payment ensured that on the whole, poverty prevention rather than status maintenance characterises the transfer system. Thus, despite what appears to have been the aim of policy-makers in the first flush of internationalisation, the system would ultimately remain one which looks much more Beveridgean than Bismarckian. Tracing the full workings out of these outcomes through the ups and downs of subsequent years requires more detailed historical analysis both of this and of later periods, and perhaps a very different theoretical focus.

Conclusion

Considering the events described above in relation to those of the 1940s and 1950s points us to discontinuities in the policy context of social security which are so numerous that it is difficult to summarise them concisely. It is useful to divide them into policy aims and policy processes. In terms of aims, we might note that social security policy becomes visibly instrumental in this period. Policy-makers clearly recognised that the emerging economy would need to be underpinned by social policy initiatives. As McCashin (2004) has argued, 'there was a clear recognition that the introduction of certain social security reforms . . . would actively facilitate improved productivity and economic restructuring' (McCashin, 2004: 42). In this sense, distributional policies were clearly complementary to the wider developmental goals of the state (Ó Riain and O'Connell, 2000). Of course, social policy was instrumental in some important respects in the earlier period too, in so far as it was motivated by the electoral considerations of politicians, and tailored around social and economic conditions. But, although consideration was certainly given to the impact of expenditure on the balance of payments, or the costs to employers and producers, it was not designed to underpin macro-economic policy.

The shift towards the explicit use of social policy as a tool to facilitate broader economic goals is linked to shifts in the policy process too, in particular the development of an embryonic corporatism. Although full blown social partnership lay many years in the future, it is clear that social security policy-making would no longer be the exclusive domain of politicians and civil servants. The emergence and consolidation of the peak organisations of farmers, trade unions and business over the period from the mid-1950s on would profoundly change the policy process in the long term. Interests would access and influence the policy process very differently in the years ahead. To a large extent, it is this complex of shifts in aims and processes which underpin the state centred perspectives examined in Chapter 1, and these shifts are so fundamental that the insights of this book may seem irrelevant to later events. Thus, for example, while agrarianism might continue to exert an influence, it would clearly do so very differently, through more explicit modes of interest representation, and with an international rather than a national focus.

However, although there were sharp discontinuities in the move from agrarian protectionism to export-oriented industrialisation, there are surprising continuities too. In particular, we can see how the incremental nature of the policy process gives policy legacies enormous weight. This is extremely clear in the emergence of and subsequent development of the Irish pensions system. The current pension system ensures that 'retired middle-class employees, former public servants, and middle and high income self-employed enjoy considerably enhanced incomes compared to retirees from other social classes' (Ó Riain and O'Connell, 2000: 327). As described above, in some important respects these outcomes can be traced back to the decisions taken in 1960. However, they can also be traced even further back, to decisions in 1952.

The structure of the social insurance code laid down in 1952 meant that the OACP was intended for a very specific group: manual workers, and non-manual workers below a certain income limit. It was not intended to apply to the self-employed, public sector workers, or better-off white-collar workers. As Lemass himself remarked, it was explicitly aimed at those who did not have occupational or private pension coverage. The subsequent extension of social insurance does not seem, at that point, to have been envisioned, and the long-term distributional outcomes of the decisions in 1961 could not have been fully foreseen. When social insurance was gradually extended over the succeeding thirty years, the distributional decisions made in 1952, built on and extended in 1960, would merge with later decisions in taxation (and indeed, social assistance) to create the current pensions system. There is therefore no one point in time at which distributional outcomes were conclusively decided. However, it is very clear that decisions *prior to* the expansionary period, and shaped by a very different policy environment, continued to exert an influence. The nature of occupational and private pension development needs to be located in the context of the initial decision to have a non-universal, flat-rate and segmented social insurance system. Thus, no account of the welfare state which begins in the 1960s can provide a full explanation of its character, and the 1952 Act can be seen to have long lasting implications across many dimensions of the social security system. In that sense, the influences which shaped it are fundamental to understanding the contemporary welfare state, despite the enormity of the subsequent transformation.

There is a second sense, however, in which the arguments developed around the case-study of the 1952 Act continue to apply, even to the very different Ireland of post-1958. As I have just argued, outcomes in social security reflect decisions at multiple points in time in the context of inherited policy legacies, but what is striking is that the cumulative impact of these decisions seems to tend inexorably towards non-redistributive or minimally redistributive outcomes. Clearly, policy outcomes during the period of *both* agrarian protectionism and export oriented industrialisation share this feature, and thus the explanation must, to some extent, lie in the wider character of the political system which gave rise to both modes of production and governance.

From the 1960s onwards, social security policy occurred in the context of an active interventionist state, consciously located as part of the wider Europe, with an evolving style of corporatist decision making, and the role of the state in subsequently shaping distributional outcomes has been rightly highlighted. However, the political context which shaped the *emergence* of the activist state cannot be ignored. Thus, for example, Sinnott notes that the origins of the Irish party system around a centre–periphery cleavage gave them a 'pattern of programmatic flexibility' which means that 'they are not historically and institutionally committed to entrenched positions' on the standard Church–state, agrarian–industrial and left–right cleavages (1995: 285). Thus he notes that, for a long time, 'the interests of the agrarian economy were seen as the interests of the state' (p. 284). However, when economic circumstances required a shift to facilitate industrial development, this was done with remarkable ease. The non-programmatic character of Irish political parties, drawn attention to elsewhere in the book, is part of the explanation for the swift transformation of the state in this period, and might be said to partially explain the 'flexibility' of the developmental state (Ó Riain and O'Connell, 2000; NESC, 2005). It also, however, helps explain distinctive distributional outcomes. One important aspect of Irish party politics is that their origins do not commit them to particular distributive outcomes: they lack the social-democratic push to egalitarianism or, equally, the Christian-democratic push to status maintenance. As we've seen, this programmatic flexibility, in the context of particular patterns of party competition, allowed policy-makers to juggle insurance and assistance to assuage distributional conflicts in ways which were only nominally solidaristic. This adroitness did not end when, in the modern period, factory workers rather than farmers became a key target for social policy.

Conclusion

The Irish social security system reveals in microcosm some of the puzzling aspects of the Irish welfare state, both in its hybridity, and in respect of problems in the application of some standard theories of the welfare state. 'Ireland's current welfare state has disparate elements that resemble, respectively, the citizen-based Nordic welfare model, the social-insurance Continental European model and the residual Anglo-Saxon welfare model' (NESC, 2005: xvii). In the sphere of income maintenance, 1952 marks the point at which this hybridity solidified. Although the 1952 Social Welfare Act was clearly Beveridgean in its inception, and retained the stamp of this influence in several respects, nevertheless it differed considerably from the contemporaneous UK developments. At the same time, it clearly did not go down the paths taken in other countries. On one level, the explanation for this is relatively straightforward. In Ireland, the core processes of industrialisation, democratisation and state formation, so fundamental in shaping welfare state outcomes generally, were all shaped by the intersection between colonialism and indigenous features. This intersection, and its diffuse, complex and tangential outcomes, are crucial for understanding the atypical nature of social and economic development in Ireland and, consequently, for understanding atypical welfare outcomes. It explains, too, why many standard theoretical experiences struggle to explain Irish outcomes.

This insight is not new: it is in many respects that of Cousins, who suggested that dominant approaches to the welfare state 'are core-centric and adopt – either implicitly or explicitly – a modernization approach, thereby marginalizing the experiences of peripheral countries' (1997: 223). However, this large-scale, overarching insight becomes clearer when applied to a very specific policy area. Moreover, this micro-level study also clarifies that the Irish case can in fact be illuminated by comparative theory, once we switch our attention from pointing to what it does not explain, to considering instead what it can account for. The best illustration of the first of these points – the problems with the implicit assumptions of comparative theory – was revealed by considering the puzzle of why Catholicism, generally acknowledged as so influential in shaping welfare outcomes in Ireland and elsewhere, appears to have had a negligible impact on income-maintenance outcomes in the period.

It is not surprising that many have concluded that the Irish welfare state as a whole is a 'Catholic corporatist' welfare state, and that welfare outcomes generally have been shaped by the nature of Catholic social thought (McLaughlin, 1993, 2001; Adshead and Millar, 2004, *inter alia*). The apparent dominance of the Church in the period, its undeniable activism in health, and the growing consensus in the international literature that Catholicism and corporatism are interlinked phenomena, make it an intuitively satisfying conclusion. It does not however appear to be a sustainable conclusion. Catholic activism in Ireland has certainly not resulted in corporatist outcomes in social security, nor does the health system appear classically corporatist either. The link between Catholicism and corporatism is contingent on the wider processes involved in the transformation of European societies which started with the industrial revolution and the French revolution (Flora, 1986: XII) and the precise manner in which Catholicism 'makes a difference' can thus vary substantially across countries (Castles, 1994; Daly, 1999). Perhaps one of the central lessons to be drawn from this example is that it is possible to be blinded rather than illuminated by theoretical perspectives which have attempted to universalise the experiences of what in reality are a limited number of countries.

If the role of the Church has sometimes been either overestimated or misinterpreted, agrarian actors have been generally underestimated or ignored (Fahey, 2002). The dominance of theories stressing industrialisation, and political theories which focused on the industrial working class, has meant that industrial workers and their interests have been prioritised in the comparative literature. This is perhaps no less true for Irish scholars, fixated on the 'problem' of the weakness of the Irish left. However, this analysis, in tandem with that of Cousins (1997) and Fahey (1998a, 2002) has pointed to the importance of an agrarian paradigm which has fundamentally influenced distributive outcomes in Ireland. Once it is accepted that there may be variation in how fundamental transformations are experienced, it is also clear that the actors and interests shaping welfare outcomes can also vary. The Irish case directs our attention to a less acknowledged but increasingly visible body of work stressing agrarian influences in other countries, and thus points to unrecognised commonalities (Petersen, 1990; Esping-Andersen, 1990; Baldwin; 1990; Dutton; 2000; *inter alia*). Delineating the precise nature of agrarian influences across diverse countries seems likely to be a profitable area for future research.

The structure of the agrarian sector in Ireland reflects its particular history and, consequently, the precise outcomes described reflect both the specific Irish circumstances and the particular policy sector studied. Having said this, it is possible to identify potentially important features of agrarianism. Amongst other features, patterns of land ownership, the nature of employment relationships in agriculture, and the way in which agrarian interests are mediated politically and institutionally need to be encompassed in any account of how agrarianism might influence welfare states (Esping-Andersen, 1990). However, the need for attention to variation in the structure and organisation of social movements merely echoes what has long been taken for granted in relation to urban working-class movements (Carey, 2005).

Accounting for the mediation of diverse interests, agrarian and other, requires that attention be paid to the distinctive character of the Irish party system. Political theories of the welfare state have seemed problematic in Ireland, since the assumption in the comparative literature is that politics is expressed in very particular kinds of party systems. It is well known that the Irish party system is, if not *sui generis*, at least very different from other European party systems (Whyte, 1974; Mair, 1992). Thus one assumption has been that political parties have mattered little for the nature of Irish welfare state outcomes, and thus political theories of the welfare state are generally deemed inapplicable (Maguire, 1986; Curry, 1980; O'Connell and Rottman, 1992). On reflection, it is not at all surprising that if one attempts to assess the impact of Irish parties on welfare outcomes using measures designed around concepts such as 'social democracy' or 'Christian democracy', you find that the impact is not measurable. It is not measurable, because the tools have been designed to capture a very different kind of politics. A distinctive party political system however might translate into distinctive welfare state outcomes that standard accounts obscure rather than reveal.

The perception that political theories of the welfare state fare poorly in Ireland seems to imply that politics has mattered profoundly in shaping welfare states everywhere but Ireland. Unsurprisingly, a close examination of the policy process around social security revealed that politics was as fundamental in Ireland as elsewhere. The way in which interests are reflected in political parties, expressed through battles over partisan control of government, and appear in the actions of interest groups and other organizations has indeed structured distributional outcomes. The events examined here reveal that when we look beneath the macro-level concept of total public social expenditure, and examine the detail of who pays and who benefits at the micro-level of social security, it becomes clear that the Irish party system has shaped the nature of the Irish welfare state in several important respects. However, insights from the comparative political literature which increasingly focus on qualitative as well as quantitative differences in outcome seem applicable here (Esping-Andersen, 1990; Huber, Ragin and Stephens; 1993). If the cross-class nature of Christian democracy is now recognised as fundamental to the particular nature of certain welfare states, it seems unproblematic to assert that the particular cross-class nature of the Irish party system (conceptualized as a whole) likewise fosters very distinctive outcomes. Other authors have recognised the impact of Irish political life on the welfare state, but perhaps because the party system has seemed so adrift from the comparative literature, have suggested that political factors are best subsumed into statist accounts (O'Connell and Rottman, 1992). This implicitly downplays the impact of politics and risks missing valuable insights generated by political theories of the welfare state. Having said this, it is clear that explaining outcomes in the 1952 Social Welfare Act requires insights from different theoretical perspectives, and cannot be understood by focusing only on how politics has mattered.

Understanding how politics has mattered in Ireland directs our attention to the nature of the party system – itself an institutional structure influencing how individual political parties define their electoral interests. At many points, the analysis here has drawn on institutionalist themes to explain outcomes. The explanation for the lack of corporatism drew heavily on the legacies of distinctive patterns of state formation, the impact of particular modes of government and the continuing effect of past policy choices in shaping the administrative structure of social insurance. Indeed, the weight of policy legacies was described as fundamental not to just explaining outcomes in 1952, but to understanding how contemporary distributional outcomes can be traced back to the period before the expansionary phase of the welfare state. Thus, while stressing that political factors have often been underestimated, it is clear that the way in which interests are mediated in very specific institutional configurations is crucial.

The necessity for combining different kinds of explanations might seem to have its origins in the distinctiveness of Irish social and political history, but this is not the case. Increasingly, contemporary welfare theory has had to juggle convergence and divergence in a manner that has pointed to the value of combining explanations (Huber, Ragin and Stephens, 1993; Amenta, 1998; Huber and Stephens, 2001; Amenta et al., 2001; Myles and Quadagno, 2002). The enthusiasm with which the insights of institutionalists have been taken up reflects the fact that issues of difference have become central to contemporary theory. Regime theory, for example, has been struggling under the weight of competing claims that there are other worlds, unique cases, hybrid states, or neglected dimensions (Lewis, 1992; Castles and Mitchell, 1992; Ferrera, 1996; Esping-Andersen, 1997; Kasza 2002). These tensions apply, too, to what has been termed 'neo-convergence', where the retrenchment literature increasingly points to different responses to similar economic pressures (Pierson, 1994 and 2001). Institutionalist insights are central, but have not displaced explanations predicated on politics. Hence, Myles and Quadagno point to a multi-faceted explanation of the development of income-security schemes in affluent democracies: 'Crossnational differences in class-based organizations and parties as well as the electoral and administrative institutions that structure and mediate the democratic class struggle were especially crucial' (2002: 51). The shift in focus towards combining mid-range theories reflects struggles to defuse the tensions between convergence and divergence. The consequence is a declining enthusiasm for the claims of 'grand theory'; the most recent contender, globalisation, has been shown to promise rather more than it delivered in terms of generalisability. While much of this book has grappled with the problematic aspects of contemporary theory, it nevertheless suggests that 'additional one-of-a-kind interpretations' are not necessary (Amenta et al., 2001: 228). Instead, it argues that the Irish case points to the value of theoretical eclecticism, echoing wider concerns within contemporary welfare state theory. A central conclusion, then, is that while no *one* grand theory seems to easily fit the Irish case, this is a problem for welfare state theory in general, rather than reflecting unique aspects of Irish experiences.

This nature of this conclusion, stressing as it does the multi-dimensional and complex causes underpinning outcomes in social security, is reflective of the case-oriented methodology of this study. As Heclo, one of the earliest forerunners of this approach, pointed out: 'Understanding how, or whether, politics has affected the advent of modern social policy seems to depend less on statistically unearthing and more on inductively building up generalizations from detailed if somewhat less tidy accounts' (1974: 12). Untidy as this account may be, it points, I hope, to the value of giving detailed consideration to the dynamics within particular policy sectors (Green-Pedersen and Haverland, 2002; Kasza, 2002; O'Sullivan, 2004). The value of this approach is that it reveals that mono-causal explanations of the entire Irish welfare state cannot be unproblematically applied to very specific policy sectors. Its limitation is that, of course, this almost certainly applies in reverse also.

Notes

CHAPTER ONE

1 Overviews of social service provision generally can be found in Curry (2003) and Kiely et al. (eds) (1999). For studies of specific policy areas see Farley, 1964; Hensey, 1979; Baker and O'Brien, 1979; Coolahan, 1981; Barrington, 1987; Cousins, 2003; McCashin, 2004 *inter alia*. See Timonen (2003, 2005) for an overview of social expenditure in a comparative context, and NESC (2005) for a policy-oriented account of future prospects for the welfare state.

2 Esping-Anderson suggested a threefold regime typology: social democratic, conservative and liberal. Subsequently, the 'welfare modelling business' (Abrahamson, 1999) has generated a large literature, contesting either the basic concept that ideal-typical regime types exist, or positing additional or alternative worlds (For overviews see Abrahamson, 1999; Arts and Gelissen, 2002; Powell and Barrientos, 2002).

3 The logic of industrialism is thus often considered in tandem with other functionalist accounts; in particular neo- Marxist perspectives which might be said to argue that there is a 'logic of capitalism'. Neo-Marxists accounts have stressed that welfare states are both functional and dysfunctional for capitalism, but share with the logic of industrialism this perspective that outcomes result from broad and impersonal economic forces (Gough, 1979; Offe, 1984; O'Connor, 1973).

4 They point too to the assumption of the logic of industrialism that the role of the state is determined by socioeconomic forces, and I discuss this in more detail below.

5 It is important to note that they suggest that the 'level of spending on welfare state functions, conventionally measured, is underpredicted by level of development' (p. 207). However, the bulk of their account is concerned with the impact of this spending.

6 Industrialisation and modernisation have not always been treated as one process but since Flora and Heidenheimer (1981) the bulk of welfare state theory has not distinguished much between the two, probably because political accounts took precedence in the literature from this point on.

7 A key current question is whether political partisanship still matters (Allan and Scruggs, 2004; Starke, 2006).

8 Two recent accounts point to the role of Protestant denominations, and to distinctions between Lutheran and Reformed Protestantism, which may have been neglected in the literature (Manow, 2004; Kahl, 2005).

9   The argument that Irish politics are 'politics without social bases' was first made
    by Whyte (1974) and endorsed by Carty (1981). The topic has been the subject
    of much subsequent debate. (Laver, 1992; Mair, 1992; Adshead, 2004 *inter
    alia.*)

10 Initially, the NHIS was run by a provisional committee appointed by the
    Minister for Local Government and Public Health. This committee was
    composed of civil servants (Cousins, 2003).

11 Esping-Andersen argued that welfare state variation was 'not linearly
    distributed, but clustered by regime-type' (1990: 26). These regimes typified
    qualitatively different interactions between state, market and family, rather than
    variations around ideas of 'more' or 'less'. As Green-Pedersen (2004) notes, this
    insight was 'theory-internal' in so far as it implied that expenditure was not
    necessarily a useful measure from the perspective of the power resources theory.
    Hence expenditure may still be a useful measure, depending on the theoretical
    perspective or research question (Green-Pedersen, 2004: 5).

CHAPTER TWO

1   D/Taoiseach S13053A, Henderson, R., 'World Trends in Social Security', speech
    dated 8 December 1943, forwarded to Taoiseach 4 January 1944.

2   The Mother and Child Scheme is a shorthand term for a complex series of
    events centred on Church and medical resistance to proposed reforms of the
    health services. Briefly, a scheme to provide free health care to mothers and
    children emerged from the processes of administrative reform (discussed in more
    detail later in the chapter). The scheme, drafted as part of a proposed radical
    reform of the health services generally and in response to very high rates of
    infant mortality, envisioned a non-means-tested health service. The government
    of the day came under intense behind the scenes pressure to amend the scheme,
    putting further pressure on an uneasy coalition of five, diverse parties. The
    decision by the Minister for Health responsible for the scheme to release details
    of the correspondence with the hierarchy (having lost the support of his cabinet
    colleagues for its implementation) brought the affair into the public gaze and
    raised questions about the relationship between Church and state in Ireland
    which continue to be debated today.

3   In van Kersbergen's discussion of post-war Christian democracy in Europe, Fine
    Gael is included as Ireland's Christian democratic party. Van Kersbergen
    acknowledges Hanley's (1994) suggestion that Fianna Fáil may have as many
    Christian democratic features. However, the fact the Fine Gael sits in the
    Christian democratic group in the EU, and 'was most committed to Catholic
    social policy' is cited in defence of his attribution (1995: 50 fn).

4   I consider his reasons in more detail below.

5   His analysis here, however, may be flawed. While social insurance in southern
    Europe superficially resembles Continental schemes, there are also profound
    differences in outcome and, in particular, in the factors shaping administrative
    structures. Clientelist and patronage-oriented political systems, for example,
    seem likely to be a central part of the explanation for 'dualism and polarisation'
    in social insurance (Rhodes (ed.), 1997).

6 As Chapter 7 discusses, experimentation with pay-related benefits occurred from the 1970s, but was reversed in the 1990s. It should also be noted that there is some occupational differentiation *within* the administratively centralised Irish scheme. But, as I discuss below, the central focus from the perspective of Catholic social teaching in Ireland was on the administrative structure of social insurance, arguing for institutions which were not centralised under the control of government departments, rather than on issues relating to occupational differentiation. The existence of different categories within social insurance reflects factors other than Catholicism, and I return to these in more detail in later chapters.

7 The reliance on means-testing has been said to be a distinctive feature of the welfare state as a whole. Thus NESC (2005) suggest that 'Ireland is exceptional for the high proportion of its social protection expenditure which is means-tested'. In 2001, the degree of reliance on means-testing was more than nine times higher then Belgium, the country which least resorted to it (NESC, 2005: 98).

8 This analysis is based on the argument that a range of 'women's programmes' introduced by the state in the 1970s were a direct intervention in family life (1999: 117).

9 I return and consider these ideas in more detail in chapters 4 and 5, arguing that both the dependence on social assistance, and the willingness to introduce categorical or particularistic schemes reflect the way in which social class interests are embedded in the Irish party system.

10 DD, 18 February 1942, vol. 85, col. 1818.

11 DD, 18 February 1942, vol. 85, col. 1930.

12 DD, 18 February 1942, vol. 85, col. 1940.

13 DD, 16 June, Vol. 87, col. 1068

14 MacEntee collection P67/257 (2), *Observations on the Dignan Report.*

15 D/Taoiseach S13384A, dated 2 December 1943.

16 D/Taoiseach S13384A, dated May 1944.

17 DD, 16 June 1942 vol. 87, col. 1068.

18 DD, 3 June 1942 vol. 87, col. 898.

CHAPTER THREE

1 Appendix C, *Report of the Committee of Inquiry into Widows' and Orphans' Pensions.*

2 DD, 4 June 1935, vol. 56, col. 2277.

3 D/Taoiseach S11109A. 'Extract regarding objections to and defects in Dr Dignan's plan.'

4 The Plan was published as a Pamphlet in 1945. Dignan remarked that its publication was 'due to a general demand'. He commented that: 'A few changes are made in the original but they are so few and of such minor importance that it is not necessary to draw attention to them' (Dignan, 1945: Foreword).

5 There are interesting parallels here to two other responses from departments overseen by MacEntee to movements influenced by Catholic social thought, as O'Driscoll (2000) outlines. In 1936, MacEntee, unhappy at criticism directed

against his policies by an organisation known as the 'League Against Poverty' requested that the Department of Justice identify the group behind it. The special branch made enquiries, and reported with a full dossier on the group in 1936. The file remained open till 1938 (O'Driscoll, 2000: 135). In 1938, when he was Minister for Finance, the publication of the Third Minority Report of the Banking Commission, strongly influenced by Catholic social thinkers of the time, aroused the alarm of the department and 'some officials within the Department acted in a questionable manner when an unsuccessful attempt was made to gain an injunction against the printing company through the Chief Solicitor's Office' (ibid.: 138). The department, it seems, continued to develop an extended tabular comparison on the Third Minority Report and 'purported to show the similarity of the two reports to the Labour Party Programme and the proposals of the IRA' (ibid.: 139). MacEntee, however, was not the only minister to use state resources to investigate movements linked with Catholic social teaching. Delaney (2001) in his discussion of the *Maria Duce* movement notes that 'the state security apparatus had been instructed by the department of industry and commerce to inquire how Marie Duce was obtaining newsprint for its publication, *Fiat*, when it was rationed for specific purposes at the time.' (2001: 497) In the process, Special Branch made unsuccessful attempts to obtain a list of members of the organisation.

6   MacEntee collection, P67/257, letter dated 21 October 1944.
7   MacEntee collection, P67/257, letter dated 2 November, 1944, marked 'copy'. Henderson's account of events was disputed by MacEntee, and I return to this in more detail below.
8   MacEntee collection, P67/257 (3).
9   MacEntee collection, P67/257, letter dated 2 November, 1944, marked 'copy'.
10 MacEntee collection, P67/258 (1).
11 MacEntee collection, P67/258 (2), letter dated 25 October, 1944, marked 'copy'.
12 McQuaid papers, DDA AB/8/8/B/XV.
13 The extract below suggests that An Rioghacht had asked him to speak. This was a federation of study circles founded in 1926 by Father Edward Cahill, and was part of the grouping of Catholic social thinkers discussed by O'Driscoll (2000), above. As noted there, their thinking was not always endorsed by the hierarchy. Whyte points out that the Annual Conference of An Rioghacht had welcomed the Dignan plan (1980: 117).
14 McQuaid papers, DDA AB/8/8/B/XV: 'The Labour people are not to be trusted in their desire to hear a Bishop: Political opportunism is always to be suspected, in view of the divisions in their ranks. This judgement may seem severe, but the recent disputes and some utterances of the two Larkins indicate the attitude of some members. The vast bulk of labouring men in Dublin is genuinely Catholic: so, too, some of the most prominent leaders. To have explained sound social policy must always be a benefit to these decent people.'
15 Ibid.
16 Dignan papers, X111.K.17. The doctors informed Dignan that at one of their local meetings many of the dispensary doctors were prepared to work it, 'attracted undoubtedly by the large salaries promised'. But they were 'reliably' informed by one of the principal doctors present that the bishop had condemned it and consequently they voted for its rejection.

17 Unfortunately, much of this is illegible and, consequently, the suggestion that it is a draft letter is speculative. However, this interpretation is supported by a letter (dated 6 April 1951) in the Dignan papers from Bishop Staunton (secretary to the hierarchy) which remarks: 'I received your letter and read it very carefully both before the Standing Committee (twice) and before the General Meeting of the Bishops. I read also a letter from the Minister in which he announced a change which he proposed to make in the Mother and Child scheme, by which the choice of doctor would be in the hands of the mother . . . The reading of these letters did not move the Bishops to approve the scheme . . . '

18 Ibid.

19 Whyte does indicate this when he suggests this bureaucratic approach derived from 'the British-derived doctrine of ministerial responsibility', but he does not address this further.

20 MacEntee collection, P67/257 (3)/27: In January 1945, in reply to a Dáil question, MacEntee rejected the Dignan plan as impractical 'under almost every heading'. Dignan wrote to MacEntee: 'I worked hard for a long time on the "Outlines" and I can assure you I realised the "several very complex fundamental difficulties" involved and I did my best to take "due cognisance" of them.' He asks if MacEntee would be good enough to send him the reasons and the grounds for the department's verdict. 'I may have no right to them, but as Chairman of the Committee of Management I persuade myself I am entitled to have them. And the reason I wish to have them is to answer them – if I am able!'

21 D/Taoiseach S11109A, 'Extract regarding objections to and defects in Dr Dignan's Plan'.

22 D/Taoiseach S13384A 'Memorandum on Income Maintenance Services', dated 11 November, 1946.

23 D/Taoiseach S13384A. memo dated 10 June 1948

24 D/Taoiseach S13384A, undated memo, handwritten note giving date of 13 June 1948.

25 D/Taoiseach S13384A: A decision was forwarded to Social Welfare on 12 July, a revised decision on 13th July, and the following month Finance was asked to return 'as requested orally' the decision transmitted on 12 July. The 12 July decision records that 'it might be accepted' that at a later date, 'the government will agree' to the abolition of the NHIS. The second (13 July) decision records that the government 'approved in principle' of the abolition of the NHIS. This seems an example of McCullagh's (1998) elastic government within the inter-party government, but it is interesting that the second decision is much more clearly in Norton's favour.

26 *The Leader*, December 15 1945.

27 D/Taoiseach S13384C, letter dated 13 February 1950.

28 McQuaid papers, DDA AB8/B/XV111.

29 Whyte notes that this under-represents the involvement of the hierarchy since it includes only legislation, and also is probably incomplete. He includes on his list the 1953 Health Act outlined above, but not the 1952 Social Welfare Act.

30 MacEntee collection, P67/257 (3)/19, letter marked 'Draft'.

31 However, it should be noted that the Dignan papers suggest that Dignan's views represented a minority perspective within the hierarchy.

CHAPTER FOUR

1 D/Taoiseach S13884B, D/Agriculture memo on draft White Paper, 25 August 1949.
2 As Cousins notes, this motion was put down in October but adjourned twelve times in October, November, and December (2003: 138)
3 MacEntee collection, P67/261 (169), note dated 20 November 1944.
4 Key to Watson's argument is that outcomes reflected conflicts between parties and unions, and welfare policy was primarily aimed at weakening communist union power in favour of the socialist party. Thus her argument focuses on issues relating to class mobilisation and party organisation.
5 Watson's general argument examines how policy outcomes were designed by socialists as part of a struggle within the left to control groups (p. 27).
6 They argue that New Deal agricultural policy has been a key case for state-centred analyses.
7 His unpublished (1998b) paper deals more fully with these conflicts, and I refer to it below.
8 The functions of the Congested District Board were transferred to the reconstituted Land Commission in 1923 (Dooley, 2004b: 181).
9 The extent to which there is a uniformity of interest among 'urban' workers is discussed in Chapter 6. The bitterest dispute of the inter-party government after the Mother and Child Scheme was the question of higher-paid versus lower-paid workers.
10 Article 45.2.v.
11 Usually translated as children (or party) of the soil.
12 Feeney notes that MacEntee's attacks on all the opposition parties in the period led to worry amongst some Fianna Fáil politicians, prompting Lemass to write to him asking him to tone down his comments (Feeney, 2001: 65).
13 'Considerations attending the problems of extending Social Insurance in Ireland with special reference to the Rural Community', MacEntee collection, P67/261 (68)
14 Eleven members signed the majority report, two the first minority report, and one the second minority report.
15 DD, 4 June 1935, vol. 56, col. 2235.
16 MacEntee collection, P67/261 (68), 'Considerations attending the problems of extending Social Insurance in Ireland with special reference to the Rural Community'.
17 However, the dimensions of farm size, type of farming and regional location continued to be a source of diversity at the end of the twentieth century (Hannan and Breen, 1987).

CHAPTER FIVE

1 DD, 12 September 1922, vol. 1, col. 136. Cited in Bradley, 1988: 17–18.
2 MacEntee collection, P67 261 (68), 'Considerations attending the problem of extending Social Insurance in Ireland with special reference to the Rural Community', (Appendix 111), undated.

3 MacEntee collection P67/261 (170), memo dated 20 Jan. 1945. Dr James Deeny was chief medical officer of the Department of Local Government and Public Health from 1944–46, and was influential in shaping health policy in the period (Barrington, 1987).

4 MacEntee collection P67/261, undated.

5 Census of Population, 1946, vol. 11.

6 DD, 28 February, 1950, vol. 119, col.851.

7 The explanatory notes to vol. 11 of the 1946 Census (p. vi) draws attention to the problem of defining agricultural occupations. Noting that only the principal occupation was recorded, it points out that the numbers of farmers returned was smaller than the actual numbers of persons owning land. 'Large numbers of persons holding small farms work, for instance as labourers on larger farms or for local authorities, etc. In describing themselves on the Census schedule such persons would properly return their occupation as 'agricultural labourer' in the first place and as "local authority labourer" in the second if such was their principal occupation.'

8 DD 8 November 1950, vol. 123, col. 490.

9 Cousins attributes authorship to P.J.Keady, who had been a member of the provisional committee of management of the NHIS, and subsequently chair. He had chaired the Committee of Inquiry into Widows' and Orphans' Pensions in the 1930s, and had served on variety of social security related committees. He was to become Secretary of the Department in 1954 (Cousins, 2003: 149–150).

10 DD, 2 March 1951, vol. 124, col. 1075.

11 Hogan was Minister for Agriculture from 1922 to 1932. He took the view that 'national development in Ireland, for our generation at least, is synonymous with agricultural development' (quoted in Daly, 2002: 124). Lee comments that Hogan equated the welfare of the agricultural community with the welfare of the farmer and, moreover, with that of large farmers (1989: 112–08). Daly (2002) broadly concurs with this assessment.

12 *Report of the Administrative Council of the Labour Party* 1943. The members of the sub-committee were L. Bennett, E. O'Brien, S. Kyle, F. Foley, Arnold Marsh, Mark Daly, George Pollock, A. Heron, and R.J. Connolly.

13 *Report of the Administrative Council of the Labour Party* 1943

14 'Imterim Report of the Sub-Committee on Social Services' Appendix 111, *Report of the Administrative Council of the Labour Party*, 1944.

15 NAI: TU/ICTU/2/247

16 NAI: TU/ICTU/2/247, letter from L.J.Duffy, dated 7 March, 1947.

17 Report of the Adminstartive Council of the Labour Party, 1946–47

18 'Interim Report of the Sub-Committee on Social Services' Appendix 111, *Report of the Administrative Council of the Labour Party* 1944.

19 Ibid, p. 32.

20 NAI: TU/ICTU/2/247: 'The Financing of Health and Social Security Services'.

21 *Report of the Administrative Council of the Labour Party 1946–47.*

22 Norton Papers, Box 7: 106, dated 15 August, 1947.

23 Thus it remarked that it differed on this from the Beveridge Plan which 'was based on the assumption that unemployment in Great Britain would be static at $8^1/_2$ per cent. A preposterous figure evidently emanating from a Tory Chancellor and completely abandoned by Beveridge himself three years later.'

24 *Report of the Administrative Council* 1947–8, p.40
25 Memo signed W.A.H. (Honohan), dated 12 June 1948, Norton papers, box 7:108.
26 An early draft of the White Paper in the Norton Papers indicates an intention to bring them in time, an aspiration which had vanished from the final draft. Box: 120, undated.
27 While the Dáil debate focused on broad-brush conflicts between 'privileged trade unionists' and impoverished small farmers, the internal debate within the inter-party government focused equally as much on the issue of privilege within the employed class. Chapter 6 explores this in more detail.
28 D/Taoiseach S13384B, D/Agriculture memo dated 29 June 1949.
29 Dillon's commitment to the land rehabilitation project is clear. He appears to have fought a minor turf war to ensure that it would be run by the Department of Agriculture rather than a proposed land-development authority. He launched the scheme in the same hotel used to launch the Land League in 1879, and unveiled a commemorative plaque linking the two events. By 1969, 1.75 million acres had been reclaimed at a cost of £30 million. Dillon had estimated in 1949 that 4 million acres could be reclaimed in ten–twelve years (Daly, 2002: 282–86).
30 D/Taoiseach S13384B, D/Agriculture memo dated 25 August 1949.
31 D/Taoiseach S13384B, D/Finance memo dated 7 June 1949.
32 D/Taoiseach S13384B D/Social Welfare memo dated 10 June 1949
33 D/Taoiseach S13384B, D/Social Welfare memo 25 June 1949.
34 D/Taoiseach S13384D, Cabinet Minute dated 1 December 1950.
35 *Irish Times*, 11 December 1950.
36 Norton papers, box 7: 114, letter dated 18 March 1950.
37 Norton papers, box 7: 114.
38 DD, 2 March 1951, vol. 124, col. 1131.
39 DD, 4 April 1951, vol. 125, col. 83.
40 DD, 2 March 1951, vol. 124, col. 1080.
41 *Irish Independent*, 5 February 1951.
42 DD, 4 April 1951, vol. 125, col. 61.
43 DD, 4 April 1951, vol. 125, col. 61–2.
44 DD, 4 April 1951, vol. 125, col. 77.
45 *Irish Times*, 7 October 1950.
46 He was simultaneously Minister for Health, between 22 January and 18 February 1947.
47 DD, 2 March1951, vol. 124, col. 1099.
48 Ibid.
49 DD, 2 March 1951, vol. 124, col. 1100.
50 DD, 2 March 1951, vol. 124, col. 1107.
51 D/Taoiseach S13616B, memo dated 28 December 1951.
52 D/Social Welfare 1A 170/53, note dated 10 July 1951.
53 D/Taoiseach S13384F, D/Finance memo dated 5 January 1952.
54 D/Taoiseach S13384F, dated 10 January 1952.
55 Ibid
56 D/Taoiseach S13384F, D/Finance memo dated 5 January 1952.
57 D/Taoiseach S13384F, dated 17 January 1952. Ryan now said that he was prepared to exclude private domestic servants from unemployment benefit, keep

the contributory widows' and orphans' pension, and postpone the pension at 65 for women. He suggested that he would retain a free of means test pension for insured workers: this was dropped at some point though I have found no record of when this decision was made.

58 DD, 27 March 1952, vol. 130, col. 632.

59 DD, 27 March 1952, vol. 130, col. 636: Ryan's second stage speech on the 1952 Act.

60 The provision for farmers to insure themselves through co-operatives vanished from the Ryan proposals, but this does not seem to appear in the departmental debate. The reason for its omission is perhaps is that initially this would have been unnecessary given Ryan's first proposals, and subsequently, the narrower basis of the 1952 Act and the more favourable treatment of agriculture generally made it less of an issue.

CHAPTER SIX

1 D/Taoiseach S13384F, D/Social Welfare memo dated 27 June, 1950, Appendix. This is discussed in more detail below.

2 DD, 27 March 1952, vol. 130, col. 633, Minister for Social Welfare, Jim Ryan, on the 1952 Social Welfare Act.

3 A memo from Finance on the Draft Heads of a Bill based on the White Paper begins: 'Accepting that a Social Security Scheme is to be introduced', D/Taoiseach S13384D, dated 29 June 1950.

4 D/Social Welfare 1A 170/53, dated 20 June 1949.

5 D/Taoiseach S13384B.

6 For example: 'It is observed that the proposed scheme makes no distinction between single men and single women, on the grounds that both have to provide for similar needs. An official pronouncement to that effect might be taken as a pronouncement on the controversial issue of equal pay for equal work and should, therefore, be avoided.' D/Taoiseach S13384B, D/Finance memo dated 7 June 1949.

7 D/Taoiseach S13384B, D/Social Welfare dated 10 June 1949.

8 D/Social Welfare 1A 132/53. CIE was the state transport body.

9 D/Social Welfare 1A 132/53.

10 William Norton papers, box 8:116.

11 William Norton papers, box 8:116.

12 D/Taoiseach S13384B, dated 25 June 1949.

13 D/Social Welfare 1A 137/53, dated 7 October 1949.

14 D/Social Welfare 1A 132/53, dated 19 November 1949.

15 Ibid.

16 D/Taoiseach S13384D: dated 27 June 1950, with Appendix containing extract from minute of 12 May accompanying Draft Heads of Bill.

17 Ibid.

18 Ibid.

19 D/Taoiseach S13384D, D/Finance memo 29 June 1950. The memo noted that 'It is understood that the Department of Defence are putting forward the views

of their Minister [on exemptions of members of the Defence Forces].' McCullagh notes that it appears that party colleagues had discussed their response in advance (1998: 192).

20 D/Taoiseach S13384D, D/Defence memo 29/6/50.
21 Ibid.
22 D/Taoiseach S13384D, D/Finance memo 29 June 1950.
23 D/Taoiseach S13384D.
24 D/Taoiseach S13384D, D/Finance memo dated 24 November 1950.
25 D/Taoiseach S13384D, letter dated 26 September, 1950.
26 D/Taoiseach S13384D letters dated 4 October and 20 November 1950.
27 D/Taoiseach S13384D letter dated 9 November 1950.
28 *Civil Service Review*, October 1950.
29 D/Social Welfare 1A 137/53, letter dated 22 June 1950.
30 *Irish Times*, 7 October 1950.
31 D/Social Welfare 1A 137/53, note dated 1 July 1950.
32 *Irish Independent*, 15 November 1950.
33 Costello told civil servants that he had approved the arrangements informally (McCullagh, 1998: 193).
34 McCullagh points out that with four Fine Gael members, plus Dillon, the composition was heavily weighted against Norton (McCullagh, 1998: 301, note 80).
35 D/Taoiseach S13384D, cabinet minute dated 1 December 1950.
36 As noted in Chapter 5, additional amendments concerned farmers.
37 DD, 4 April 1951, vol. 125, col. 90.
38 D/Social Welfare 1A 170/53, dated 10 July 1951.
39 *Irish Times*, 7 October 1950.
40 D/Taoiseach S13384F, memo dated 28 December 1951.
41 D/Social Welfare 1A 170/53, 10 July 1951.
42 D/Taoiseach S13384G, memo dated 3 May 1952
43 DD, vol. 124, 2 Mar. 1961, col. 1123.
44 DD 27 March 1952 vol. 130, col. 638
45 D/Taoiseach S13384F, D/Finance, dated 10 March 1952.
46 D/Social Welfare 1A 123/53, note dated 15 October 1947.

EPILOGUE

1 Kennedy points out that economic activity in the period was very depressed.
2 D/Social Welfare, 1A 52/59A, letter dated 29 June 1959. The extract from the speech, marked 'copy' has been annotated by hand, apparently to indicate the text of the speech as actually made. The speech was not given till September: *Irish Press*, 6 September 1959.
3 D/Social Welfare 1A 52/59. In May of 1959, a Social Welfare Bill was introduced in the Dáil which provided for an increase in social assistance payments. MacEntee was worried that these increases would erode the differential between contributory and non-contributory benefits, and suggested that contributory benefits should be increased to maintain these differentials. This was problematic, since the increases did not map neatly onto contributory benefits. During

the consideration of the issue, MacEntee expressed his desire to continue widows and disability pensions after 70.

4 D/Social Welfare 1A 52/59. Memo entitled 'Increases in Social Insurance Benefits.' Undated, but handwritten note that revised memorandum was submitted on 23 June 1959.

5 D/Social Welfare 1A 52/59A, memo of discussion dated 28 May 1959. As the previous chapter discussed, Keady was active throughout the period under discussion. His suggestion here was to raise the level of the old age pension to that of other (insurance) benefits 'if the country could afford it.'

6 D/Social Welfare, 1A 52/59A. Lemass' letter to MacEntee begins: 'As you know, I am interested in getting started . . . [on examining the OACP].'

7 DSW 1A 52/59. Note dated 30 June 1959. 'Extreme' is a handwritten insert.

8 Ibid.

9 D/Social Welfare 1A 52/59A, note from MacEntee dated 8 February, 1960.

10 DSW 1A 52/59 Letters 16 December and 21 December, memo to all Departments 29 December. The term 'extreme urgency' is also used by MacEntee at a number of points in the drafting process.

11 D/Social Welfare 1A 52/59, letter dated 20 December.

12 ICTU, *Report of the Executive Council for 1959–60.*

13 D/Social Welfare 1A/ 52/59A, memorandum of discussion held on 1 July 1959.

14 D/Taoiseach S13616B, letter dated 3 July 1959. In addition, a memo from the Parliamentary Secretary, dated 2 July 1959 remarks: 'I am aware that during your predecessors term in Office, that consultations were held with the Irish Transport and General Workers' Union in relation to the whole question.' He remarks that due to very fundamental disagreements no conclusions were reached, and the proposal appears not to have been proceeded with.

15 *Irish Press,* 6 September 1959.

16 DD, 14 June 1960, vol. 182, col.1192.

17 D/Taoiseach S17474F. An Interdepartmental Group which had been set up to examine the question of financing Social Welfare, Health and Education on the tripartite insurance principle reported in February 1967. The group suggested a social development tax instead of an insurance basis for financing future developments. The Report seems to have been largely ignored until a year later, when it was submitted to government by the Minister for Finance (Cabinet minute 18 April 1968). At the same time, the Minister for Finance received permission to have an insurance scheme prepared which would cover middle-income groups in respect of health services. This seems to be the genesis of the 1971 Health Contributions Act which imposed flat-rate contributions on people with limited eligibility. However, the question of developments in health lies outside the scope of this work.

18 DD, 23 November 1965, vol. 219, col.115–116.

19 D/Taoiseach S17474F, 29 September 1967 and 29 February 1968.

20 D/Taoiseach S17474F, 27 March 1968.

21 D/Taoiseach S17474F, 'Draft Policy Statement on Social Welfare', forwarded to Taoiseach on 29 February 1967.

22 D/Taoiseach S17474F, letter dated 29 September 1967.

23 Ibid. The letter suggests that Brennan's predecessor in office may have made an earlier suggestion, but gaps in the social welfare files make this impossible to corroborate at present.

24 D/Taoiseach S17474F, letter dated December 1967.

25 DD, 7 November 1978, vol. 309, col. 277–8.

26 DD, 7 November 1978, vol. 309, col. 278.

27 Letter dated 29 September, 1967.

28 D/Taoiseach S17474F, 'Draft Policy Statement on Social Welfare', forwarded to Taoiseach on 29 February 1967.

29 DD, 24 October 1974, vol. 275, col. 286. I am indebted to Tony McCashin for drawing my attention to this scheme.

Income maintenance schemes before 1952

The 1838 Poor Relief (Ireland) Act is generally taken to be the first national statutory system of welfare in Ireland (Burke, 1987). This established a network of workhouses throughout the country, run by Boards of Guardians and financed by a Poor Law rate levied on property owners. Initially relief was only granted inside the workhouse, but under the impetus of the Famine the 1847 Poor Relief (Ireland) Act allowed for outdoor relief, generally deemed to be the first state income maintenance payment. What cash payments were made under the scheme of outdoor relief, however, were locally based, discretionary and stigmatised (McCashin, 2004). The system of outdoor relief was renamed Home Assistance after independence, but it effectively continued as a localised and discretionary payment until replaced by the Supplementary Welfare Allowance introduced in 1975. The nineteenth century also saw the introduction in 1897 of the Workmen's Compensation Act, which required employers to pay compensation to employees injured in the course of their work. This applied only to workplaces deemed to be especially hazardous. The scheme was gradually broadened to include other workers, and a 1906 Act extended its application to almost all employees engaged in manual labour, and non-manual employees whose remuneration did not exceed £250 (Commission on Social Welfare, 1986: 28).

There were two key developments in the years just before independence, the 1908 Old Age Pension Act and the 1911 National Insurance Act. The 1908 Act introduced a means-tested pension at age 70, financed by general taxation, which came into effect in 1909. Perhaps its most important feature was that 'it established the principle of a right to support from the State, where the qualifying conditions were met' (Commission on Social Welfare, 1986: 29). In addition to the means test, the qualifying conditions included some deterrent clauses, such as non receipt of poor relief for a specified period, and some generalised character clause (McCashin, 2004). The

Act was particularly important in Ireland because, being set at income levels current in Britain, it had a high replacement value in Ireland (McCashin, 2004). In 1920, a Blind Person's Pension for those between 50 and 70 was introduced, with eligibility criteria linked to those of the 1908 Act and subsequent amending legislation.

The 1911 National Insurance Act was the first compulsory social insurance scheme in both Britain and Ireland. It was financed by employer and employee contributions, plus a state contribution. Contributions were flat-rate, as were the benefits paid under the scheme. The scheme was supervised by the Irish Insurance Commissioners, who oversaw the operation of the scheme by 'approved societies' most of whom were pre-existing trade unions and friendly societies (Farley, 1964). For those who were not members of such societies, a system whereby contributions could be paid through the Post Office was put in place. The Act provided for unemployment benefit and sickness benefit for insured workers. Health insurance, covered by Part 1 of the Act, insured most manual workers over the age of 16, and non-manual workers below a certain income limit. It provided cash payments for short-term and long-term illness, as well as maternity and sanatorium benefit. In Britain the Act also provided for medical benefit, that is, treatment by a doctor and the cost of prescriptions. However, medical benefit was omitted from the Irish scheme following opposition from the Catholic hierarchy, the medical profession and the Irish parliamentary party. Its omission reflected the existence of a free dispensary system for the poor which operated under the aegis of the Poor Law (Barrington, 1987. See also Chapter 3).

Unemployment insurance, covered by Part 11 of the Act, had a more limited scope initially, and applied only to trades 'known to have severe periodic fluctuation of employment' (Department of Social Welfare, 1949: 5). However, it was extended in 1920 to cover all manual workers, and non-manual workers below a certain income limit, with the exception of workers in agriculture or private domestic service. Contribution and benefit rates differentiated between men and women, and girls and boys. Contribution and benefit rates were raised over time, and the conditions for benefit adjusted. Dependency allowances were introduced in 1921. The approved societies which operated the scheme were amalgamated into one national society, the National Health Insurance Society (NHIS) in 1933.

Post-independence developments largely built on the pre-existing inherited schemes. Thus for example the widows' and orphans' pension introduced in 1935 covered all those insured under the National Health Insurance Acts, and also certain employees of the state and local authorities who had not previously had provision for this risk. The pension converted into an old age pension at age 70 without a means, nationality or residence test. The scheme contained provision for a dependent child's allowance up to age 14, or 16 if still in school or ill. At the same time, provision was made for a non-contributory widows' and orphans' pension. There were some initiatives which reflected gaps in provisions, in particular the inauguration of an unemployment assistance scheme in 1933, reflecting unemployment problems in the 1930s. The Act was intended to apply to those who were either not covered by unemployment insurance, or who had exhausted their right to benefit. It was a means-tested benefit, with payment rates which varied by area of residence, family circumstances and means. Although agricultural workers and smallholders were included, the Act allowed for their exclusion during periods when it was thought that employment would be plentiful. Finally, a Children's Allowance was introduced in 1944.

(Further information can be found in Farley, 1964; Burke, 1987; Commission on Social Welfare, 1986; Cousins, 1995 and 2003; McCashin, 2004.)

The 1952 Social Welfare Act

The 1952 Social Welfare Act came into effect on 5 January 1953. The Act replaced the separate schemes for unemployment, national health and widows' and orphans' pensions with a single coordinated social insurance scheme, and all those between the ages of 16 and 70 employed under a contract of service were insured. Male employees in agriculture and private domestic service were insured against unemployment for the first time, but female employees were not (though they were insured for other benefits). Power was given to modify the scheme in the case of civil servants, members of the defence forces, employees of local or public authorities, teachers in National or secondary school, seamen or airmen, and persons employed in statutory transport undertakings. This modification, once made, insured the bulk of these groups for limited coverage for widows' or orphans' pensions at a reduced contribution rate. An income limit of £600 initially applied to all employees, but this was quickly amended by regulation to apply only to non-manual employees. Provision was also made for those who, having been previously insured, subsequently went outside the scope of insurable employment to become voluntary contributors for the purposes of widows' and orphans' pensions only if they had a requisite number of contributions.

Flat-rate contributions were payable by employers and employees. However, there were both ordinary and special rates of contributions, as well as rates for voluntary contributors. Special reduced rates applied to contributions from both the employer and the employee where the man was employed in agriculture, or a woman in agriculture or domestic service, but the latter did not cover for unemployment benefit.

The same rate of benefit was now to be paid for sickness, unemployment, maternity and widowhood. Both disability and unemployment benefit qualified for adult and child dependency rates, and a child dependency allowance was payable for the widows' pension. Single men and women received the same rate of benefit, but different arrangements applied to married women. Married women ceased to be entitled to benefit after marriage unless they continued in employment and made at least twenty-six contributions subsequently. The rates payable to married women who remained in employment were, depending on circumstances, lower than those payable to single women. However, on marriage insured women could qualify for marriage benefit, a lump sum payable in compensation for the termination of their insurance rights, and could continue as voluntary contributors if they met the requirements for this scheme.

Table 1: Differences between the Social Welfare (Insurance)
(no. 2) Bill and the 1952 Social Welfare Act

Social Welfare (Insurance) (no. 2) Bill	*1952 Social Welfare Act*
No salary limit.	£600 limit.
All employees in agriculture/domestic service insured for unemployment benefit for first time.	Only male employees so insured.
Power to modify in respect of civil servants, local-authority employees and miscellaneous other groups.	Power to modify in respect of civil servants, local-authority employees and miscellaneous other groups.
Provision for farmer members of co-operatives to insure.	No provision for farmer members of co-operatives.
Low-waged group (£3.10.0s) with lower contributions and benefits.	Agricultural workers only, lower contribution from employees and employers. No reduction in benefits.
Old-age pension at 65 for men and 60 for women.	No pension. Over 65/60 can draw unemployment benefit without limit.
Death grant.	No death grant.
In general, contributions and benefits higher.	Lower contributions and benefits.

(Adapted from Cousins, 2003: 174–5, and D/Taoiseach, S13384D, note dated 10th April 1952)

Bibliography

PRIMARY SOURCES

Archival sources

National Archives of Ireland: Department of Taoiseach files; Department of Social Welfare files; ICTU records.
University College Dublin Archives: MacEntee Papers.
Irish Labour History Museum and Archives: Norton Papers.
Archive of the Diocese of Clonfert: Dignan Papers.
Dublin Diocesan Archives: McQuaid Papers.

Newspapers and periodicals

Irish Times
Irish Independent
Irish Press

Other unpublished sources

Dáil Éireann: Public Debates.

SECONDARY SOURCES

Abrahamson, P. (1999), 'The Welfare Modelling Business', *Social Policy and Administration*, 33, 4, pp. 394–415.
Adshead, M. (2004), 'Still the counter-factual? Lipset and Rokkan cleavages in Ireland', paper presented to the 54th Political Studies Association Annual Conference, University of Lincoln, 6–8 April.
Adshead, M. and Millar, M. (2004), 'Health care in Ireland: applying Esping-Andersen's typology of welfare to the Irish case', paper presented to the 54th Political Studies Association Annual Conference, University of Lincoln, 6–8 April.
Allan, J.P. and Scruggs, L. (2004), 'Political Partisanship and Welfare State Reform in Advanced Industrial Societies', *American Journal of Political Science*, 48, 3, July, pp. 496–512.

Allen, K. (1997), *Fianna Fáil and Irish Labour: 1926 to the Present*, London: Pluto Press.

Alston, L.J. and Ferrie, J.P. (1985), 'Labor Costs, Paternalism and Loyalty in Southern Agriculture: A Constraint on the Growth of the Welfare State', *Journal of Economic History*, xlv, 1, March, pp. 95–117.

Amenta, E. and Skocpol, T. (1986), 'States and Social Policies', *Annual Review of Sociology*, 12, pp. 131–57

Amenta, E. (1993), 'The State of the Art in Welfare State Research on Social Spending Efforts in Capitalist Democracies since 1960', *American Journal of Sociology*, 99, 3, pp. 750–63.

Amenta, E. (1998), *Bold Relief: Institutional Politics and the Origins of Modern American Social Policy*, Princeton, NJ: Princeton University Press.

Amenta, E., Bonastia, C. and Caren, N. (2001), 'U.S. Social Policy in Comparative and Historical Perspective: Concepts, Images, Arguments and Research Strategies', *Annual Review of Sociology*, 27, pp. 213–14.

Arts, W., and Gelissen, J. (2002), 'Three Worlds of Welfare Capitalism or More? A State-of-the-art Report', *Journal of European Social Policy*, 12, 2, pp. 137–58.

Baker, T.J. and O'Brien, L.M. (1979), *The Irish Housing System: A Critical Overview*, Dublin: Economic and Social Research Institute.

Baldwin, P. (1990), *The Politics of Social Solidarity*, Cambridge: Cambridge University Press.

Baldwin P. (1994), 'Beveridge in the *Longue Durée*', in Hills, J., Ditch, J. and Glennerster, H. (eds), *Beveridge and Social Security: An International Retrospective*, Oxford: Clarendon Press, pp. 37–55.

Bambra, C. (2004), 'The Worlds of Welfare: Illusory and Gender Blind?', *Social Policy and Society*, 3, 3, pp. 201–11.

Barrington, R. (1987), *Health, Medicine, and Politics in Ireland 1900–1970*, Dublin: Institute of Public Administration.

Barrington, R. (2003), 'Catholic Influences on the Health Services 1830–2000', in Mackay, J. and McDonogh, E. (eds), *Religion and Politics in Ireland at the turn of the millennium*, Dublin, Columba Press, pp. 152–65.

Bartlett, T. (2002), 'Church and State in Modern Ireland: An Appraisal Reappraised', in Bradshaw, B. and Keogh, D. (eds), *Christianity in Ireland: Revisiting the Story*, Dublin: Columba Press, pp. 248–58.

Béland, D. and Hacker, J.S. (2004), 'Ideas, Private Institutions and American Welfare State "Exceptionalism": The Case of Health and Old-age Insurance, 1915–1965', *International Journal of Social Welfare*, 13, 1, pp. 42–54.

Beveridge, W. (1942), *Social Insurance and Allied Services*, London: HMSO.

Bew, P. and Patterson, H. (1982), *Sean Lemass and the Making of Modern Ireland*, Dublin: Gill and Macmillan.

Bolderson, H. and Mabbett, D. (1995), 'Mongrels or Thoroughbreds: A Cross-national Look at Social Security Systems', *European Journal of Political Research*, 28, pp. 119–39.

Bradley, D. (1988), *Farm Labourers: Irish Struggle 1900–1976*, Belfast: Athol Books.

Breen, R. (1983), 'Farm Servanthood in Ireland, 1900–1940', *Economic History Review*, 36, 1, pp. 87–102.

Breen, R., Hannan, D., Rottman, D.B. and Whelan, C.T. (1990), *Understanding Contemporary Ireland: State, Class and Development in the Republic of Ireland*, London: Macmillan.

Browne, N. (1986), *Against the Tide*, Dublin: Gill and Macmillan.

Bull, P. (1996), *Land, Politics and Nationalism: A Study of the Irish Land Question*, Dublin: Gill and Macmillan.

Burke, H. (1987), *The People and the Poor Law in 19th Century Ireland*, Littlehampton: Womens' Educational Bureau.

Cameron, D.R. (1978), 'The Expansion of the Public Economy: A Comparative Analysis', *American Political Science Review*, 72, 4, Dec., pp. 1243–61.

Carey, S., (2005), 'Land, Labour and Politics: Social Insurance in Post-War Ireland', *Social Policy and Society*, 4, 3, pp. 303–11.

Carty, R.K. (1981), *Party and Parish Pump: Electoral Politics in Ireland*, Waterloo (Ontario): Wilfrid Laurier University Press.

Castles, F.G. (1978), *The Social Democratic Image of Society*, London: Routledge and Kegan Paul.

Castles, F.G. (1982), 'The Impact of Parties on Public Expenditure', in Castles, F.G. (ed.), *The Impact of Parties: Politics and Policies in Democratic Capitalist States*, London: Sage Publications , pp. 21–96.

Castles, F.G. and Mitchell, D. (1993), 'Worlds of Welfare and Families of Nations', in Castles, F.G. (ed.), *Families of Nations: Patterns of Public Policy in Western Democracies*, Aldershot: Dartmouth Publishing Company, pp. 93–118.

Castles, F.G (ed.), (1993), *Families of Nations: Patterns of Public Policy in Western Democracies*, Aldershot: Dartmouth Publishing Company.

Castles, F.G. (1994), 'On Religion and Public Policy: Does Catholicism Make a Difference?', *European Journal of Political Research*, 25, pp. 19–40.

Central Statistics Office (1960), *Agricultural Statistics 1934–1956*, Dublin: Government Stationery Office.

Chubb, B. (1992), *The Government and Politics of Ireland* (3rd edn), London: Longman.

Clasen, J. (1994), 'Beveridge or Bismarck for the Unemployed?', in Morgan, W.J. (ed.), *The Beveridge Plan 1942–1992: Fifty Years On*, Nottingham: Centre for Research into the Education of Adults, University of Nottingham, pp. 63–81.

Clasen, J. (2002), 'Changing Principles in European Social Security', *European Journal of Social Security*, 4, 2, pp. 89–115.

Cleary, J. (2003), 'Misplaced Ideas? Colonialism, Location and Dislocation in Irish Studies', in Connolly, C. (ed.), *Theorising Ireland (Readers in Cultural Criticism)*, London: Palgrave Macmillan.

Coakley, J. (1990), 'Minor Parties in Irish Political Life, 1922–1989', *Economic and Social Review*, 21, 3, April, pp. 269–97.

Coakley, J. (1999), 'The Foundations of Statehood' in Coakley, J. and Gallagher, M., *Politics in the Republic of Ireland*, London: Routledge, pp. 1–32.

Commission on Social Welfare (1986), *Report*, Dublin: Stationery Office.

Committee on Widows' and Orphans' Pensions (1933), *Report*, Dublin: Stationery Office.

Connolly, E. and O'Halpin, E. (1999), 'The Government and the Governmental System', in Coakley, J. and Gallagher, M. (eds), *Politics in the Republic of Ireland*, London: Routledge, pp. 249–70.

Cook, G. (1982–83), 'The Irish Social Security System in Perspective: The Growth and Development of the Social Security System in the Republic of Ireland', *Social Studies*, 7, pp. 127–42.

Cook, G. and McCashin, A. (1997), 'Male Breadwinner: A Case-study of Gender and Social Security in the Republic of Ireland', in Byrne, A. and Leonard, M. (eds), *Women in Irish Society: A Sociological Reader*, Belfast: Beyond the Pale Publications, pp. 167–80.

Coolahan, J. (1981), *Irish Education: Its History and Structure*, Dublin: Institute of Public Administration.

Cooney, J. (1999), *John Charles McQuaid: Ruler of Catholic Ireland*, Dublin: The O'Brien Press.

Coughlan, A. (1984), 'Ireland's Welfare State in Time of Crisis', *Administration*, 32, 1, pp. 37–54.

Cousins, M. (1995), *The Irish Social Welfare System: Law and Social Policy*, Dublin: Round Hall Press.

Cousins, M. (1997), 'Ireland's Place in the Worlds of Welfare Capitalism', *Journal of European Social Policy*, 7, 3, pp. 223–35.

Cousins, M. (1999), 'The Introduction of Children's Allowances in Ireland 1939–1944', *Irish Economic and Social History*, xxvi, pp. 35–53.

Cousins, M. (2003), *The Birth of Social Welfare*, Dublin: Four Courts Press.

Cousins, M., (2005), *Explaining the Irish Welfare State: An Historical, Comparative and Political Analysis*,Lewiston:Edwin Mellen Press.

Curry, J. (1980; 1998, 3rd edn; 2003, 4th edn), *Irish Social Services*, Dublin: Institute of Public Administration.

Cutright, P. (1965), 'Political Structure, Economic Development, and National Social Security Programs', *American Journal of Sociology*, 70, pp. 537–50.

Daly, M. (1994), 'Comparing Welfare States: Towards a Gender Friendly Approach', in Sainsbury, D. (ed.), *Gendering Welfare States*, London: Sage Publications, pp. 101–17.

Daly, M. (1999), 'The Functioning Family: Catholicism and Social Policy in Germany and Ireland' in *Comparative Social Research*, 18, pp. 105–33.

Daly, M. (2001), 'Globalization and the Bismarckian Welfare States' in Sykes, R., Palier, B. and Prior, P.M. (eds), *Globalization and European Welfare States: Challenges and Change*, Basingstoke: Palgrave, pp. 79–102.

Daly, M.E. (2002), *The First Department: A History of the Department of Agriculture*, Dublin: Institute of Public Administration.

Daly, M.E. (1992), *Industrial Development and Irish National Identity, 1922–1939*, Dublin: Gill and Macmillan.

Daly, M. and Yeates, N. (2003), 'Common Origins, Different Paths: Adaptation and Change in Social Security in Britain and Ireland', *Policy and Politics*, 31, 1, pp. 85–97.

Deeny, J. (1989), *To Cure and To Care: Memoirs of a Chief Medical Officer*, Dublin: Glendale Press.

De Deken, J.J. (2002) 'Christian Democracy, Social Democracy and the Paradoxes of Earnings-related Social Security', *International Journal of Social Welfare*, vol. 11, pp. 22–39.

Delaney, E. (2001), 'Political Catholicism in Post-War Ireland: The Revd Denis Fahey and *Maria Duce*, 1945-54', *Journal of Ecclesiastical History*, 52, 3, July, pp. 487-511.

Department of Social Welfare (1949), *Social Security*, Dublin, Stationery Office.

Department of Social Welfare (1978), *Social Insurance for the Self-employed: A Discussion Paper*, Dublin: Stationery Office.

Department of Social Welfare (1996), *Social Insurance in Ireland*, Dublin: Department of Social Welfare.

Department of Social and Family Affairs (2005), *Developing a Fully Inclusive Social Insurance Model: A Review by the Social Partners of Pointers to Reform Social Insurance in a Changing Work and Social Context*, Dublin: Department of Social and Family Affairs.

Dignan, Rev. J. (1945), *Social Security: Outlines of a Scheme of National Health Insurance*, Sligo: The Champion Publications.

Dignan, Rev. J. (1950), 'The Government Proposals for Social Security', *Christus Rex*, 4, April, pp. 102–12.

Dooley, T. (2004a), *The Land for the People: The Land Question in Independent Ireland*, Dublin: UCD Press.

Dooley, T. (2004b), 'Land and Politics in independent Ireland, 1923–48: the case for reappraisal', *Irish Historical Studies*, xxxiv, 134, November, pp. 175–97.

Dooney, S. and O'Toole, J. (1998), *Irish Government Today*, Dublin: Gill and Macmillan.

Duggan, E. (2004), *The Ploughman on the Pound Note: Farmer Politics in County Galway during the Twentieth Century: The United Irish League, the Galway Farmers' Association, N.F.A, Clann na Talmhan, IFA*, Athenry, Co. Galway : Eugene Duggan.

Dunphy, R. (1995), *The Making of Fianna Fáil Power in Ireland, 1923–1948*, Oxford: Oxford University Press.

Dutton, P.V. (2000), 'An Overlooked Source of Social Reform: Family Policy in French Agriculture, 1936–1945', *Journal of Modern History*, 72, pp. 375–412.

Erskine, A and Clasen, J. (1997), 'Social Insurance in Europe – Adapting to Change?', in Clasen, J. (ed.), *Social Insurance in Europe*, Bristol: The Policy Press, pp. 241–50.

Esping-Andersen, G. and Korpi, W. (1984), 'Social Policy as Class Politics in Post-War Capitalism: Scandinavia, Austria and Germany', in Goldthorpe, J.H. (ed.), *Order and Conflict in Contemporary Capitalism*, Clarendon: Press Oxford, pp. 179–208.

Esping-Andersen, G. (1985), *Politics Against Markets: The Social Democratic Road to Power*, Princeton, NJ: Princeton University Press.

Esping-Andersen, G. (1990), *The Three Worlds of Welfare Capitalism*, Cambridge: Polity Press.

Esping-Andersen, G. (1997), 'Hybrid or Unique? The Japanese Welfare State Between Europe and America', *Journal of European Social Policy*, 7, 3, pp. 179–89.

Esping-Andersen, G. and van Kersbergen, K. (1992), 'Contemporary Research on Social Democracy', *Annual Review of Sociology*, 18, pp. 187–208.

Evans, P., Rueschemeyer, D. and Skocpol, T. (1985), *Bringing the State Back In*, Cambridge: Cambridge University Press.

Fahey, T. (1998a), 'The Catholic Church and Social Policy', in Healy, S. and Reynolds, B. (eds), *Social Policy in Ireland: Principles, Practice and Problems*, Dublin: Oak Tree Press, pp. 411–30.

Fahey, T. (1998b), 'The Agrarian Dimension in the History of the Irish Welfare State', unpublished ESRI seminar paper, 28 May.

Fahey, T. (2002), 'The Family Economy in the Development of Welfare Regimes: A Case Study', *European Sociological Review*, 18, 1, pp. 51–64.

Fanning, R. (1978), *The Irish Department of Finance 1922–58*, Dublin: Institute of Public Administration.

Fanning, B. (2004), 'Locating Irish Social Policy' in Fanning, B., Kennedy, P., Kiely, G. and Quin, S., (eds), *Theorising Irish Social Policy*, Dublin: UCD Press, pp. 6–22.

Farley, D. (1964), *Social Insurance and Social Assistance in Ireland*, Dublin: Institute of Public Administration.

Farrell, B. (1988), 'From First Dáil through Irish Free State', in Farrell, B. (ed.), *De Valera's Constitution and Ours*, Dublin: Gill and MacMillan, pp. 18–32.

Farrell, B. (1993), 'The Government', in Coakley, J. and Gallagher, M. (eds), *Politics in the Republic of Ireland*, (2nd edn), Dublin: Folens/PSAI Press, pp. 167–89.

Feeney, T. (2001), 'The Road to Serfdom: Sean MacEntee, "Beveridgeism" and the Development of Irish Social Policy', *The History Review*, journal of UCD History Society, xii, pp. 63–72.

Ferrera, M. (1996), 'The "Southern Model" of Welfare in Social Europe', *Journal of European Social Policy*, 6, 1, pp. 17–37.

Finegold, K. (1988), 'Agriculture and the Politics of U.S. Social Provision: Social Insurance and Food Stamps', in Weir, M., Orloff, A. S. and Skocpol, T., *The Politics of Social Policy in the United States*, Princeton,NJ: Princeton University Press, pp. 199–234.

Fitzpatrick, D. (1980), 'The Disappearance of the Irish Agricultural Labourer, 1841–1912', *Irish Economic and Social History*, vii, pp. 66–92.

Flora, P. and Alber, J. (1981), 'Modernization, Democratisation and the Development of Welfare States in Western Europe', in Flora, P., and Heidenheimer, A.J. (eds), *The Development of the Welfare States in Europe and America*, London: Transaction Publishers, pp. 37–80.

Flora, P. and Heidenheimer, A.J. (1981), 'The Historical Core and Changing Boundaries of the Welfare State', in Flora, P. and Heidenheimer, A.J. (eds), *The Development of the Welfare States in Europe and America*, London: Transaction Publishers, pp. 17–34.

Flora, P. (1986), 'Introduction', in Flora, P. (ed.), *Growth to Limits: The Western European Welfare States Since World War II*, Berlin: Walter de Gruyter, pp. xii–xxxvi.

Gallagher, M. (1976), *Electoral Support for Irish Political Parties, 1927–73*, London: Sage Publications.

Gallagher, M. (1982), *The Irish Labour Party in Transition, 1957–1982*, Dublin: Gill and Macmillan.

Gallagher, M. (1999), 'Parliament', in Coakley, J. and Gallagher, M. (eds), *Politics in the Republic of Ireland*, (3rd edn), Dublin: Routledge/PSAI Press, pp. 177–205.

Gallagher, M., Laver, M. and Mair, P. (2001), *Representative Government in Modern Europe* (3rd edn), London: McGraw-Hill.

Gilbert, J. and Howe, C. (1991), 'Beyond "State vs. Society": Theories of the State and New Deal Agricultural Policies', *American Sociological Review*, 56, 2, April, pp. 204–20.

Girvin, B. (1989), *Between Two Worlds: Politics and Economy in Independent Ireland*, Dublin: Gill and Macmillan.

Glennerster, H. and Evans, M. (1994), 'Beveridge and his Assumptive Worlds: The Incompatibilities of a Flawed Design' in Hills, J., Ditch, J. and Glennerster, H. (eds), *Beveridge and Social Security:*

An International Retrospective, Oxford: Clarendon Press, pp. 56–72.

Goldthorpe, J.H. and Whelan, C.T. (eds) (1992), *The Development of Industrial Society in Ireland*, Oxford: Oxford University Press.

Goldthorpe, J.H. (1992), 'The Theory of Industrialisation and the Irish Case', in Goldthorpe, J.H. and Whelan, C.T. (eds), *The Development of Industrial Society in Ireland*, Oxford: Oxford University Press, pp. 411–32.

Goodin, R.E. and Mitchell, D. (2000), 'Foundations of the Welfare State: An Overview', in Goodin, R.E. and Mitchell, D. (eds), *Foundations of the Welfare State*, Cheltenham: Edward Elgar, vols. 1–3, pp. ix–xxi.

Gough, I. (1979), *The Political Economy of the Welfare State*, London: Macmillan.

Government of Ireland (1969), *Third Programme for Economic and Social Development, 1969–72*, Dublin: Stationery Office.

Green-Pedersen, C. and Haverland, M. (2002), 'The New Politics and Scholarship of the Welfare State', *Journal of European Social Policy*, 12, 1, pp. 43–51.

Green-Pedersen, C. (2004), 'The Dependent Variable Problem within the Study of Welfare State Retrenchment: Defining the Problem and Looking for Solutions', *Journal of Comparative Policy Analysis: Research and Practice*, 6, 1, April, pp. 3–14.

Guy Peters, B. (1996), 'Political Institutions, Old and New', in Goodin, R.E. and Klingemann, H. (eds), *A New Handbook of Political Science*, Oxford: Oxford University Press, pp. 205–22.

Guy Peters, B., Pierre, J. and King, D.S. (2005), 'The Politics of Path Dependency: Political Conflict in Historical Institutionalism', *Journal of Politics*, 67, 4, Nov., pp 1275–1300.

Hall, P.A. (1993), 'Policy Paradigms, Social Learning, and the State: The Case of Economic Policymaking in Britain', *Comparative Politics*, 25, 3, April, pp. 275–96.

Hall, P.A. and Taylor, R.C.R. (1996), 'Political Science and the Three New Institutionalisms', *Political Studies*, 44, 5, pp. 936–57.

Hannan, D.F. (1979), *Displacement and Development: Class, Kinship and Social Change in Irish Rural Communities*, Dublin: ESRI.

Hannan, D.F. and Breen, R. (1987) 'Family Farming in Ireland', in Galeski, B. and Wilkenning, E. (eds), *Family Farming in Europe and America*, Boulder, CO: Westview Press, pp. 39–69.

Hannan, D.F. and Commins, P. (1992), 'The Significance of Small-scale Landholders in Ireland's Socio-economic Transformation', in Goldthorpe, J.H. and Whelan, C.T. (eds), *The Development of Industrial Society in Ireland*, Oxford: Oxford University Press, pp. 79–104.

Hardiman, N. (1988), *Pay, Politics and Economic Performance in Ireland 1970–1987*, Oxford: Clarendon Press.

Healy, K. (1998), 'The New Institutionalism and Irish Social Policy', in Healy, S. and Reynolds, B. (eds), *Social Policy in Ireland: Principles, Practice, and Problems*, Dublin: Oak Tree Press, pp. 59–83.

Heclo, H. (1974), *Modern Social Politics in Britain and Sweden: From Relief to Income Maintenance*, New Haven, CT and London: Yale University Press.

Heidenheimer, A.J., Heclo, H. and Adams, C.T. (1990), *Comparative Public Policy: The Politics of Social Choice in America, Europe and Japan*, London: Macmillan.

Hegarty, Rev. E.J. (1950), 'The Principles Against State Welfare Schemes', *Christus Rex*, Oct., pp. 1–19.

Hensey, B. (1979), *The Health Services of Ireland*, Dublin: Institute of Public Administration.

Hewitt, C. (1977), 'The Effect of Political Democracy and Social Democracy on Equality in Industrial Societies: A Cross-National Comparison', *American Sociological Review*, 42, 3, June, pp. 450–64.

Hicks, A. and Misra, J. (1993), 'Political Resources and the Growth of Welfare in Affluent Capitalist Democracies, 1960–1982', *American Journal of Sociology*, 99, 3, Nov., pp. 668–710.

Hicks, A.M. and Swank, D.H. (1992), 'Politics, Institutions, and Welfare Spending in Industrialized Democracies, 1960–1982', *American Political Science Review*, 86, 3, Sep., pp. 658–74.

Hill, M. (2000), 'Introduction', in Hill, M. (ed.), *Income Maintenance Policy*, Cheltenham:Edward Elgar, pp. xi–xix.

Honohan, W.A. (1959–60) 'Providing for Old Age through Private Channels', *Journal of the Statistical and Social Inquiry Society of Ireland*, Vol. XX, Part III.

Hogan, J. (2005), 'Testing for a Critical Juncture: Change in the ICTU's Influence over Public Policy in 1959', *Irish Political Studies*, 20, 3, Sept., pp. 271–295.

Horgan, J. (2000), *Noel Browne: Passionate Outsider*, Dublin: Gill and Macmillan.

Hornsby-Smith, M. and Whelan, C. (1994), 'Religious and Moral Values', in Whelan, C.T., *Values and Social Change in Ireland*, Dublin: Gill and Macmillan, pp. 7–44.

Huber, E., Ragin, C. and Stephens, J.D. (1993), 'Social Democracy, Christian Democracy, Constitutional Structure and the Welfare State', *American Journal of Sociology*, 99, 3, Nov., pp. 711–49.

Huber, E. and Stephens, J.D. (2001), *Development and Crisis of the Welfare State: Parties and Policies in Global Markets*, Chicago, IL: University of Chicago Press.

Hughes, G. (1988), *The Irish Civil Service Superannuation Scheme*, Dublin: Economic and Social Research Institute.

Immergut, E.M. (1992), *Health Politics: Interests and Institutions in Western Europe*, Cambridge: Cambridge University Press.

Immergut, E.M. (1998), 'The Theoretical Core of the New Institutionalism', *Politics and Society*, 6, 1, pp. 5–35.

International Labour Office (1955), *Unemployment Insurance Schemes*, Geneva: ILO.

Johnston, H. (1999), 'Poverty in Ireland', in Kiely, G., O'Donnell, A., Kennedy, P. and Quin, S. (eds), *Irish Social Policy in Context*, Dublin: UCD Press, pp. 210–30.

Jones, C. (1985), *Patterns of Social Policy: An Introduction to Comparative Analysis*, London: Tavistock.

Jones, D.S., (2001), 'Divisions within the Irish government over land-distribution policy, 1940–70', *Eire-Ireland*, xxxvi, Fall/Winter, pp. 83–109.

Kahl, S. (2005), 'The Religious Roots of Modern Poverty Policy: Catholic, Lutheran and Reformed Protestant Traditions Compared', *Archives Européennes de Sociologie*, 46, 1, pp. 91–126.

Kaim-Caudle, P. (1967), *Social Policy in the Republic of Ireland*, London: Routledge and Kegan Paul.

Kaim-Caudle, P.R. and Byrne, J.G. (1971), *Irish Pension Schemes, 1969*, Dublin: E.S.R.I.

Kasza, Gregory J. (2002), 'The Illusion of Welfare "Regimes"', *Journal of Social Policy*, 31, 2, pp. 271–87.

Kennedy, F. (1975), *Public Social Expenditure in Ireland*, Dublin: Economic and Social Research Institute.

Kennedy, F. (1997), 'The Course of the Irish Welfare State', in Ó Muircheartaigh, F. (ed.), *Ireland in the Coming Times: Essays to Celebrate T.K. Whitaker's 80 Years*, Dublin: IPA, pp. 129–155.

Kennedy, L. (1989), *The Modern Industrialisation of Ireland 1940–1988*, Dublin: Economic and Social History Society of Ireland.

Keogh, D. (1994), 'Foundation and Early Years of the Irish TUC 1894–1912', in Nevin, D. (ed.), *Trade Union Century*, Dublin: Mercier Press, pp. 19–32.

Keogh, D. (1996), 'The Role of the Catholic Church in the Republic of Ireland 1922–1995', in *Building Trust in Ireland: Studies Commissioned by the Forum for Peace and Reconciliation*, Belfast: Blackhall Press, pp. 85–213.

Kerr, C., Dunlop, J., Harbison, F., and Myers, C. (1973) *Industrialism and Industrial Man*, Harmondsworth: Penguin.

Kiely, G. (1999), 'Introduction: From Colonial Paternalism to National Partnership: An Overview of Irish Social Policy', in Kiely, G., O'Donnell, A., Kennedy, P. and Quin, S. (eds), *Irish Social Policy in Context*, Dublin: UCD Press, pp. 1–10.

Kiely, G., O'Donnell, A., Kennedy, P. and Quin, S. (eds), (1999), *Irish Social Policy in Context*, Dublin: UCD Press.

King, D.S. (1986), 'The Public Sector Growth and State Autonomy in Western Europe: The Changing Role and Scope of the State in Ireland since 1950', *West European Politics*, 9, 1, pp. 81–96.

Korpi, W. (1978), *The Working Class in Welfare Capitalism: Work, Unions and Politics in Sweden*, London: Routledge and Kegan Paul.

Korpi, W. (1992), *Welfare State Development in Europe Since 1930: Ireland in Comparative Perspective*, Dublin: ESRI.

Laver, M. (1992), 'Are Irish Parties Peculiar?' in Goldthorpe, J.H. and Whelan, C.T. (eds), *The Development of Industrial Society in Ireland*, Oxford: Oxford University Press, pp. 359–82.

Lee, J. (1979), 'Aspects of Corporatist Thought in Ireland: The Commission on Vocational Organisation, 1939–43', in Cosgrave, A. and McCartney, D. (eds), *Studies in Irish History* Dublin: University College, Dublin, pp. 324–46.

Lee, J. (1989), *Ireland 1912–1985: Politics and Society*, Cambridge: Cambridge University Press.

Lewis, J. (1992), 'Gender and the Development of Welfare Regimes', *Journal of European Social Policy*, 2, 3, pp. 159–73.

Liebfried, S. (1993), 'Towards a European Welfare State?', in Jones, C. (ed.), *New Perspectives on the Welfare State*, London: Routledge, pp. 133–56.

Lipset, S.M. and Rokkan, S. (1967), 'Cleavage Structures, Party Systems and Voter Alignments: An Introduction', in Lipset, S.M. and Rokkan, S. (eds), *Party Systems and Voter Alignments*, New York: The Free Press, pp. 1–64.

Lucey, Rev. Professor (1943), 'The Beveridge Report and Eire', *Studies*, pp. 36–44.

Mabbett, D. and Bolderson, H. (1999), 'Theories and Methods in Comparative Social Policy', in Clasen, J. (ed.), *Comparative*

Social Policy: Concepts, Theories and Methods, Oxford: Blackwell, pp. 34–56.

McCashin, A. (1982), 'Social Policy: 1957–82', *Administration*, 30, 1–2, pp. 203–24.

McCashin, A. (2004), *Social Security in Ireland*, Dublin: Gill and Macmillan.

McCullagh, D. (1998), *A Makeshift Majority: The First Inter-Party Government 1948–51*, Dublin: Institute of Public Administration.

McKee, E. (1986), 'Church–State Relations and the Development of Irish Health Policy: The Mother and Child Scheme 1944–53', *Irish Historical Studies*, xxv, 98, pp. 159–94.

McLaughlin, E. (1993), 'Ireland: Catholic Corporatism', in Cochrane, A. and Clarke, J. (eds), *Comparing Welfare States: Britain in International Context*, London: Sage Publications, pp. 205–38.

McLaughlin, E. (2001), 'Ireland: From Catholic Corporatism to Social Partnership', in Cochrane, A., Clarke, J. and Gewirtz, S. (eds), *Comparing Welfare States*, London: Sage Publications, pp. 223–59.

Maguire, M. (1986), 'Ireland', in P. Flora (ed.), *Growth to Limits: The Western European Welfare States Since World War II*, Berlin: Walter de Gruyter, vol. 2, pp. 244–384.

Maioni, A. (1997), 'Parting at the Crossroads: The Development of Health Insurance in Canada and the United States 1940–1965', *Comparative Politics*, 29, 4, July, pp. 411–32.

Mair, P. (1987), *The Changing Irish Party System: Organisation, Ideology and Electoral Competition*, London: Pinter Publications.

Mair, P. (1992), 'Explaining the Absence of Class Politics in Ireland', in Goldthorpe, J.H. and Whelan, C.T. (eds), *The Development of Industrial Society in Ireland*, Oxford: Oxford University Press, pp. 383–410.

Mair, P. (1993), 'The Party System and Party Competition', in Coakley, J. and Gallagher, M. (eds), *Politics in the Republic of Ireland*, Dublin: Folens/PSAI Press.

Mair, P. (1999), 'Party Competition and the changing Irish Party System', in Coakley, J. and Gallagher, M. (eds), *Politics in the Republic of Ireland*, (3rd edn) Dublin: Routledge/PSAI Press, pp. 127–151.

Manning, M. (1979) 'The Farmers' in Lee, J.J. (ed.), *Ireland: 1945–70,* Dublin: Gill and Macmillan, pp. 48–60.

Manning, M. (1999), *James Dillon: A Biography*, Dublin: Wolfhound Press.

Manow, P. (2004), *The Good, the Bad and the Ugly: Esping-Andersen's Regime Typology and the Religious Roots of the Western Welfare State*, Max-Planck Institute of the Study of Societies Working paper 04/3, Cologne: MPIFfG.

Marshall, T.H. (1950), *Citizenship and Social Class and Other Essays*, Cambridge: Cambridge University Press.

Mishra, R. (1984), *The Welfare State in Crisis: Social Thought and Social Change*, Brighton: Wheatsheaf Books.

Millar, M. (2003), 'Institutionalism "old" and new: Exploring the Mother and Child Scheme', in Adshead, M. and Millar, M. (eds), *Public Administration and Public Policy in Ireland: Theory and Methods*, London: Routledge, pp. 129–146.

Murphy, G. (1999), 'Toward a Corporate State? Seán Lemass and the Realignment of Interest Groups in the Policy Process 1948–1964', *Administration*, 47, 1, Spring, pp. 86–102.

Murphy, G. (2003), *Economic Realignment and the Politics of EEC Entry*, Dublin and Bethesda, MD : Maunsel & Co.

Murray, C.H. (1990) *The Civil Service Observed*. Dublin: Institute of Public Administration

Myles, J. and Quadagno, J. (2002), 'Political Theories of the Welfare State', *Social Service Review*, March, pp. 34–57.

NESC (2003), *An Investment in Quality: Services, Inclusion and Enterprise*, Dublin: Government Publications Office.

NESC, (2005), *The Developmental Welfare State*, Dublin: Government Publications Office.

OECD (1994) *Private Pensions in OECD Countries: Ireland*, OECD Social Policy Studies No. 13

Ó Cearbhaill, T. (1983), 'The Civil Service in its Place', Administration, 31, 1, pp. 8–33.

Ó Cinnéide, S. (1969), 'The Development of the Home Assistance Service', *Administration*, 17, 3, pp. 284–308.

Ó Cinnéide, S. (1970), *A Law for the Poor: A Study of Home Assistance in Ireland*, Dublin: Institute of Public Administration.

Ó Cinnéide, S. (1999), 'The 1949 White Paper and the Foundations of Social Welfare', in Lavan, A. (ed.), *50 Years of Social Welfare Policy*, Dublin: Department of Social, Community and Family Affairs, pp. 18–30.

O'Connell, P. (1982), 'The Distribution and Redistribution of Income in the Republic of Ireland', *The Economic and Social Review*, 13, pp. 251–278.

O'Connell, P.J. and Rottman, D.B. (1992), 'The Irish Welfare State in Comparative Perspective', in Goldthorpe, J.H. and Whelan, C.T. (eds), *The Development of Industrial Society in Ireland*, Oxford: Oxford University Press, pp. 205–40.

O'Connor, J. (1973), *The Fiscal Crisis of the State*, New York: St Martin's Press.

O'Connor, J.S. (1988), 'Convergence or Divergence?: Change in Welfare Effort in OECD Countries 1960–1980', *European Journal of Political Research*, 16, pp. 277–99.

O'Connor, J.S. (2003), 'Welfare state development in the context of European integration and economic convergence: situating Ireland within the European Union context', *Policy and Politics*, 31, 3, pp. 387–404.

O'Donnell, A. (1999), 'Comparing Welfare States: Considering the Case of Ireland', in Kiely, G., O'Donnell, A., Kennedy, P. and Quin, S. (eds), *Irish Social Policy in Context*, Dublin: UCD Press, pp. 70–89.

O'Driscoll, F. (2000), 'Social Catholicism and the Social Question in Independent Ireland: The Challenge to the Fiscal System', in Cronin, M. and Regan, J. (eds), *Ireland: The Politics of Independence, 1922–1949*, Basingstoke: Macmillan.

O'Halpin, E. (1991), 'The Civil Service and the Political System', *Administration*, 38, 3, pp. 283–302.

O'Hearn, D. (1989), 'The Irish Case of Dependency: An Exception to the Exceptions?', *American Sociological Review*, vol. 54, Aug., pp. 578–96.

O'Hearn, D. (1995), 'Global Restructuring and the Irish Political Economy', in Clancy, P. (ed.), *Irish Society: Sociological Perspectives*, Dublin: Institute of Public Administration, pp. 90–131.

O'Hearn, D. (1998), *Inside the Celtic Tiger: the Irish Economy and the Asian Model*, London: Pluto.

O'Leary, C. (1979), *Irish Elections 1918–1977: Parties, Voters and Proportional Representation*, Dublin: Gill and Macmillan.

O'Leary, D. (2000), *Vocationalism and Social Catholicism in Twentieth-Century Ireland: The Search for a Christian Social Order*, Dublin: Irish Academic Press.

O'Malley, E. (1985), 'The Problem of Late Industrialisation and the Experience of the Republic of Ireland', *Cambridge Journal of Economics*, 9, pp. 141–154.

O'Malley, E. (1989), *The Challenge for the Latecomer*, Dublin: Gill and Macmillan.

O Mathúna, S. (1956), 'The Christian Brothers and the Civil Service', *Administration*, 3, 2, pp. 69–74.

Ó Riáin, S. and O'Connell, P.J. (2000), 'The Role of the State in Growth and Welfare' in Nolan et al. (eds), *Bust to Boom? The Irish Experience of Growth and Inequality*, Dublin: IPA.

O'Sullivan, E. (2004), 'Welfare Regimes, Housing and Homelessness in the Republic of Ireland', *European Journal of Housing Policy*, 4, 3, December, pp. 323–343.

O'Sullivan, E. (2005) 'Book Review', *Studies*, 94 (376), Winter, pp. 425–427.

Ó Tuathaigh, M.A.G. (1982), 'The Land Question, Politics, and Irish Society 1922–1960', in Drudy, P.J. (ed.), *Ireland: Land, People and Politics*, Cambridge: Cambridge University Press, pp. 167–89.

Offe, C. (1984), *Contradictions of the Welfare State*, London: Hutchinson Education.

Orloff, A.S. (1993), *The Politics of Pensions*, London: University of Wisconsin Press.

Pateman, C. (1988), 'The Patriarchal Welfare State', in Gutmann, A. (ed.), *Democracy and the Welfare State*, Oxford: Princeton University Press, pp. 231–60.

Payne, D. and McCashin, A. (2005), 'Welfare State Legitimacy: The Republic of Ireland in Comparative Perspective', paper presented to the ESPAnet05 Conference, University of Fribourg, Switzerland, 22–24 September.

Peillon, M. (1994), 'Placing Ireland in a Comparative Context', *Economic and Social Review*, 25, 2, pp. 179–95.

Peillon, M. (1996), 'Welfare and State Autonomy in Ireland', paper presented to the annual conference of the Political Studies Association of Ireland.

Petersen, J.H. (1990), 'The Danish 1891 Act on Old Age Relief: A Response to Agrarian Demand and Pressure', *Journal of Social Policy*, 19, 1, Jan, pp. 69–92.

Pierson, C. (1991), *Beyond the Welfare State?*, Cambridge: Polity Press.

Pierson, P. (1993), 'When Effect Becomes Cause: Policy Feedback and Political Change', *World Politics*, July, pp. 595–628.

Pierson, P. (1996), 'The New Politics of the Welfare State', *World Politics*, 48, January, pp. 143–79.

Pierson, P. (2001), 'Coping With Permanent Austerity: Welfare State Restructuring in Affluent Democracies', in Pierson, P. (ed.), *The New Politics of The Welfare State* Oxford: Oxford University Press, pp. 410–56.

Pierson, P. (2004), *Politics in Time: History, Institutions and Social Analysis*, Princeton,NJ: Princeton University Press.

Ploug, N. and Kvist, J. (1996), *Social Security in Europe: Development or Dismantlement?*, London: Kluwer Law International.

Powell, F.W. (1992), *The Politics of Irish Social Policy 1600–1990*, Lewiston: Edwin Mellen Press.

Powell, M. and Barrientos, A. (2002), 'Theory and Method in the Welfare Modelling Business', paper presented to COST A15 Conference, Oslo, 5–6 April.

Puirséil, N. (2002), 'Labour and Coalition: The Impact of the First Inter-Party Government, 1948–1951', *Saothar*, 27, pp. 55–64.

Quadagno, J. (1987), 'Theories of the Welfare State', *Annual Review of Sociology*, 13, pp. 109–28.

Rhodes, M. (1997), *Southern European Welfare State: Between Crisis and Reform*, London: Frank Cass.

Rimlinger, G. (1971), *Welfare Policy and Industrialization in Europe, America and Russia*, New York and London: John Wiley and Sons.

Riordan, S. (2000), 'A Political Blackthorn: Seán MacEntee, The Dignan Plan and the Principle of Ministerial Responsibility', *Economic and Social History*, xxvii, pp. 44–62.

Rosenberry, S.A. (1982), 'Social Insurance, Distributive Criteria and the Welfare Backlash: A Comparative Analysis', *British Journal of Political Science*, 12, pp. 421–47.

Rottman, D. and O.'Connell, P. (1982), 'The Changing Social Structure of Ireland', *Administration*, 30, 3, pp. 63–88.

Rottman, D. and Reidy, M. (1988), *Redistribution Through State Social Expenditure in the Republic of Ireland: 1973–1980*, Dublin: National Economic and Social Council.

Rothstein, B. (1996), 'Political Institutions: An Overview', in Goodin, R.E. and Klingemann, H. (eds), *A New Handbook of Political Science*, Oxford: Oxford University Press, pp. 133–66.

Rumpf, E. and Hepburn, A.C. (1977), *Nationalism and Socialism in Twentieth Century Ireland*, Liverpool: Liverpool University Press.

Saltman, R.B., Busse, R. and Figueras, J., (eds), *Social Health Insurance Systems in Western Europe*, Maidenhead: Open University Press.

Sartori, G. (1976), *Parties and Party Systems: a Framework For Analysis*, Cambridge: Cambridge University Press.

Schmid, G., Reissert, B. and Bruche, G. (1992), *Unemployment Insurance and Active Labor Market Policy: An International Comparison of Financing Systems*, Detroit: Wayne State University Press.

Schmid, J. (1996), 'Two Steps Forward – One Step Back? Some Critical Comments on F.G. Castles' "On Religion and Public Policy: Does Catholicism Make a Difference?"', *European Journal of Political Research*, 30, pp. 103–9.

Schmidt, M.G. (2002), 'The Impact of Political Parties, Constitutional Structures and Veto Players on Public Policy', in Keman, H (ed.), *Comparative Democratic Politics: A Guide to Contemporary Theory and Research*, London: Sage Publications, pp. 166–84.

Shalev, M. (1983), 'The Social Democratic Model and Beyond: Two "Generations" of Comparative Research on the Welfare State', *Comparative Social Research*, 6, pp. 315–51.

Sinnott, R. (1995), *Irish Voters Decide: Voting Behaviour in Elections and Referendums Since 1918*, Manchester: Manchester University Press.

Skocpol, T. (1985), 'Bringing the State Back In: Strategies of Analysis in Current Research', in Evans, P., Rueschemeyer, D. and Skocpol, T., *Bringing the State Back In*, Cambridge: Cambridge University Press, pp. 3–37.

Skocpol, T. and Amenta, E. (1986), 'States and Social Policies', *Annual Review of Sociology*, 12, pp. 131–57.

Skocpol, T. (1992), 'State Formation and Social Policy in the United States', *American Behavioural Scientist*, 35, 4/5, pp. 559–73.

Skocpol, T. (1995), *Social Policy in the United States: Future Possibilities in Historical Perspective*, Princeton: Princeton University Press.

Starke, P. (2006), 'The Politics of Welfare State Retrenchment: A Literature Review', *Social Policy and Administration*, 40, 1, February, pp. 104-120.

Stapleton, J. (1991), 'Civil Service Reform', *Administration*, 38, 3, pp. 303–35.

Steinmo, S. (1989), 'Political Institutions and Tax Policy in the United States, Sweden and Britain', *World Politics*, xli, pp. 500–35.

Stephens, J.D. (1979), *The Transition from Capitalism to Socialism*, London: Macmillan.

Thelen, K. and Steinmo, S. (1992), 'Historical Institutionalism in Comparative Politics', in Steinmo, S., Thelen, K and Longstreth, F. (eds), *Structuring Politics: Historical Institutionalism in Comparative Analysis*, Cambridge: Cambridge University Press.

Thelen, K. (1999), 'Historical Institutionalism in Comparative Politics', *Annual Review of Political Science*, 2, pp. 369–404.

Therborn, G. (1994), 'Another Way of Taking Religion Seriously: Comment on Francis G. Castles', *European Journal of Political Research,* 26, 1, pp. 103–10.

Timonen, V. (2003), *Irish Social Expenditure in a Comparative International Context*, Dublin: IPA, Combat Poverty Agency.

Timonen, V. (2005), *Irish Social Expenditure in a Comparative International Context: Epilogue*, Dublin: IPA, Combat Poverty Agency.

Titmuss, R.M. (1968), *Commitment to Welfare,* London: George Allen and Unwin.

Urwin, D.W. (1980), *From Ploughshare to Ballotbox: The Politics of Agrarian Defence in Europe*, Oslo: Universitetsforlaget Oslo.

Uusitalo, H. (1984), 'Comparative Research on the Determinants of the Welfare State: The State of the Art', *European Journal of Political Research*, 12, pp. 403–22.

Varley, T. and Curtin, C. (1999), 'Defending Rural Interests Against Nationalists in 20th Century Ireland: A Tale of Three Movements' in Davis, J (ed.), *Rural Change in Ireland*, Belfast: Institute of Irish Studies, pp. 58–83.

van Kersbergen, K. and Verbeek, B. (1994), 'The Politics of Subsidiarity in the European Union', *Journal of Common Market Studies*, 23, 2, pp. 215–36.

van Kersbergen, K. (1995), *Social Capitalism: A Study of Christian Democracy and the Welfare State*, London: Routledge.

van Kersbergen, K. (2001), 'Welfare State Theory and Social Quality', in Beck, W.L., van der Maesen, J.G., Thomése, F. and Walker, A., *Social Quality: A Vision for Europe*, The Hague: Kluwer Law International, pp. 87–104.

Van Kersbergen, K. and Becker, U. (2002), 'Comparative Politics and the Welfare State' in Keman, H (ed.), *Comparative Democratic Politics: A Guide to Contemporary Theory and Research*, London: Sage Publications, pp. 185–214.

Veit-Wilson, J. (2000), 'States of Welfare: A Conceptual Challenge', *Social Policy and Administration*, 34, 1, pp. 1–25.

Watson, S.E. (2005), 'Parties and the Welfare State in Late Development: Land, Social Policy, and the Solution to Southern Spain's Agrarian Social Question', paper prepared for the Annual Conference of the ISA's Research Committee 19 on Poverty, Social Welfare and Social Policy, 8–10 September, Chicago: Northwestern University.

Weir, M., Orloff, A.S. and Skocpol, T. (1988), 'Introduction: Understanding American Social Politics', in Weir, M., Orloff, A.S. and Skocpol, T. (eds), *The Politics of Social Policy in the United States*, Princeton,NJ: Princeton University Press, pp. 3–36.

Whyte, J.H. (1974), 'Ireland: Politics Without Social Bases', in Rose, R. (ed.), *Electoral Behaviour: A Comparative Handbook*, New York: The Free Press, pp. 619–51.

Whyte, J.H. (1980; 1971, 1st edn), *Church and State in Modern Ireland 1923–1979*, Dublin: Gill and Macmillan.

Wickham, J. (1983), 'Dependence and State Structure: Foreign Firms and Industrial Policy in the Republic of Ireland', in Holl, Otmar (ed.), *Small States in Europe and Dependence*, Wien: Braumüller, pp. 164–83.

Wilensky, H.L. (1975), *The Welfare State and Equality: Structural and Ideological Roots of Public Expenditures*, Berkley and Los Angeles: University of California Press.

Wilensky, H.L. (1981), 'Leftism, Catholicism and Democratic Corporatism: The Role of Political Parties in Recent Welfare State Development', in Flora, P. and Heidenheimer, A.J. (eds), *The Development of the Welfare States in Europe and America*, London: Transaction Publishers, pp. 345–82.

Williamson, P.J. (1985), *Varieties of Corporatism: Theory and Practice*, Cambridge: Cambridge University Press.

Williamson P.J. (1989), *Corporatism in Perspective: An Introductory Guide to Corporatist Theory*, London: Sage Publications Ltd.

Wrigley, E.A. (1972), 'The Process of Modernization and the Industrial Revolution in England', *Journal of Interdisciplinary History*, 3, pp. 225–59.

Yeates, N. (1997), 'Gender and the Development of the Irish Social Welfare System', in Byrne, A. and Leonard, M. (eds), *Women in Irish Society: A Sociological Reader*, Belfast: Beyond the Pale Publications, pp. 145–66.

Index

Please note that references to Notes have the letter 'n' following the page number

O'Connor, J.S., 50
O'Driscoll, F., 96
OEEC, Ireland as founder member of, 214
O'Halpin, E., 178
O'Higgins, 189
O'Kelly, S.T., 84–85, 138
Old Age (Care) Allowance, 223
Old Age Pension (1908), 4
Old Age Pension Act (1908), 247
O'Leary, D.: on Dignan plan, 88–89; on
    vocationalism/Catholicism, 68, 70, 94, 96
origins of welfare states, 19, 26
O'Sullivan, E., 50, 56

parliamentary systems, consensus
    model/majoritarian model, 45
path dependency, 45, 46, 80
Payne, D., 50
pay-related contribution system (PRSI), 221
peasant proprietorship system, 83
Peillon, M., 65, 108
pensions: Blind Person's Pension (1920), 248;
    contributory schemes, 84; and Lemass,
    212–217; O'Kelly on, 84–85; *Report of the
    Committee of Inquiry into Widows' and
    Orphans' Pensions*, 137; Revenue
    Commissioners, administered by, 71; 'three-
    tiered' nature of, 41; White Paper (*Social
    Security*, 1949), 213; Widows' and
    Orphans Pensions Act 1935, 35, 84, 137,
    155, 180
Peters, Guy: on institutions, 43, 47–48
Petersen, J.H.: on Denmark, agrarian factors,
    115, 117
policy paradigms, 170, 208
political theories, 2, 16, 231–232; cleavages,
    28–29, 173–174; continuity and change,
    52–53; divergence, 27–32; evaluation, 38;
    expenditure, 35–36; and industrialisation,
    26; Irish welfare state, 32–38; social
    democratic parties, 28, 29, 31; social
    policy, and party-political differences, 35;
    timing issues, 52; typologies, 29
Poor Law legislation: all-or-nothing principle,
    abandonment (1847), 25; Boards of
    Guardians, 82, 129, 247; and current
    welfare provision, 24; and Irish social
    services, 86; Irish/British, 82; male
    breadwinner assumption, 64; and means-
    testing, 4; and reform, 33
Poor Relief Extension Act 1847, 25
Poor Relief (Ireland) Act 1838, 14, 247
PR electoral system, 180
pre-industrial society, as 'traditional' society, 25
Prescribed Relatives Allowance, 223
private insurance schemes, social insurance
    compared, 6
private pension schemes, 216
Protestantism, 28, 235n
PRSI (pay-related contribution system), 221
Public Assistance Act 1939, 90
Purséil, N., 183

Quadagno, J., 17
Quadragesimo Anno (papal encyclical):
    corporatism, 62, 69; ideas in, 58; and social
    policy, 66; and vocationalism, 94

Ragin, C., 61–62, 110
reform, 8–10
relatives assisting farms, Ireland, 144, 145, 221
religion, 28, 56; *see also* Catholic
    Church/Catholicism; Christian democracy
*Report of the Committee of Inquiry into
    Widows' and Orphans' Pensions*, 137
*Report of the Departmental Committee on
    Health Services*, 75, 85–86
*Report of the Inter-Departmental Committee on
    the Health Services*, 100
Report on the Commission on Social Welfare,
    212
Rerum Novarum (papal encyclical):
    corporatism, 62, 69; ideas in, 58; and social
    policy, 66
Revenue Commissioners, pensions administered
    by, 71
Rimlinger, G., 81
Riordan, S., 88, 91, 97
Rokkan, S., 28, 130
Rothstein, B., 43
Rottman, D.B.: on agrarianism, neglect of in
    Ireland, 122–123; on industrialisation, 20;
    on Irish welfare state, 37; on political
    parties, 31; on 'post-colonial legacy', 33; on
    state approach, 22, 37, 41, 42
Ryan, James: on agricultural workers, 169; on
    categories of workers, 165–166; challenges
    and constraints faced by, 141; Cousins on,
    171–172; and Fianna Fáil, 164; on pension
    schemes, 216; and Social Welfare Act 1952,
    170, 200, 201–203, 209; and White Paper
    (1949), 197

Scandinavia: agrarian factors, and welfare state
    outcomes, 115–116, 118, 122, 130–131;
    'red-green' alliance, 119; 'universal' welfare
    states, 21
Schmid, J., 60
Second World War, and 'golden age' of welfare
    state, 54
self-employed, insurance for: agricultural
    interests, 147–148, 154, 164; and Beveridge
    scheme, 181; inclusion or exclusion from
    social insurance schemes, 147–148, 154,
    164, 181, 205–206; Ireland, importance in,
    221; Sweden and Denmark, 143
Shanley, Dr, 92, 93
sickness benefit, and National Insurance Act
    1911, 4
Single Woman's Allowance, 224
Sinn Féin, 128, 132
Sinnott, R., 228
Skocpol, T., 39, 40, 43
Smallholders' Unemployment Assistance –
    Notional Assessment (1965), 223–224